Policy and Practice for Multilingual Educational Settings

BILINGUAL EDUCATION & BILINGUALISM

Series Editors: **Nancy H. Hornberger** *(University of Pennsylvania, USA)* and **Wayne E. Wright** *(Purdue University, USA)*

Bilingual Education and Bilingualism is an international, multidisciplinary series publishing research on the philosophy, politics, policy, provision and practice of language planning, Indigenous and minority language education, multilingualism, multiculturalism, biliteracy, bilingualism and bilingual education. The series aims to mirror current debates and discussions. New proposals for single-authored, multiple-authored, or edited books in the series are warmly welcomed, in any of the following categories or others authors may propose: overview or introductory texts; course readers or general reference texts; focus books on particular multilingual education program types; school-based case studies; national case studies; collected cases with a clear programmatic or conceptual theme; and professional education manuals.

All books in this series are externally peer-reviewed.

Full details of all the books in this series and of all our other publications can be found on http://www.multilingual-matters.com, or by writing to Multilingual Matters, St Nicholas House, 31–34 High Street, Bristol, BS1 2AW, UK.

BILINGUAL EDUCATION & BILINGUALISM: 138

Policy and Practice for Multilingual Educational Settings

Comparisons across Contexts

Edited by
Siv Björklund and Mikaela Björklund

MULTILINGUAL MATTERS
Bristol • Jackson

DOI https://doi.org/10.21832/BJORKL2989
Library of Congress Cataloging in Publication Data
A catalog record for this book is available from the Library of Congress.
Names: Björklund, Siv, editor. | Björklund, Mikaela, editor.
Title: Policy and Practice for Multilingual Educational Settings:
  Comparisons across Contexts/Edited by Siv Björklund and Mikaela Björklund.
Description: Jackson: Multilingual Matters, [2023] | Series: Bilingual
  Education & Bilingualism: Volume 138 | Includes bibliographical
  references and index. | Summary: "Exploring multilingualism as a
  complex, context-related, societal and individual phenomenon, this book
  centres around perspectives on how multiple languages are made
  (in)visible within educational settings. The chapters compare findings
  across geographical contexts in the areas of language policy and
  planning, multilingual practices and identity"— Provided by publisher.
Identifiers: LCCN 2022050578 (print) | LCCN 2022050579 (ebook) | ISBN
  9781800412996 (paperback) | ISBN 9781800412989 (hardback) | ISBN
  9781800413016 (epub) | ISBN 9781800413009 (pdf)
Subjects: LCSH: Multilingual education—Cross-cultural studies. | Education
  and state—Cross-cultural studies. | Language and languages—Study and
  teaching—Cross-cultural studies. | Multicultural
  education—Cross-cultural studies.
Classification: LCC LC3715 .P66 2023 (print) | LCC LC3715 (ebook) | DDC
  370.117/5—dc23/eng/20221115 LC record available at https://lccn.loc.gov/2022050578
LC ebook record available at https://lccn.loc.gov/2022050579

British Library Cataloguing in Publication Data
A catalogue entry for this book is available from the British Library.

ISBN-13: 978-1-80041-298-9 (hbk)
ISBN-13: 978-1-80041-299-6 (pbk)
ISBN-13: 978-1-80041-300-9 (pdf)
ISBN-13: 978-1-80041-301-6 (epub)

Open Access

Except where otherwise noted, this work is licensed under the Creative Commons Attribution-NoDerivatives 4.0 International License. To view a copy of this license, visit http://creativecommons.org/licenses/by-nd/4.0/ or send a letter to Creative Commons, PO Box 1866, Mountain View, CA 94042, USA.

Multilingual Matters
UK: St Nicholas House, 31–34 High Street, Bristol, BS1 2AW, UK.
USA: Ingram, Jackson, TN, USA.

Website: www.multilingual-matters.com
Twitter: Multi_Ling_Mat
Facebook: https://www.facebook.com/multilingualmatters
Blog: www.channelviewpublications.wordpress.com

Copyright © 2023 Siv Björklund, Mikaela Björklund and the authors of individual chapters.

All rights reserved. No part of this work may be reproduced in any form or by any means without permission in writing from the publisher.

The policy of Multilingual Matters/Channel View Publications is to use papers that are natural, renewable and recyclable products, made from wood grown in sustainable forests. In the manufacturing process of our books, and to further support our policy, preference is given to printers that have FSC and PEFC Chain of Custody certification. The FSC and/or PEFC logos will appear on those books where full certification has been granted to the printer concerned.

Typeset by Nova Techset Private Limited, Bengaluru and Chennai, India.

Contents

	Contributors	vii
	Introduction *Siv Björklund and Mikaela Björklund*	1
1	A Comparison of Swedish and Canadian Educational Policies and Instructional Practices: The Case of Multilingual Language Learners *Jim Cummins and Jarmo Lainio*	11
2	National Curriculum Reforms and Their Impact on Indigenous and Minority Languages: The Sami in Norway and Welsh in Wales in Comparative Perspective *Kamil Özerk and Colin H. Williams*	39
3	Languaging and Language Policies among Multilingual Children and Youth Groups in Finland and Denmark *Anna Slotte, Janus Spindler Møller and Tuuli From*	68
4	'I Am a Plurilingual Speaker, but Can I Teach Plurilingual Speakers?' Contradictions in Student Teacher Discourses on Plurilingualism in Spain, Slovenia and Finland *Júlia Llompart, Tjaša Dražnik and Mari Bergroth*	95
5	In Search of Dominant Language Constellations among Multilingual Young Adults in Cyprus and Finland: The Influence of Multiple Language Use and Practices on Linguistic Identity and Trajectories as Future Teachers *Sviatlana Karpava, Mikaela Björklund and Siv Björklund*	121
6	Supporting Multilingual Learning in Educational Contexts: Lessons from Poland, Finland and California *Agnieszka Otwinowska, Mari Bergroth and Eve Zyzik*	147

7 Researching Adolescents' Linguistic Repertoires in Multilingual
   Areas: Case Studies from South Tyrol and Finland   173
   *Lorenzo Zanasi, Karita Mård-Miettinen and
   Verena Platzgummer*

   Creating Synergies in Comparative Multilingualism:
   An Epilogue   198
   Colin H. Williams

   Index   213

Contributors

Editors

Mikaela Björklund has worked as a university lecturer in foreign language education at the Faculty of Education and Welfare Studies at Åbo Akademi University. Her main research interests focus on content and language integrated learning (CLIL), linguistic and cultural integration patterns in primary school contexts, including teacher beliefs, pupils' patterns of multilingual language use and linguistic schoolscapes. Her most recent research interest is teacher education as an arena for language awareness and multilingual language use. She is one of the initiators of the Workshop on Multilingualism network and has co-edited several academic volumes.

Siv Björklund is Professor of Swedish immersion and multilingualism at the Faculty of Education and Welfare Studies at Åbo Akademi University. Her research encompasses Swedish as a second language, bilingual and multilingual learning, CLIL and minority studies. Recent research projects focus on the relation between multilingualism and identity in immersion programs, pedagogical practices for language-diverse classes and the development of participatory writing among students with Swedish as a first or second language in different classroom settings. Björklund is also one of the founders of the *Journal of Immersion and Content-Based Language Education*.

Authors

Mari Bergroth (PhD) works as senior lecturer in educational sciences at the University of Helsinki, Finland. She holds a title of Associate Professor in education: immersion education and linguistic diversity at Åbo Akademi University, Finland. Her research interests include multilingualism, multilingual learning and teaching. Her recent published work focuses on educational policy, language-in-education policy, family language policy, developing language aware initial and in-service teacher education for both bilingual and mainstream education.

Jim Cummins is Professor Emeritus at the Ontario Institute for Studies in Education of University of Toronto and was Adjunct Professor at Åbo Akademi University in Finland from 2015 to 2019. His research focuses on literacy development in educational contexts characterized by linguistic diversity. In numerous articles and books, he has explored the nature of language proficiency and its relationship to literacy development, with particular emphasis on the intersections of societal power relations, teacher–student identity negotiation and literacy attainment in multilingual classrooms.

Tjaša Dražnik (MA) is a doctoral candidate at the Faculty of Education and Welfare Studies at Åbo Akademi University, Finland. She has recently been working in an international Erasmus+ project, Linguistically Sensitive Teaching in All Classrooms (Listiac), as a member of a research group at the Faculty of Education of the University of Ljubljana, Slovenia. She holds a Master's degree in Teaching English and French as a Foreign Language.

Tuuli From is a project researcher at the Faculty of Education and Welfare Sciences, Åbo Akademi University, Finland, in the project Citizen Science research on co-located schools in Finland and Italy. In her PhD thesis (University of Helsinki, 2020) she examined how language policies operate through symbolic and material spaces in bilingual educational settings, particularly in co-located Finnish- and Swedish-medium schools in Finland and bilingual Sweden–Finnish schools in Sweden. From's research interests include studying questions related to language, power and social difference in education using critical and ethnographic approaches.

Sviatlana Karpava is a lecturer in Applied Linguistics/TESOL and Linguistics Section Coordinator at the Department of English Studies, University of Cyprus. She is also Co-coordinator of the Testing, Teaching and Translation Lab. Dr Karpava has presented her research at numerous international conferences and her research work has been published in various peer-reviewed journals. Her areas of research are applied linguistics, syntax, semantics and pragmatics, phonetics and phonology, speech perception and production, orthography, first and second language acquisition, bilingualism, multilingualism, sociolinguistics, teaching and education, critical digital literacy, heritage language use, maintenance and transmission, language loss, shift and attrition, family language policy, home literacy environment and intercultural communication.

Jarmo Lainio is Professor of Finnish at Stockholm University (2008–). His research covers sociolinguistics, sociology of language, minority languages, language policy and (bilingual) educational linguistics. He is the co-founder of a network of teacher training educators of national minority languages (Nätmin) and the Swedish member of the Council of Europe's Committee of Experts since 2005, monitoring the European Charter for Regional or Minority Languages. In 2017 he was a Special Inquirer for the Swedish Government, regarding the instruction of national minority languages (SOU 2017:91). He has been widely published in the fields mentioned above.

Júlia Llompart is a postdoctoral researcher and principal investigator for the CULT project (Constructing a collaborative understanding of learning and teaching for the XXI century, Ministerio de Ciencia e Innovación, PID2020-115446RJ-I00) at the Universitat Autònoma de Barcelona and a member of the GREIP. Her research focuses on plurilingual practices in education, language mediation and teaching and learning in non-formal settings. Her work combines ethnography, collaborative and participatory action research and conversation analysis. She has participated in national and international projects and has several published articles related to her research interests.

Karita Mård-Miettinen is Professor in Applied Linguistics at the University of Jyväskylä, Finland. Her research focuses especially on practices and policies in early language learning and teaching, and multiple language learning in bilingual education and additional language teaching settings. She applies ethnographic, collaborative and visual methods and adopts content and discourse analytic approaches.

Janus Spindler Møller is Associate Professor at the Department of Nordic Studies and Linguistics (NorS) at the University of Copenhagen. In 2009, he earned a PhD with a thesis on the longitudinal development of polylingual practices among a group of Danes with Turkish background. His main fields of interest are languaging, interactional sociolinguistics and language ideology. He is currently leading the Everyday Languaging Project, which studies languaging among school students in a culturally diverse area of Copenhagen, and is participating in the SoMeFamily Project, dealing with social media activities within families viewed across generations. His work has been published in a range of journals.

Agnieszka Otwinowska (MA, PhD, Habil.) is Associate Professor at the Faculty of Modern Languages, University of Warsaw, Poland. Her research involves multilingual language acquisition, cross-linguistic influences, child bilingualism, foreign language teaching and CLIL (bilingual) education. She is a teacher trainer and an author of course books and syllabuses for English language teaching approved by the Polish Ministry of Education; she also worked as an external expert for the Polish Educational Research Institute. She has been an active member of European academic networks: the International Association of Multilingualism, the Network on Multilingualism organized by the University of Vaasa and Åbo Akademi, COST Action IS0804 Language Impairment in a Multilingual Society and COST Action IS1306 New Speakers in a Multilingual Europe: Opportunities and Challenges.

Verena Platzgummer holds a PhD from the University of Vienna and is member of a research team on multilingualism at the Institute for Applied Linguistics at Eurac Research in Bozen-Bolzano. Her interests lie primarily in linguistic repertoires, language ideologies and language in education, which she investigates with sociolinguistic and linguistic ethnographic methods.

Anna Slotte has the title of Docent and works as a senior university lecturer at the Swedish teacher education program at the University of Helsinki, Finland. Her primary fields of research are multilingualism, video ethnography and digital literacy. She is especially interested in language sensitive teaching, digitalized text practices in school and language-crossing activities in the everyday lives of children and youth. She is a member of the Nordic Center of Excellence, Quality in Nordic Teaching (QUINT) (2018–2024).

Colin H. Williams was Research Professor in Sociolinguistics, now an Honorary Professor, in the School of Welsh, Cardiff University, UK. Currently he is a Visiting Fellow, and a Senior Research Associate of the Von Hügel Institute at St Edmund's College, the University of Cambridge, UK where he specializes in post-conflict reconstruction and reconciliation. His main scholarly interests are sociolinguistics and language policy in multicultural societies, ethnic and minority relations and political geography. Williams has advised government agencies in Europe and North America on minority issues and currently advises the Welsh Government on its Official Language Strategies.

Lorenzo Zanasi is a senior researcher at the Institute for Applied Linguistics at Eurac Research in Bozen-Bolzano, Italy. He holds a PhD in linguistics from the University for Foreigners, Siena, Italy, and has also studied at the Sapienza University of Rome. He has taught Italian as a second language in Italy as well as in France, Morocco and Sri Lanka. His research interests lie in the fields of Italian linguistics, educational linguistics and plurilingual teaching methodology.

Eve Zyzik (PhD, University of California, Davis) is Professor in the Department of Languages and Applied Linguistics at the University of California, Santa Cruz. She has published on a variety of topics related to second language acquisition, heritage language development and issues related to language pedagogy in content-based courses. She has published two books: the advanced-level textbook *El español y la lingüística aplicada* (Georgetown University Press) with Robert Blake and *Authentic Materials Myths: Applying Second Language Research to Classroom Teaching* (University of Michigan Press) with Charlene Polio. She currently serves as Executive Director of Language Learning.

Kamil Özerk is Professor of Education at the University of Oslo and Sami University of Applied Sciences, Norway. He teaches classes on teaching and learning, curriculum development, educational counselling, bilingualism, language revitalization, reading and autism. Dr Özerk served as Vice Chair for academic issues at the Department of Education and as a member of the steering committee of the Norwegian Language Council. His recent books are on bilingual development and learning, reading comprehension strategies, autism and pedagogy.

Introduction

Siv Björklund and Mikaela Björklund

Multilingualism should be studied and observed as a dynamic phenomenon that is constructed and reconstructed over time. Due to its dynamicity and complexity 'multilingualism' (e.g. Singleton & Aronin, 2019) is a phenomenon that does not lend itself to be fully described and explored in single research studies. Even though the in-built dynamicity requires individual researchers and research teams to choose approaches and positioning within the multidisciplinary research field, a growing number of studies on multilingualism worldwide clearly indicates that researchers view multilingualism *per se* as a benefit and a worthwhile aim to strive for. One consequence of this consensus within the research field is that many researchers try to reach outside the research field to normalise multilingualism as part of (monolingual) societies and point out its general benefit for different stakeholders and actors in society.

This manner of promoting multilingualism was part of a joint Finnish initiative to establish an international Workshop on Multilingualism network (see Figure 0.1 and the next section). Another consequence of the consensus on the benefits of multilingualism was more inside oriented within the network and aimed to deepen the knowledge of the realities of languages observed in different contexts. This context-dependency is closely intertwined with the notion that multilingualism itself is not neutral (Duchêne, 2020). In line with Heller (2020), who calls for new sociolinguistic priorities within sociolinguistics to answer questions about why language 'has served, and continues to serve, as a terrain for the making of social difference and social inequality' (Heller, 2020: 125) and 'what emancipation and equality might look like, for whom, when, and where' (Heller, 2020: 125), the presence of two or more languages needs an explorative perspective as to investigate how languages are operationalised and made (in)visible in different contexts. This volume is the result of an explicit attempt to go beyond single, contextualised case studies to compare and contrast two or more contexts, and thus optimally function as an eye-opener to detect general and specific conditions under which multiple languages are (un)used. The primarily intended audience of the volume consists of a rather broad range of researchers on and of multilingualism as a complex, context-related, societal and individual phenomenon. This audience should benefit from both the variety of methodological approaches and the gained results. The secondary audience is administrators, practitioners and university students within the fields of multilingual education, sociolinguistics, youth culture and identity studies.

One of the starting points for defining dynamic multilingualism in this volume is that it develops and adjusts at different levels according to the needs of individuals, organisations/institutions and societies across different contexts, at the same time as it sets requirements and creates opportunities at all three levels. Comparisons and possible tensions between different domains and contexts are also of interest to learn from each other's experiences and from evidence-based practices and to be able to develop functioning and coherent policies and strategies for a globalising world and diversifying communities. The question of minority versus majority languages within the frame of multilingualism, the experienced status of languages and different usage domains may be offered as examples.

The Workshop on Multilingualism Network

This volume emanates from the jointly developed lines of thought throughout the international Workshop on Multilingualism network, and from the wide and diverse past and ongoing research within the field of multilingualism conducted by the participating researchers. It is one of the results of the cross-disciplinary researcher network established in 2014 and initiated by researchers from Åbo Akademi University and the University of Vaasa in Finland.

The starting point of the network was the assumption that linguistically and culturally diverse challenges of individuals, organisations and society are closely interwoven. Thus, it would be fruitful to bring related researchers together in a search for common interfaces and reflections on how the field of research can be enriched by identifying cross-disciplinary and cross-contextualised commonalities and challenges. Research-oriented discussions on planning for multilingual sustainability, language needs and multilingual patterns of behaviour from individual, societal and organisational perspectives offer new opportunities to create a shared research agenda. Consequently, the purpose of the network was to identify coherent approaches to current issues of multilingualism and to develop a holistic research perspective on multilingualism. In order to achieve that aim, an international and cross-disciplinary group of both distinguished and junior researchers on multilingualism was invited to four seminars. The seminar themes encompassed diachronic and synchronic aspects of language needs from the perspectives of individuals, business and society, professional multilingualism, policy and practice, and finally the possibilities of developing a shared research agenda on multilingualism.

The participants in the network were mainly European, but scholars from North America also participated in the workshops. The scientific fields represented among the participants cover the fields of education, linguistics, sociology, communication studies, social studies and economics. The most prominent outcomes of the network were to share ideas and develop new knowledge together, with colleagues sharing the same interest in multilingualism but from slightly different perspectives/disciplines and quite differing contexts. The widespread misconceptions about multilingualism and multilingual societies among central stakeholders and the public turned out to be a shared challenge. Some key aspects for supporting (the development of) functional multilingualism were identified and an attempt to spread these to central stakeholders and the general public in an easily accessible form was made in the form of a postcard (see Figure 0.1).

The aim was to show that limited concrete action within central domains in society, education and business can contribute to functional multilingualism. Furthermore, the shared insights on professional multilingualism, multilingual policy and practice, and the possibility of developing shared research perspectives on multilingualism led the network members to ask for the possibility of publishing some of their mutual insights together. For that purpose, a writers' workshop was organised in January 2018 and the network members were asked to pair up for joint

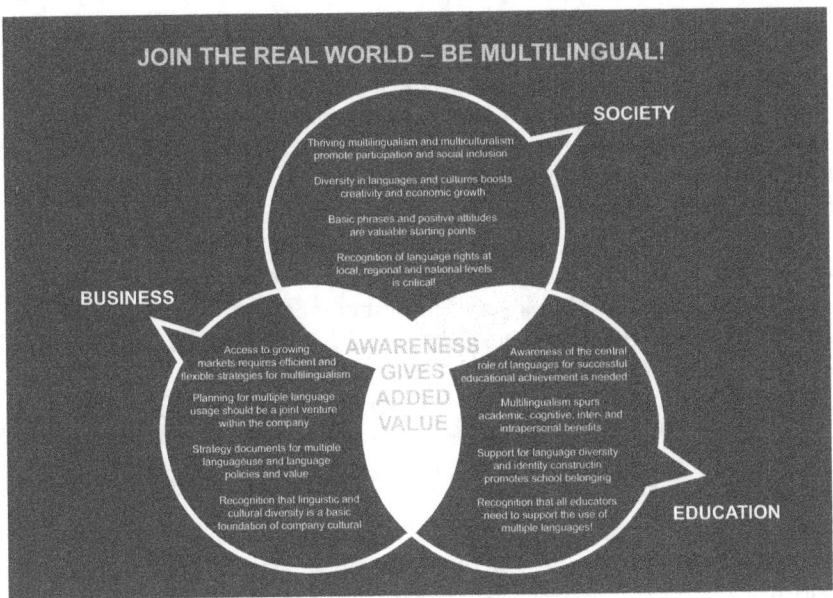

Figure 0.1 Awareness gives added value to stakeholders in society, business and education

(research and) writing efforts. Some of these efforts have been published in other fora but, for this volume, the editors compiled and brought together contributions that relate to education as one of the three central domains in Figure 0.1. All the contributions in this volume contain at least one author who was originally part of the Workshop on Multilingualism network to ensure the maintenance of the comparative and contrastive dimensions that the network members envisioned at the core of the network's shared research agenda. These original network authors have been given the opportunity to invite other co-authors to contribute to the individual chapters if deemed necessary, as a couple of planned studies could not be executed when members of the network could unexpectedly not gain access to schools due to the spread of Covid-19.

About This Volume

The particular add-ons of this volume are the joint efforts of the network researchers to go beyond their own context and, together with co-authors of the same chapter, compare and contrast across discipline and geographical context in the search for layers of multilingualism that, on the one hand, conform across context and, on the other, diverge context-specifically. As editors, we claim that there is added value in exploring multilingualism across contexts. For researchers on multilingualism who wish to increase their societal impact, it is necessary to consider comparisons across contexts and disciplines – that is, more holistic or ecological approaches to research (see also Björklund *et al.*, 2013). This volume is thus an attempt by the Workshop on Multilingualism network to provide such an example. Our dual role as editors and authors of a chapter in this volume confirmed that a consistent comparative perspective has brought challenges as well as enrichments to the fore in each chapter. In addition to the international and multidisciplinary nature of this volume, we thus claim that the thorough context-comparative perspective positions this volume in a unique way and we hope that the initiatives of the network will inspire similar future approaches across relevant fields.

In our search for a book series to best comply with this approach and set-up, we found that the series *Bilingual Education and Bilingualism* by Multilingual Matters expresses the ambition to be an international forum for interdisciplinary research on linguistic diversity and to facilitate the exchange of information and experience between academics and practitioners in different domains in combination with an explicit focus on multilingualism.

The choice of education as the domain of focus in this volume is based on the fact that many of the network members actively conduct research within this field. Furthermore, it is a very multilayered and dynamic domain that, according to Spolsky (2017), is one of the most important domains of language management. Education encompasses virtually every individual, irrespective of whether individual views on multilingualism in school are based upon current experiences, retrospective associations or future expectations. It is a domain where many active agents add to the complexity of the domain and where researchers today are more oriented toward understanding underlying language management consequences and evolving socio- and psycholinguistic aspects than towards merely introducing new methods and observing actual language practices (Spolsky, 2017).

The chapters of the book are case studies and consistently include comparative elements. Thus, the volume as such does not naturally cover all possible cases but hopes to present reasonably diverse language settings to centre around perspectives on multilingual language use and the identity of individuals in different domains within educational settings. The chapters predominantly build on empirical data and include perspectives on linguistic diversity in social life and language use in several languages in educational domains. Since the individual chapters present case studies from a multitude of contexts and researchers from different disciplines, definitions and use of terminology alone would lend itself to lengthy discussions in each chapter. We have therefore chosen not to take this approach. The reader will notice that 'multilingualism' is used in a very broad sense, sometimes including more bilingual set-ups, and mostly covering both individual and societal multilingualism. If 'plurilingualism' is used, it is the individual choice of the authors and stems from projects where plurilingualism is used to make the individual dimension explicit, whereas multilingualism is limited to the societal perspective. Since there is no English spelling unanimously agreed upon, we have chosen a consequent use of 'Sami' for both Sami languages and cultures even though we are aware that there are arguments also for other spelling conventions.

The chapters range from contributions with a clear focus on national/state planning for the development of sustainable multilingual and intercultural educational policies to contributions that deal with multilingual practices, identities and their subsequent consequences for the maintenance of multilingual practices, language strategies and policies for multilingual and diversifying educational settings and societies. The chapters of the book present macro-, meso- and micro-level studies of educational planning and practices in several contexts and thus, via comparative perspectives, aim to generate new knowledge about the complex connectedness of the three levels and the main methods linked to investigating them.

The Individual Chapters in This Volume

The focus on the three-level internal relationships (macro-, meso- and micro-level) within the Workshop on Multilingualism network is reflected in all contributions of this volume. The three levels do not exclude each other and are often implicitly embedded within the presented case studies. Comparative perspectives in the case studies presented in the individual chapters automatically pave the way for including a macro-level perspective, where the authors minimally present the linguistic landscape nationally, regionally or locally to contextualise their cases. This macro-level perspective is mostly accompanied by a micro-level perspective as most chapters address multilingual learners to highlight beliefs, attitudes, use, practices or identity in connection to them. In addition, a meso-level can more implicitly be identified in some of the chapters. Even though school as such can serve as a meso-level between society and individuals we, as editors, have chosen initial teacher education (ITE)/teacher training as representative for this level in the volume. Accordingly, the chapters are presented in an order where the macro-level perspective is most prevalent in the first chapters and the volume ends with chapters where the micro-level perspective is dominant. When identifying the dominant perspectives, we have also been guided by the choices of methods and theoretical frames of individual chapters.

Chapter 1 (A Comparison of Swedish and Canadian Educational Policies and Instructional Practices: The Case of Multilingual Language Learners, by Cummins and Lainio) and Chapter 2 (National Curriculum Reforms and Their Impact on Indigenous and Minority Languages: The Sami in Norway and Welsh in Wales in Comparative Perspective, by Özerk and Williams) use close readings of textual data such as educational steering documents, educational reports/guidelines and research studies to analyse and interpret the impact of and ideological underpinnings of national documents in relation to implementation in schools.

Cummins and Lainio show that there is no straightforward path for continued awareness of the multilingual realities in schools, even though their contexts are well-known for initiating an early sensitivity towards promoting bilingualism in Canada (French immersion) and the need for home language instruction for migrant language students in Sweden. In Canada, the maintenance of indigenous and heritage languages, as well as local educational support for migrant languages, have been overshadowed by the bilingualism predominantly occupied with the provincial main languages English and French. It is not until recently, and more within the western than eastern parts of Canada, that those other language groups have been made visible via bilingual programmes, and bi- and multilingual pedagogies have slowly gained ground to support language diversity in the classroom and the language identities of individual students. In Sweden, the home language (nowadays mother tongue instruction) reform was never fully completed, due to local resistance, and did not develop into bilingual programmes. Bilingual programmes are today mainly pursued by independent schools, which risks developing elitist bilingualism, while parents and students tend to leave multilingual public schools if given the choice. Lately, mother tongue instruction has had a slight increase among students and now has a critically central position alongside the recognition of the five national minority languages (in 2009) as a means to maintain bilingualism when bilingual education is provided almost exclusively by independent schools.

In Chapter 2, Özerk and Williams focus on established minority and indigenous languages in education and scrutinise how Sami and Welsh are directly or indirectly influenced by frames given in curricula and by educational authorities. As in Chapter 1, the process Özerk and Williams describe is not linear but can be described as a pattern of backward and forward steps. They conclude that the centrality of consistent revitalisation efforts must be fully supported at all levels if the ideologies behind documents are to be overtly and transparently expressed and understood. Furthermore, local actors have to engage and raise their voices to improve and develop bi- and multilingual education in relation to central regional or state authorities and vice versa. An ongoing dialogue is vital since educational documents have a direct impact on how minority languages are used in education and on the status of students' second languages (L2s).

Overall, both chapters mention differing views on national levels as to the expected language competence among L1 and L2 students. In some contexts, L2 students are defined at beginner level and in other contexts at the near-native language level. In addition, the discourse that seems to classify students in A or B categories has negative impacts on the choice of L2 education among students, while reclassification from L2 to L1 remains static and inflexible in some contexts (also see Chapter 6 in this volume). On the other hand, if the classification of L1 and L2 students is not upheld in the curriculum, it may have consequences for minority L1 students in bilingual and multilingual education with majority students with the same language as L2, as pointed out by Williams and Özerk. Another way to deal with the multifaceted competence level among students is to develop several syllabi for different levels in the language, as exemplified in Finland (see Chapter 6).

An explicit orientation towards the macro-level perspective is also maintained in Chapter 3 (Languaging and Language Policies among Multilingual Children and Youth Groups in Finland and Denmark, by Slotte, Møller and From). Contrary to the first two chapters, Slotte, Møller and From reverse their point of departure for the analysis and use interviews with students, video/audio recordings from bilingual workshops and student group conversations to show how language management policies in Finland and Denmark are visible among the participants of the study. The results clearly indicate that language ideologies behind the two national systems are reflected in the language use of the students. The authors exemplify how students from Finnish- and Swedish-medium schools meet for bilingually arranged workshops and how they revert to the monolingual norm of their own school institution by identifying other students as either monolingual Finnish- or Swedish-speaking, neglecting the bilingual experience many of the students have. Bilingual use was considered time-consuming and peculiar and – for the Danish participants – even a disadvantage in a classroom context, where standard Danish was associated with 'nice', 'polite' and enforced by the teachers. Furthermore, the Danish students described a division between standard Danish and what they call 'slang' and an awareness of how they manoeuvre between the use of polylingual practices and strategical avoidance of them.

Chapter 4 ('I Am a Plurilingual Speaker, but Can I Teach Plurilingual Speakers?' Contradictions in Student Teacher Discourses on Plurilingualism in Spain, Slovenia and Finland, by Llompart, Dražnik and Bergroth) represents the meso-level perspective together with the more implicitly derived professional multilingualism deployed in Chapter 5 (In Search of Dominant Language Constellations among Multilingual Young Adults in Cyprus and Finland: The Influence of Multiple Language Use and Practices on Linguistic Identity and Trajectories as Future Teachers, by Karpava, Björklund and Björklund).

In Chapter 4, Llompart, Dražnik and Bergroth compare ITE in three contexts (Spain, Slovenia and Finland) by investigating how multilingualism is part of student teachers' ($n = 173$) identity and profession. The meso-level of the chapter is enhanced by a state-of-the-art description of multilingualism in ITE in each context and the choice of linguistic ideologies and teacher thinking as theoretical frames. Their data is unique for this volume as it was collected within a joint project that addresses ITE and linguistically sensitive teaching. The results show a coherent trend within all three contexts. In all contexts, ITE has taken the first steps to adapt to language diversity in classrooms but the authors call for more systematic and sensitive pedagogies to be addressed in steering documents and training to be developed for teacher educators and in-service teachers. The strengths, weaknesses, opportunities and threats (SWOT) analysis performed within the project showed that participating student teachers are confident in being multilingual speakers and have an overall positive attitude towards multilingualism as a phenomenon in school institutions, whereas discourses of threats and challenges are concerned with topics such as student teachers' own knowledge of and readiness to make use of classroom teaching practices that are linguistically sensitive and support pupils' cultural and linguistic identity.

Student teachers are also targeted in the subsequent chapter by Karpava, Björklund and Björklund. Their analysis is based on questionnaires, group discussions and written assignments, and contains two parts. The first part focuses on the identification of dominant language constellations (DLCs) among student teachers in Cyprus and Finland who communicate daily in several languages. The second part seeks to use the DLC patterns of the participants to identify future trajectories as multilingual professionals in education. The authors conclude that the participants express hybrid, dynamic and varied linguistic identities and that there is necessarily no clear consistency between linguistic self-identification and reported daily and frequent use of languages. In accordance with the results reported by Llompart, Dražnik and Bergroth in Chapter 4, the student teachers in this study have a positive view of multilingualism in school, which they believe they can implement in relevant multilingual pedagogies in the future. However, the student teacher groups in both Cyprus and Finland seem to strongly associate their future multilingual pedagogies with their own DLCs (i.e. the languages, in particular English as a support language, they feel comfortable using). References to strategies learned for professional multilingual pedagogies within ITE are not mentioned (cf. Chapter 4).

In the last two chapters, the micro-level dominates since individual multilingual learners are analysed as key persons of the studies. Chapter 6 (Supporting Multilingual Learning in Educational Contexts: Lessons from Poland, Finland and California, by Otwinowska, Bergroth and Zyzik) outlines childhood multilingualism as a theoretical frame, especially pointing out the risks of intellectual helplessness, cognitive overload and resentment for individual multilingual learners in linguistically non-aware schools. The analysis is backed up with excerpts that illustrate experiences from individual students, teachers and teacher educators. Otwinowska, Bergroth and Zyzik conclude that an understanding of background issues is necessary to situate educational practices, that building relationships in classes and schools must be prioritised, and that valuing learners' multilingual repertoire and identity function as a good starting point even though teachers may fear cultural clashes.

Chapter 7 (Researching Adolescents' Linguistic Repertoires in Multilingual Areas: Case Studies from South Tyrol and Finland, by Zanasi, Mård-Miettinen and Platzgummer) exemplifies two contexts with long-established bi- and multilingualism and parallel school systems where one language is the main language of instruction but is complemented with additional languages as languages of instruction to enhance individual students' bi- and multilingualism. The educational language policies in both contexts are thus built on language separation, which often results in rather complex regulations. This system is further complicated by a recent increase in the immigrant population. On the other hand, in both contexts, there is a tradition of research studies on bi- and multilingualism. This is highlighted in the chapter by the way the authors identify different theoretical approaches to their research objective, the students' linguistic repertoires and how they combine different methods to study the objective. The chapter discusses how linguistic repertoires in representation (questionnaires, language portraits, language trees, interviews) and in use (photographs, observations of interaction and trajectories, language-biographical interviews) have been investigated in the two cases and how multiple methods of data contribute to a versatile, objective and holistic understanding of individual linguistic repertoires in bi- and multilingual settings.

The volume ends with an epilogue by Williams, who reconnects to the macro-perspective on multilingualism and minority languages and highlights some of the aspects brought forth in the individual chapters. Williams also manages a necessary critical stance in relation to the contributions made and the potential limitations of the individual chapters and the volume.

All in all, our goal is that this volume will contribute to the understanding of multilingual educational contexts, further the interest to join the investigation of multilingualism across contexts and thus develop tools for a functional multilingual future.

All the funders and members of the Workshop on Multilingualism network make up the fertile soil from where this publication has sprung. Special thanks go to Aktiastiftelsen i Vasa for providing funding for the actual publication process and thus contributing to more open access research. We also express our gratitude to PhD Sanna Pakarinen for her valuable assistance with technical editing and managing communication through all phases of the editing process, and to Julia Björklund for assistance with some of the visual representations.

References

Björklund, M., Björklund, S. and Sjöholm, K. (2013) Multilingual policies and multilingual education in the Nordic countries. *International Electronic Journal of Elementary Education* 6, 1–22.

Duchêne, A. (2020) Multilingualism: An insufficient answer to sociolinguistic inequalities. *International Journal of the Sociology of Language* 263, 91–97.

Heller, M. (2020) Sociolinguistic frontiers: Emancipation and equality. *International Journal of the Sociology of Language* 263, 121–126.

Singleton, D. and Aronin, L. (eds) (2019) *Twelve Lectures on Multilingualism*. Bristol: Multilingual Matters.

Spolsky, B. (2017) Language policy in education: history, theory, praxis. In T. McCarty and S. May (eds) *Language Policy and Political Issues in Education. Encyclopedia of Language and Education* (3rd edn, pp. 3–16). Cham: Springer.

1 A Comparison of Swedish and Canadian Educational Policies and Instructional Practices: The Case of Multilingual Language Learners

Jim Cummins and Jarmo Lainio

This chapter is based on long-term experiences of language policy development, primarily within heritage and minority language education, in Sweden and Canada. In the case of Sweden, two recent inquiries on national minority and national minority education are used to summarise the (official) situation for the five national minority languages (NMLs) within the language policy and educational fields. In the case of Canada, the many overviews and critical publications on multilingual education are used in a similar way. The international standards forming language rights, and set up by the Council of Europe (CoE), also work as a frame of reference for the comparison of the possibilities for the heritage and minority languages within the educational systems of Sweden and Canada.

Introduction

In several respects, but for quite different reasons, Canada and Sweden have been perceived as role models for the development of bilingual and mother tongue/first language educational programmes at the international level. Canada attracted global attention through the introduction of French immersion programmes, introduced in the Montreal area in the mid-1960s with the goal of enabling English-speaking children to develop fluency in French. These programmes spread rapidly across Canada in the 1970s and are now firmly established as an educational option in every province and territory.

Around the same time, Sweden attracted wide attention by instituting a legal structure for the provision of home language instruction for migrant and other minority languages. The Swedish Riksdag first enacted a formal policy in relation to migration and integration in 1975 following extensive discussion of these issues from the late 1960s. The policy rejected cultural assimilation in favour of a multicultural orientation that recognised the freedom of immigrant communities to choose the extent to which they wanted to retain their cultures and languages of origin. In 1977, the home language reform was formally adopted, to give immigrant and minority children a legal basis for mother tongue instruction (typically 1–2 hours per week).

These pioneering initiatives in both countries have continued over the past 40 years but, in both contexts, issues have been raised about the ideological underpinnings and pedagogical effectiveness of these programmes. Problematic issues related to broader language-in-education policies have also been debated – for example, do Canadian French immersion programmes serve the interests of a socially advantaged middle-class elite to the exclusion of socially disadvantaged and multilingual students? Why are there so few bilingual programmes implemented involving indigenous and heritage languages? In the Swedish context, indigenous languages (i.e. Sami languages) and national minority languages (NMLs; Finnish, Meänkieli, Romani, Sami and Yiddish) have, until recently, been largely marginalised with respect to promotion within the educational system. Bilingual options for children with a minority background have not been implemented, except for the Finnish minority, but even for this group bilingual programmes have declined significantly in recent decades.

Our focus in this chapter is on a subset that we are calling multilingual language learners (MLLs), which we define as students who speak or sign a minority or migrant or heritage language at home (for at least part of the time) and who are learning the majority or dominant language within the context of the preschool or school environment. The MLLs in this paper do not include Swedish L1 learners of English and/or other languages in school, or Canadian L1 speakers of English or French who are learning the other official language in school (either as a subject or in bilingual/L2 immersion programmes). In the following sections, we describe the education of MLLs in Swedish and Canadian schools, focusing on both instructional programmes designed to promote multilingual learning and specific initiatives implemented by educators designed to acknowledge, engage and promote the multilingual repertoires of students in linguistically diverse schools.

Swedish Language Policies and Instructional Initiatives

Social context

The development and effects of indigenous, minority or migrant language policies in Sweden, including Swedish as a second language, have received widespread attention among sociolinguists, educationists, historians and social scientists (Boyd & Huss, 2001; Ganuza & Hyltenstam, 2020; Hyltenstam & Milani, 2012; Lainio, 2015; Milani, 2007; Municio, 1994; Salö et al., 2018; Wickström, 2015). Up to the Second World War (WWII), Sweden was, similarly to Canada, endorsing segregation or assimilation policies towards indigenous and national minority groups. In Sweden, race biological ideologies quickly rooted in the early 1900s (Hagerman, 2015). The segregation of the Sami had clearly colonial features. Sami and Tornedalian children were placed away from home, in so-called working lodges, in which punishments and prohibition to use the ancestral language were recurrent. The Roma were not allowed to enrol in the public school system before the 1960s and had experienced a long-term expulsion from Sweden until the mid-1950s.

After WWII, Sweden benefitted from an international reputation as a modern, democratic and progressive society, based on the long-term dominance of Social Democrats. Two core principles were established: universalism and the idea of a people's home; basic needs and equal standards of living should apply to all, which became the foundations of the welfare state (Lainio, 2015). These principles now conflict with the promotion of equity within education: the strict, equal treatment of all has blocked attempts to achieve improvements in the quality and availability of educational programmes for bi- or multilingual children (Bajqinca, 2019; NAE, 2008).

After WWII, Swedish industry was comparatively intact and needed a labour force. This was largely imported; Nordic citizens benefitted from the open Nordic labour market and the abolishment of passport controls in the mid-1950s. Finns made extensive use of this opportunity: more than 600,000 people have moved from Finland to Sweden since WWII. Migration from southern Europe also increased, which changed views on educational priorities during the first post-war decades. Since the 1970s, migration has also had global dimensions. This (refugee) migration put additional strain on Sweden's ability to integrate migrant communities.

The domestic population needed to reconsider the earlier position demanding assimilation from newcomers. The inquiry on immigration (SOU 1974: 69, 1974) outlined new principles: migrants and the majority population should exchange experiences, targeting equality, freedom of choice and cooperation. The 1970s introduced policies that referred to multiculturalism, not assimilation (Bajqinca, 2019). Language policy issues are, however, not losing importance. According to estimations, approximately 2 million of Sweden's 10 million inhabitants have Swedish as L2.

Language policies

The inquiry on immigration (SOU 1974: 69, 1974) paved the way for a major change within the field of education in the form of the home language instruction (HLI) reform of 1977. Until the early 1990s, education was state-governed, which facilitated coherent national policies for education. The principles for HLI and bilingual education were influenced by the threat of double semilingualism – an issue originally raised by Hansegård (1968) and promoted by Skutnabb-Kangas (1981). Wickström described semilingualism as 'a game-changing concept in the struggle to legitimise mother tongue teaching' (2015: 185). It highlighted gaps in both L1 and L2 academic language proficiency that 'legitimised the whole home language reform, [...] in the name of equality' (2015: 188). One main principle was that learning the mother tongue should precede the introduction of the second, majority language. The languages were to be kept separate. Such ideas were under attack from researchers and debaters promoting Swedish only or transitional language shift models (Bratt Paulston, 1983; Ekstrand, 1978). In the early 1980s, many researchers, both in Sweden and internationally, distanced themselves from the idea of semilingualism (Hansegård, 1991; Hyltenstam & Stroud, 1982; Martin-Jones & Romaine, 1986).

The HLI reform was never fully implemented (Ganuza & Hyltenstam, 2020; Salö et al., 2018). It was resisted at the local administration level (Municio, 1987, 1994). Neither HLI nor various forms of bilingual education have been extensively evaluated. It is thus difficult to state what effects bilingual education or HLI (mother tongue instruction (MTI) from 1997), have had on the educational and social careers of children participating in them. Still, some studies on identity, language use and educational progression have been made (e.g. Avery, 2011; Axelsson & Magnusson, 2012; Ganuza & Hedman, 2018, 2019; Hill, 1996; Janulf, 1998; Mehlbye et al., 2011; NAE, 2008; Tuomela, 2001).

The late 1980s and 1990s saw a backlash in the progressive reasoning on language-connected educational issues. The abolition of a specific home language teacher training in the late 1980s and the structural changes of the early 1990s – when compulsory education was transferred from the state to the municipalities – have had a major negative impact on bilingual education and HLI. The general shift in ideologies during the 1990s also covered aspects of new public management and the transfer of societal responsibilities to the individual, for example for social integration and language learning (Bajqinca, 2019; cf. Sayers & Lawson, 2016). In the early 1990s, other regulations were established: the possibility to found independent schools and the introduction of free school choice. Independent schools are optional, funded by society, have defined educational profiles and follow public curricula. Their competition with the public school system has become controversial; independent schools combined with the free school choice have contributed to an ongoing segregation of Swedish society. The establishment of confessional schools has raised claims about migrants' failed integration and adaptation to Swedish values. Families with high educational, socioeconomic and linguistic resources tend to leave public multilingual schools in segregated suburbs. For the bilingual aspirations of, for example, Sweden Finns, however, the independent school system has almost completely taken over the responsibility of providing bilingual education. The same applies to some Muslim schools, which provide part of education in Arabic (Mohme, 2016) and for Spanish–Swedish bilingual school in the Stockholm region. The independent school system is a prerequisite for large consortia of schools teaching in Swedish and English according to CLIL (content and language integrated learning) principles (Yoxsimer Paulsrud, 2014; Toth, 2018). These schools increasingly enrol children with minority language backgrounds.

In the early 1990s, when Sweden approached the EU, it needed to clarify its view on domestic minorities and minority languages. The Sami were already recognised as an indigenous population in the Constitution, and the Sametinget started its work in 1993 (Sametingslagen 1992: 1433). In 1994, Finnish was recognised by the government as a 'domestic language' (Regeringens skrivelse 1994: 1). During the late 1990s, an inquiry (SOU 1997: 192, 1997; SOU 1997: 193, 1997) proposed a choice of NMLs for ratification in two minority and minority language conventions of the Council of Europe (CoE), which covered Finnish, Meänkieli, Romani Chib, Sami and Yiddish. In this process, Meänkieli was recognised as a separate language from Finnish. Sign language could not be covered by the CoE conventions.

As a result of the official recognition of the NMLs in the ratification of the European Charter for Regional or Minority Languages (ECRML), voices were raised that Swedish needed to become declared as the official language (Boyd & Huss, 2001; Hult, 2012). Until this was confirmed in the Language Act (2009), Swedish was not a *de jure* official language, but clearly so *de facto*, contested only by the strong position of English. Swedish was declared the main language in the Language Act (2009), with sign language and the five NMLs possible to use, develop and learn. The position of migrant languages was weaker: these languages could be used and developed, but not taught as mainstream school subjects. The Language Act is thus in conflict with the School Act, which guarantees MTI under certain circumstances also for migrant languages. As a reaction to the repeated critique from the CoE regarding Sweden's failure to fulfil its obligations under the two conventions, a law on national minorities and NMLs was adopted in 2009 (Lag 2009: 724, 2009).

The development in the Swedish context has resulted in the following three main overlapping MLLs, among whom the degree of multilingualism acquired at home has grown steadily.

(1) Sami children, with Swedish, Sami language(s) and other languages in their family surrounding. The Sami are both indigenous and covered by the ECRML as NMLs. Sami children have MTI within and outside Sami state schools.
(2) NML children with Finnish, Meänkieli, Romani, Sami and Yiddish language background, whose languages are recognised as NMLs or are simultaneously NMLs and migrant languages.
(3) Migrant languages, that are not recognised as NMLs, constitute about 180 languages in terms of MTI at the national level.

This creates a complex web of educational challenges for society and language groups. The autonomous municipal governance (290 municipalities) further complicates the educational position of MLLs.

During the 1990s and the early 2000s, MTI was on its way to be fully abolished (Hyltenstam & Milani, 2012; NAE, 2002). Today, it regularly consists of one hour per week, after school hours (SOU 2017: 91, 2017; SOU 2019: 18, 2019). The number of students receiving MTI seems to be growing, however. Views on mother tongue language issues remain politically highly conflictual and societally ambivalent (Hult, 2012; Lainio, 2015; Reierstam, 2020; Wingstedt, 1998).

Evaluating the teaching of Sami, NMLs and migrant languages

The Swedish focus in evaluating the results of MLLs and educational models has been on statistical 'output' – that is, marks, merit points, participation in and statistics on how many proceed to a higher level of education. Long-term evaluations of 'outcomes' are missing in terms of educational content, careers and language abilities for MLLs. The focus has been on regulations rather than on quality and content of instruction (cf. Ganuza & Hyltenstam, 2020; Hyltenstam & Milani, 2012).

MTI is sometimes referred to as bilingual teaching by authorities or providers. Otherwise, bilingual education refers to educational models and teaching that cover other subjects than language, in more than one language. The proportion of bilingual education in a mother tongue other than Swedish must remain under 50% during primary school. These matters combined make evaluations of bilingual education problematic. Reliable statistics are missing regarding bilingual education targeting the promotion of MLLs. If preschool, primary school and upper secondary school are considered, there is a handful of bilingual programme types. They cover options for public and independent schools, for Sami children, NML background children and migrant language background children. Additional options target majority population children, in foreign languages and

English, the latter of which may cover from preschool to upper secondary school, as CLIL teaching in municipal and independent schools. Bilingual alternatives that target national minority and migrant language children are not eligible at upper secondary level.

Most MLLs thus have to rely on MTI for their wishes to learn the mother tongue and become MLLs in school. A main outcome of the existing MTI system is that it does not suffice to develop a high level of biliteracy. MTI is a non-prioritised aspect of education in municipalities, as has been stated by the Schools Inspectorate (2012, 2020), the Institutet för språk och folkminnen (ISOF) (Spetz, 2012, 2019) and the National Agency of Education (NAE, 2008; also cf. SOU 2019: 18, 2019), and bilingual education even less so. The views of the larger public on MTI are paradoxical: strong personal opposition and liberal support are presented side by side, occasionally by the same individuals (Wingstedt, 1998). Bilingual education proper is now so rare that the majority of the public is unaware of its potential positive effects (Reierstam, 2020).

Teaching indigenous, national minority and migrant languages in Sweden

Sami

The first forms of education for Sami children were based on the idea of making them 'good Christians' (cf. Hyltenstam *et al.*, 1999; Belančić, 2020: 7 ff.). In 1913, the Swedish Riksdag decided that Sami children would receive teaching from travelling teachers for the first three years and then be transferred to local Lapp schools. Although not regulated, teaching was mostly in Swedish. The school targeted cultural assimilation of the Sami, but they should still remain nomadic. Non-nomadic children should attend the regular Swedish folk school for six years. In 1962, the Riksdag decided that nomadic schools be replaced by a Sami school (for six years), voluntary for all Sami children. Sami language instruction was first regulated to last for two hours per week. In 1980, the responsibility for Sami schools was transferred to the Sami School Board. A stream for Years 7–9, called Sami integration, was introduced in 1969 and formally established in 1987. This allowed the teaching of subjects about Sami culture and livelihood, offering more instruction than the regular MTI hours (Skollag 2010: 800, 2010: Chapter 10, §7a–b; SFS 2017: 620, 2017; SFS 2020: 605, 2020).

Through the creation of different segregation models, the long-term result has been a culture and language policy of erasure (Irvine & Gal, 2000). Sami is taught as an indigenous language, a NML, and is part of the MTI field. The number of pupils in a Sami state school was regularly 150–180 children, rising to 200 in 2020 (Sami School Board, 2020). In addition, during the school year 2019/2020, 443 pupils received MTI, out of 746 eligible pupils (Belančić, 2020; Table 1.1). MTI is important in municipalities where Sami is not traditionally used and there are no possibilities to attend a Sami school, for example in Stockholm. Sametinget carries the main responsibility, on behalf of the government, for Sami state schools, the Sami School Board and the Sami Language Board. It has published a language handbook for Sami (Näkkäläjärvi Utsi, 2020), which aims at an increased use of Sami in public and private life.

Language policy aspects for Sami changed with the ratification by Sweden of the CoE's ECRML in 2000. This was followed by a law on national minorities and NMLs (Lag 2009: 724, 2009) in 2010, in which Sami, Finnish and Meänkieli received a higher level of protection than Romani and Yiddish. In the field of education, however, only preschool is covered. The School Act complements these instruments.

Since 2015, a separate MTI regulation has supported all NMLs. The NMLs can be chosen both as L1 and L2, the latter meaning that it is at beginners' level. Like the other NMLs, Sami children experience discriminatory treatment regarding their language rights in schools, both from other people and authorities (Diskrimineringsombudsmannen, undated; Lainio, 2022).

The ECRML referred to Sami as one language in 2000. In Finland, Norway and Sweden, North Sami is a major Sami language, spoken in all three countries. In Sweden, four additional Sami languages are promoted in the context of the ECRML – Lule Sami, South Sami, Pite Sami (all three spoken also in Norway) and Ume Sami – all of which are severely threatened. Today's educational strivings for all Sami languages are based on the principle of revitalisation, meaning that language shift is a severe threat. Parental generations now lack competence in Sami. Aspects concerning education and Sami language use have often touched upon identification with Sami language and culture, but also a psychological language barrier to use Sami (e.g. Belančić, 2020; Fjellgren & Huss, 2019).

In the process of revitalising the Sami languages and culture, forms of educational options have been complemented by other measures. One example is the creation of Sami language centres. They promote projects that increase the use and improve the position of Sami in Swedish society and among adults who lack the capacity to use the Sami languages. Examples are apprentice–master meetings or excursions, where competent speakers of Sami communicate with learners, in domains that are traditionally Sami, such as hunting, fishing or reindeer herding (e.g. Fjellgren & Huss, 2019).

Due to the decreasing use of Sami at home, children have restricted access to it. Even teachers may share this experience. The school setting has become a major language space for the use of Sami (Belančić, 2020). Such features are also typical for the other NMLs. Much of the education takes place in North Sami and Swedish in Sami schools. One of the five Sami school units partially uses South Sami as a language of instruction. The strong presence of language shift results in Swedish, as a lingua franca, becoming dominant in all forms of Sami instruction.

National minority languages (NMLs)

Formally, the NMLs were integrated in regulations for all MTI until 2000 and the ratification of the ECRML. The national adaptation of the ECRML, Lag 2009: 724 (2009) excludes levels of education other than preschool. Furthermore, this act mainly concerns the administrative areas of Finnish, Meänkieli and Sami. Demographically, Finnish, Romani and Yiddish are both traditional and migrant community languages, which influences the number, language proficiency and language use patterns of speakers. Meänkieli is predominantly a regional language in the north of Sweden, characterised by a strong language shift process since the late 1800s, when teaching in public schools was to take place in Swedish (Wande, 1996). In 2015, the School Act (Skollag 2010: 800, 2010) was amended due to the new status of NMLs, targeting their revitalisation.

International monitoring of CoE's two conventions on minorities and minority languages since 2000 has promoted the readiness of national educational authorities to improve conditions for the teaching of NMLs, but local implementation is lagging behind. Under Part II of the ECRML there are general provisions that apply to education of all five NMLs nationwide. Under Part III, Article 8, for Finnish, Meänkieli and Sami, there are specified obligations chosen by Sweden for preschool, primary school, secondary school, vocational and adult education, higher education, teaching of the history and rights of the NMLs for all children and the establishment of a monitoring body to follow up the quality development of the teaching of and in NMLs (Lainio, 2018). In Sweden, no such national monitoring body exists for evaluating the quality of teaching and the effects of poor local implementation of the undertakings. The conflict between legislation and implementation reflects an inherited ambivalent view on MTI and bilingual education since the early 1980s (Lainio, 2001, 2015).

The School Act is valid for all languages and mother tongues, but with some exceptions for NMLs. For preschools in general, the following applies (Skollag 2010: 800, 2010: Chapter 8, §10): 'The preschool shall assist children with other mother tongues than Swedish to have a possibility to develop both Swedish and the mother tongue' (translation by Lainio). In most municipalities, provisions for preschool regarding mother tongue support are missing (Schools Inspectorate, 2020). About half of the municipalities that are covered by Lag 2009: 724 (2009), in which mother tongue provisions should be fully or to a substantial part in Finnish, Meänkieli or Sami, fail to give such services despite the law demanding it (Schools Inspectorate, 2012).

For primary schools, the CoE has repeated its critique since the early 2000s: the number of hours is too small and bilingual education should be developed. For the NMLs, there is no bilingual education for Meänkieli and Yiddish. The only bilingual class in Sweden for Romani Chib was closed in 2016. For Finnish, the decline in bilingual classes in municipal schools is dramatic – from about 400 in the 1980s to a handful today (SOU 2017: 91, 2017). From the early 1990s, five independent bilingual schools have survived – four of them in the Stockholm area and one in Eskilstuna (SOU 2017: 91, 2017). Only three are for all primary school years (Year F to Year 9, F being the intermediate year between preschool and primary school) rather than Year F to Year 6. Some municipalities aim at restarting municipal bilingual education, but similar problems persist as under the state school system before 1991 – lack of stability of instruction, poor location of the school, appropriate pedagogic and linguistic qualifications of the teachers and lack of teaching materials – all of which make parents hesitate.

For the bilingual independent schools, a few studies show that every day parallel use of Finnish and Swedish exists among pupils and by teachers. Use of English and occasionally other languages also occurs (Gynne & Bagga Gupta, 2015; Kolu, 2017; Vuorsola, 2019). Due to a lack of longitudinal studies, there is little knowledge about the long-term effects of multilingual language use on the language development or subject learning for NML children, nor of its potential impact on the language capacity at group level (cf. Lainio & Pesonen, 2021). Similar studies are missing for the other NMLs.

MTI for NMLs has contained specific regulations (see section 'Migrant languages') since 2015. Children with a NML connection may, in addition to MTI as a 'first language' require 'second language' teaching, meaning that the latter teaching concerns beginners' level and the former some fluency in the language (SOU 2017: 91, 2017). However, it is unusual to separate beginners from L1 speakers in class, and younger learners from older ones. The greatest challenges are that teaching takes place outside the regular school day in most schools and municipalities, and MTI is provided for only one hour per week (SOU 2017: 91, 2017).

During the school year 2020/2021, 46.2% of all children with a NML background who were eligible for MTI participated in it (Table 1.1). The degree to which the mother tongue is studied as a second language reflects the level of language shift and, partly, the availability of teachers. The eligibility of pupils to receive MTI no longer is valid as a criterion for

Table 1.1 Eligible pupils and participating pupils in MTI for the school year 2020/2021[a]

Mother tongue	Pupils eligible for MTI	Pupils participating in MTI	Percentage of pupils studying the language as	
			First language (L1)	Second language (L2)
Total	12,657	5846	70.7	29.3
Finnish	8992	4464	71.4	28.6
Yiddish	20	17	64.7	35.3
Meänkieli	475	162	40.7	59.3
Romani	2441	745	86.6	13.4
Sami	729	458	49.6	50.4

[a]National Agency for Education (2021-05-17), NAE (2020: Table 8G), Sami School Board (2020)

NMLs, since children may refer to heritage or identity factors and claim their right to have MTI.

Migrant languages

Teaching migrant languages in Sweden is mainly connected to MTI since few public and only a handful of independent schools provide bilingual education. According to the School Act, the following applies for MTI in primary school (Skollag 2010: 800, 2010: Chapter 10, §7). If a pupil has a caretaker with a mother tongue other than Swedish, MTI shall be offered in this language if:

(1) the language is the everyday language of communication in the home; and
(2) the pupil has a basic knowledge of the language.

The School Act also states that if a pupil belongs to one of the national minorities, the pupil shall be offered MTI in its NML. MTI may be restricted if a certain number (five) of pupils do not require it (SFS 2014: 458, 2014). This regulation does not apply to NMLs.

According to the NAE (2021, 2022), the proportion of children with a mother tongue other than Swedish was around 29% in primary school and 40% in preschool. Figures for secondary school are not available. The 10 largest languages in which MTI is provided are presented in Table 1.2.

Table 1.2 The 10 largest mother tongues receiving MTI in primary school, school year 2020/2021[b]

Ten largest mother tongue languages	Pupils eligible for MTI		Pupils participating in MTI	
	Number	Percentage of all students	Number	Percentage of all eligible in the language
Arabic	80,537	7.4	58,717	72.9
Somali	21,905	2.0	17,198	78.5
English	18,587	1.7	9,928	53.4
Bosnian/Croatian/Serbian	16,743	1.5	8,539	51.0
Kurdish	16,130	1.5	9,158	56.8
Persian	14,540	1.3	8,736	60.1
Spanish	14,222	1.3	7,083	49.8
Albanian	10,103	0.9	5,820	57.6
Polish	9,592	0.9	5,819	60.7
Finnish	8,992	0.8	4,464	49.6
Other languages (170)	101,221	9.3	51,076	50.5
Total	312,572	28.7	186,538	59.7

[b]NAE (2021: Table 8B)

There is a stable discrepancy between the number of eligible pupils and the numbers receiving MTI.

Among adults, Sweden has collected no statistics on language since 1930. Municipalities are, however, required to ask families about the languages used in the family from preschool age. For children, the main language spoken at home may be different from the one the pupil receives MTI in. One reason for children being entitled to have MTI but not receiving it (Table 1.2) is the lack of (or misleading) information from authorities to families regarding their language rights (SOU 2017: 91, 2017).

Examples of evaluations

There is no extensive, modern tradition for making research-based evaluations on educational outcomes in Sweden. A few large-scale statistical evaluations have been made, for example by the NAE, the Schools Inspectorate and ISOF (Spetz, 2012, 2019). The NAE has access to statistical data, the Schools Inspectorate has made some sample monitoring studies and the ISOF has conducted conclusive studies on the educational situation of the NMLs. Here, only the NAE (2008) report is considered.

The NAE (2008) study is based on:

(1) the results of a questionnaire directed at compulsory school administrations;
(2) a qualitative interview study carried out at 13 schools in four municipalities;
(3) a statistical follow-up study of students in Years 3–9 of compulsory (primary) school.

The study also covered the organisation of MTI and the role and organisation of Swedish as a second language. Here, we focus on the outcomes for MTI for educational success.

The NAE report states that the statistical material reflects a clearly higher average merit point rating for students who have participated in MTI. This student group's average merit rating (220 points) differs most from students who have only participated in Swedish as a second language instruction (181 points), but also from students of Swedish background (208 points). The merit rating of students who have participated both in Swedish as a second language and MTI is higher (190 points) than for students who have only taken part in Swedish as a second language.

Like other analyses (e.g. Hill, 1996) the NAE study shows that the number of years of tuition may have a positive impact. The report states that higher merit rating for students taking part in MTI cannot be explained by the students' background. A higher average merit rating generally occurs for students who have participated in MTI, irrespective of the family background. Other conditions may, however, have an influence; for instance, there may be an impact of involved parents and students who are particularly motivated to study.

Even for the small group of students with a Swedish mother or father, MTI seems to make a difference. One conclusion is that MTI is possibly more important for second-generation students since their mother tongue may be less deeply established when compared with the group of foreign-born students.

The NAE report also states that MTI has a possible impact on students' general knowledge development but, paradoxically, it takes place outside other school activities and is described as marginalised. The possible effect of participation in MTI appears almost to be 'a frontal collision with the image of the tuition's marginalised position in Swedish compulsory school'.

Evaluations of the role of Sami in educational models have not been published recently (cf. Belančić, 2020). Evaluations of NML educational models and their possible effects are rare, and the situation between the NMLs differs considerably. The number of students and the general position within Swedish society for the four NMLs of Finnish, Meänkieli, Romani and Yiddish are incompatible in practice, but legally similar (see Table 1.1; SOU 2017: 91, 2017). Earlier studies referring to the use of Finnish as a means of instruction, or as the mother tongue, reflect positive effects on the outcomes for the development of Finnish and Swedish (e.g. Janulf, 1998; Tuomela, 2001). No recent large-scale evaluations on Finnish bilingual education or MTI have been made.

Researchers' evaluations of migrant languages have been revived (e.g. Hill, 1996). In some studies of multilingual classrooms there are paradoxes between the aims of teaching and the interactional patterns of teachers and pupils in the school context. Differences between pupils' cultural traits and languages are erased, with pupils constructed as one ethnic-cultural category – immigrants. Thus, only the learning of Swedish becomes a main task for all (Haglund, 2007; Runfors, 2009). This decreases the possibilities of developing multilingualism, with mother tongues as one component. Additionally, some studies have been made on Arabic (Avery, 2011) and Somali (Ganuza & Hedman, 2018, 2019). The research on Somali is now summarised.

Ganuza and Hedman (2018, 2019) carried out several sub-studies on Somali as a mother tongue in learning processes related to learning Swedish and other school subjects. Some focus was put on the analysis of literacy in both Somali and Swedish. Some of the sub-studies covered a larger number of pupils ($n = 120$), whereas some sub-sets were used in later analyses ($n = 36$). They used classroom recordings and surveys to understand the views and language behaviour of teachers and pupils. They were interested in whether participation in MTI influenced the bi-literacy proficiency of young bilinguals, using examples from Somali–Swedish bilinguals and Somali MTI. Biliteracy was operationalised as reading proficiency and vocabulary knowledge in Somali and Swedish, and pupils were tested with measures of word decoding, reading comprehension and vocabulary breadth and depth. The study used cross-sectional, longitudinal and cross-linguistic analyses of the data.

The results indicated that participation in MTI contributed positively to participants' results on Somali reading comprehension, also including the influence of age, age of arrival, reported home language and literacy use. Higher results in Somali were related to higher results on the same measures in Swedish, in particular for reading capacities. The results showed that, despite the restricted time (one hour per week) allotted to MTI, the teaching has an impact on some aspects of literacy proficiency in Somali. Furthermore, the results showed that MTI may benefit some proficiencies in Swedish. These findings are consistent with the findings reported by NAE (2008).

Canadian Language Policies and Instructional Initiatives

Social context

Although only two languages are recognised as 'official' with specified legal protections across the country, Canada has always been highly multilingual as a result of the many languages of indigenous communities and the ongoing flow of immigrants from around the world. Most indigenous languages are currently endangered, with very few languages expected to continue cross-generational transmission into the middle of this century. The loss of indigenous languages is directly attributable to Canadian government policies that, over the course of 150 years, set out to destroy the languages, cultures and identities of indigenous children in residential schools – a process labelled 'cultural genocide' by the Truth and Reconciliation Commission of Canada (2015). In these schools, children were shamed and physically beaten for speaking their languages, and many experienced sexual abuse and torture at the hands of the Catholic and Protestant religious orders that operated the schools (Truth and Reconciliation Commission of Canada, 2015). Many students died while attending these residential schools and were buried in unmarked graves on the school site (Honderich, 2021).

The legacy of residential schools and the racism that gave rise to them is large-scale underachievement among indigenous students across Canada. Although most indigenous students speak English (or a dialectal variety of English) as their home language (L1), many do not acquire sufficiently strong levels of English academic skills in school to pursue college or university qualifications (Statistics Canada, 2011).

Over the past 30 years, a variety of indigenous language teaching and bilingual education initiatives has been undertaken by communities across Canada, many with an explicit focus on decolonisation (e.g. Aitken & Robinson, 2020; Battiste, 2013; Chambers, 2014; Giesbrecht, 2020; Gomashie, 2019; Usborne *et al.*, 2009; Walton & O'Leary, 2015). Unfortunately, up to this point, structural challenges such as the shortage of formally qualified indigenous teachers have constrained the impact and scalability of these projects. The creation of an Indigenous Languages Commissioner's office by the federal government in June 2021 represents a positive step, but one that is probably too little and too late to significantly alter the downward trajectory of indigenous language maintenance and learning across Canada.

Until the late 1960s, racist policies restricted immigration from countries outside of Europe, but large numbers of immigrants from around the world have entered Canada since the early 1970s. In 2018 and 2019, more than 300,000 immigrants (including refugees and asylum-seekers) arrived in Canada. In 2019, 58% were 'economic class' immigrants (selected on the basis of skills judged to be relevant to the Canadian economy), 27% were 'family class' (admitted based on family reunification criteria) and 15% were refugees or admitted based on humanitarian criteria (Immigration, Refugees and Citizenship Canada, 2020). In contrast to the anti-immigrant rhetoric in many European countries and in the USA, many Canadian provinces compete to attract and retain immigrants. Although Canada's racist past is clear in the historical record, and xenophobic and racist sentiments are regularly expressed in social media, the expression of racism is generally more muted than in many other countries. All the major political parties are on record as supportive of immigration and they actively seek to attract votes from immigrant communities.

The educational consequences of long-term significant levels of immigration are that Canadian classrooms are increasingly multilingual and multicultural in the makeup of their student populations. In the Vancouver School Board, for example, 60% of the school population speak a language other than English at home (Ellyson *et al.*, 2015). Other large Canadian municipalities also have significant and growing populations of multilingual students.

Language policies (or lack thereof)

As noted in the introduction to this chapter, Canada's strong international reputation as a leader in the area of second language teaching derives primarily from the implementation of French immersion programmes in the 1960s. However, the development of language teaching policies at both federal and provincial levels has been largely incoherent. Because education falls under provincial jurisdiction, language teaching policies and instructional programmes vary considerably across different provinces. All provinces strongly support the learning of the second official language (French in English Canada and English in Quebec) and they also provide support for immigrant-background newcomer students to learn the language of school instruction, but neither federal nor provincial governments have developed coherent policies regarding the multilingual realities of schools and communities.

At the federal level, the 1971 policy of multiculturalism within a bilingual framework omitted any meaningful consideration of languages other than the two official languages. In the 1970s and 1980s, the federal government provided some financial support directly to community groups for the purposes of heritage language teaching but discontinued this support in the early 1990s. No province has articulated an educational language policy that addresses, in a positive way, the multilingual realities of its schools, although Alberta (usually considered the most conservative Canadian province) at least considered the issue in the 1980s (Alberta Government, 1988).

Teaching heritage and indigenous languages

In Canada, the term 'heritage languages' usually refers to all languages other than the two official languages (English and French), the languages of indigenous (First Nations and Inuit) communities and the languages of the deaf community (American sign language, ASL) and Langue des signes Québécoise (LSQ). The term 'heritage languages' came into widespread use in 1977 when the Ontario provincial government established and funded the Heritage Languages Program. This has continued largely unchanged to the present day and provides support for the teaching of heritage languages for up to 2.5 hours per week outside of the regular five-hour school day. Classes are open to all students regardless of the specific language spoken at home.

In the early 1990s, the term heritage languages was changed to 'international languages' by the Ontario government, reflecting misgivings among ethnocultural communities that the notion of 'heritage' implied learning about past traditions rather than acquiring language skills that have significance for children's overall educational and personal development. Despite its ongoing commitment to funding the International Languages Program (currently involving approximately 100,000 students per year), Ontario has maintained restrictive policies in relation to multilingualism by prohibiting the use of heritage languages (other than English and French) as mediums of instruction except on a short-term transitional basis.

In Quebec, the government continues to provide funding for the Programme d'enseignement des langues d'origine (PELO); like the Ontario Heritage Languages Program, PELO was originally introduced in 1977. However, the rationale for PELO has gone beyond simply promoting skills in students' home languages. PELO is currently seen by school boards and the Quebec government as a stimulus to enable students to transfer knowledge and skills from one language to the other and from one culture to the other, thereby supporting students in learning French and succeeding academically.

In western Canadian provinces (Alberta, British Colombia, Manitoba and Saskatchewan), the term international languages is commonly used to refer to languages taught within the public school system (either as subjects of instruction or through bilingual programmes) while the term heritage languages usually refers to languages taught in programmes organised by ethnocultural communities outside of the regular school context.

A limited number of heritage languages are also taught as regular school subjects in many school systems across Canada, usually at the secondary level where they are offered for high school credit. These languages are often labelled 'modern languages' and include several European languages (e.g. German, Italian, Spanish) as well as Asian languages such as Chinese and Japanese. These language programmes are elective and are open to all students. However, they are generally not in high demand as they compete with elective options that are seen by many students as more relevant to their future career prospects (e.g. in areas related to technology and the sciences).

Considerably more openness to the use of heritage/international languages as mediums of instruction is evident in the western Canadian provinces than in eastern Canadian provinces. Bilingual programmes involving heritage/international languages exist in all four western provinces. Alberta has been a leader in actively supporting the establishment of bilingual programmes in a variety of languages. Currently, Alberta offers 50/50 English/other language bilingual programmes in ASL, Arabic, German, Hebrew, Mandarin, Polish, Spanish and Ukrainian. The Spanish programme has grown significantly in recent years and currently serves more than 4000 students. In addition to these bilingual programmes, enhanced teaching of languages is offered in language and culture programmes in Cree (the most spoken indigenous language across Canada), Filipino and Italian.

Bilingual programmes also exist in the prairie provinces of Manitoba and Saskatchewan. For example, the Seven Oaks school district in Winnipeg has approximately 100 students in each of its Ukrainian and Ojibwe (an indigenous language) programmes. The district started a bilingual programme in Filipino in 2018 to serve the large Filipino community in Winnipeg but was unable to continue it the following year due to low enrolment (Sampson, 2019).

Formal bilingual programmes for deaf students involving ASL or LSQ are relatively rare across Canada. Snoddon and Weber (2021) note that the learning and use of ASL by deaf children has been in decline for more than 40 years. Most deaf students are 'mainstreamed' in regular or special education classrooms, usually with the support of a teacher capable of using signed English (or French) or ASL/LSQ. However, they highlight the potential of a plurilingual approach, rather than a binary English and/or ASL orientation, that recognises and validates the partial competencies involving multiple modalities (sign, spoken, written), technologies and language systems that make up deaf children's multilingual repertoire.

Although, as noted previously, initiatives to teach indigenous languages as school subjects have increasingly been implemented across Canada, no formal evaluations of these initiatives have been carried out. Journalistic accounts, together with a limited number of research studies (e.g. Aitken & Robinson, 2020), have highlighted the impact of language revitalisation programmes on students' sense of identity and affiliation with indigenous communities and cultures, but systematic empirical evidence about actual learning of the indigenous language is largely non-existent. The reported impact of language revitalisation programmes on students' sense of identity is likely due to the engagement of the school with elders in the community (who are often the only ones in the community with sufficient knowledge of the language to teach it to young children).

Evaluation of heritage and indigenous language bilingual programmes

Early evaluations of bilingual programmes involving the use of heritage languages as mediums of instruction are summarised by Cummins and Danesi (1990). The findings parallel the outcomes of French–English bilingual and immersion programmes in showing that students benefit with respect to their knowledge of the heritage or minority language at no cost to their language and literacy skills in the majority language. In this section, we summarise the outcomes of two more recent bilingual programme evaluations carried out in Ontario and the findings of a bilingual programme in Quebec involving Inuktitut and either English or French as languages of instruction.

Mandarin–English and Arabic–English transitional bilingual programmes, implemented in the Ontario cities of Hamilton and Windsor, respectively, were evaluated to assess their impact on the development of students' English and heritage language academic skills (Cummins *et al.*, 2011; Koh *et al.*, 2017; Lam *et al.*, 2015). Because only transitional programmes designed primarily to support students' academic development in English were (and still are) permitted under Ontario law, these programmes operated only from kindergarten to Grade 4. The instruction was divided equally between the two languages.

Similar findings emerged from the two evaluations. Students instructed for about half the time in their heritage language made academic gains in that language in comparison to students from the same language backgrounds instructed only in English. These gains were attained at no cost to the students' oral proficiency or literacy in English, despite the fact that the bilingual programme students were instructed through English for 50% less time than their peers in monolingual English programmes. The comparison group in the Mandarin study received instruction in Mandarin as a subject in the province's International Languages Program but this instruction was outside regular school hours.

Mandarin–English bilingual programme

Lam *et al.* (2015) reported the early outcomes of the Mandarin–English bilingual programme (up to Grade 2). The evaluation found that students in the bilingual programme made stronger progress in learning Mandarin than comparison students not enrolled in the bilingual programme. These gains were made at no cost to the students' language and literacy skills in English. Lam *et al.* concluded that 'the many positive correlations between the Chinese and English measures suggests that learning two languages simultaneously may facilitate the development of both through cross-language transfer' (2015: 119).

Arabic–English bilingual programme

Cummins *et al.* (2011) concluded that the students in the bilingual programme experienced significant growth in Arabic language and literacy skills between spring 2010 and fall 2010 testing, while the comparison group of Arabic home language students in the English-only programme showed a loss in Arabic language and literacy skills over the same period. Less time spent through the medium of English did not impede the students' English language and literacy development.

Inuktitut–English bilingual programme

Usborne *et al.* (2009) carried out a 12-year longitudinal study in a remote Inuit community in Nunavik, Québec, that provided compelling evidence of the benefits of home language literacy for the development of literacy in the dominant societal language. Students, all of whom spoke Inuktitut as their home language, received instruction exclusively in Inuktitut from kindergarten to Grade 3, after which parents could choose either English-medium or French-medium instruction for their children from Grade 4 through to the end of secondary school. Using a battery of specially constructed, culturally appropriate parallel tests in the three languages, the researchers examined the relationships between students' baseline Grade 3 proficiency in Inuktitut and their growth in English or French proficiency between Grades 4 and 6. The sample included 110 students – 49 in the French stream and 61 in the English stream. The language tests assessed vocabulary knowledge (colours, numbers, letters and body parts) and sentence reading and comprehension (sentence completion task) and were individually administered. Usborne *et al.* (2009) summarised their findings as follows.

> These results indicate that for every one point increase in baseline Inuktitut, second language scores across subsequent years increased by 0.45 points when all other predictors were held constant. [...] Furthermore, for every one point increase in baseline second language scores, second language scores across subsequent years increased by 0.23 points, when all other predictors were held constant. (Usborne *et al.*, 2009: 677)

In other words, the positive cross-linguistic effect was about double the within-language effect in predicting growth in English and French language skills. Baseline Grade 3 Inuktitut scores also predicted Grades 4–6 Inuktitut proficiency. However, minimal overall growth was observed in Inuktitut proficiency between Grades 3 and 6, which the authors attribute both to possible ceiling effects in the Inuktitut proficiency measures and the fact that instruction in Grades 4–6 was exclusively in English or French. The authors concluded that 'having a strong basis in Inuktitut is predictive of later strength rather than weakness in a second language' (Usborne et al., 2009: 680).

Usborne et al. (2009) expressed concerns about the extent to which a transitional programme of the type implemented in this community is adequate to ensure survival of the indigenous language. Inuktitut scores reached a plateau after Grade 3 and no significant improvement in proficiency beyond Grade 3 levels was observed over the 12 years of the study. They recommended further efforts to include Inuktitut as a meaningful component of the curriculum throughout all years of schooling. The major reasons this direction had not been pursued by the school system was due to the challenges of generating Inuktitut curriculum materials beyond Grade 3 and the difficulty of finding certified Inuit teachers to teach in higher grade levels.

Multilingual instructional practices within the mainstream classroom

A heritage language example

During the first 20 years of heritage language provision in Canadian schools, mainstream teachers continued to use English or French exclusively in their teaching. There seemed to be no alternative to this instructional strategy because teachers did not speak the vast majority of languages present in their classrooms. The first Canadian initiative involving heritage languages to demonstrate that there were instructional alternatives to monolingual teaching was the Dual Language Showcase. This emerged from a collaborative project (Schecter & Cummins, 2003) initiated in 1998 in which university researchers (Schecter and Cummins) worked collaboratively with educators in two highly diverse elementary schools (Thornwood School and Floradale School) in the Peel Board of Education near Toronto to explore effective pedagogical practices in multilingual and multicultural contexts. The Dual Language Showcase project was initiated by Thornwood Grade 1 teacher Patricia Chow (Chow & Cummins, 2003) as a way of actively engaging students in literacy activities that involved their home languages as well as English. An additional impact of the project was the active involvement of parents in helping their children craft stories in their home languages and, in some cases, to translate between L1 and English.

Over the course of 15 years, the Thornwood students in kindergarten to Grade 5 created dual-language texts in multiple languages that were posted on the school's website. In some cases, newcomer students or those who had developed L1 literacy skills wrote initially in the home language but more frequently students drafted their stories in English and then worked with parents (and sometimes teachers who spoke their L1) to create their L1 version.

The Dual Language Showcase demonstrated that teachers could expand the instructional space beyond simply an English-only zone to include students' and parents' multilingual and multimodal repertoires even when teachers themselves did not speak the multiple languages represented in their classrooms. It opened up pedagogical possibilities for many subsequent translanguaging or multilingual pedagogy projects (e.g. Cummins & Early, 2011; Giampapa, 2010) that have taken place across Canada over the past 20 years (see Cummins, 2021, for a summary of these projects).

An indigenous language example

Aitken and Robinson (2020) documented the implementation and outcomes of a plurilingual pedagogy project that took place in a remote community school in northeastern, subarctic Québec, where students enter kindergarten with a strong oral use of the indigenous language, Naskapi. Prior to the late 1990s, English was the main language of instruction with Naskapi taught as a subject four times a week in 30-minute blocks – a programme that, according to Aitken and Robinson, was not particularly effective in developing Naskapi literacy skills. In 1997, a Naskapi medium of instruction programme was implemented with the goal of establishing Naskapi as the exclusive medium for five years including the two preschool years and Grades 1–3, with Naskapi used in Grade 4 for between 35% and 50% of the instruction. However, as the programme was implemented, Naskapi-medium instruction was reduced to only four years, with Grade 3 taught exclusively in English and minimal teaching of Naskapi beyond that point. Aitken and Robinson (2020: 85) point out that 'while the original desire of the team was to put in place a maintenance model, conditions are such that a transitional model persists [...] and subtractive bilingualism prevails in the school'. It was common to hear non-Naskapi teachers at the school (many of whom stayed in the community for only 1–2 years) express deficit perspectives in relation to the students and to voice scepticism about the value of Naskapi-medium instruction.

During the initial year that she taught in the English-only Grade 3 transition year programme, Loretta Robinson, a Naskapi teacher from the community, noticed that students used both languages to carry out literacy-related tasks:

> She began seeing an active community of learners experimenting and using different language strategies with both Naskapi and English during literacy-focused work. Students would ask each other questions for

> clarification or for translation of certain words to make meaning. She found that after explaining a learning task in English using different strategies such as hand gestures and visuals, students would collaboratively reiterate the instructions in Naskapi, or would ask peers to provide clarification in their language. (Aitken & Robinson, 2020: 86)

After she had become more established in the school, Loretta collaborated with a Grade 4 non-Naskapi-speaking teacher to design a bilingual literacy project entitled Grandparents: What Makes Grandparents Special? Loretta's goal was to enable students to create texts that would showcase and reinforce their relationships with elders whose language, experiences and ideas were largely excluded from curriculum and instruction. In turn, this would decentre the normalised monolingual, Eurocentric narratives that were infused in the everyday life of the school.

Over several weeks of discussing the central question of the project in both languages and listening to stories in Naskapi and English about grandparents, students created identity texts (Cummins & Early, 2011) in which they composed personal narratives, letters, responses to text and poetry that incorporated ideas that were important and relevant to them. Each student produced an individual scrapbook of writing in Naskapi and English that reflected his or her view of what makes one's grandparents special.

> For example, one student wrote a personal narrative of his grandmother showing him how to make his very own traditional mittens. Another wrote about a camping trip with his grandfather out on the tundra. [...] In the cases of these and other students, the writing showed new evidence of important qualities: focused ideas, details, and rich use of vocabulary related to culture. Students' final products were presented at a Tea Time event where grandparents were invited to listen to students reading their own texts. (Aitken & Robinson, 2020: 88)

Aitken and Robinson (2020) concluded that, although the grandparents project did not lead to any immediate change in the overall monolingual and Eurocentric orientation of the school, on a smaller scale it disrupted the predominance of monolingual practices, fostered teacher and community collaboration and drew attention to how language, culture, power, and identity intersect in the school setting. The simultaneous use of Naskapi and English enabled students to see themselves as competent writers. Their initial reluctance to write in English was diminished and students became more confident in sharing their own writing strategies and collaborating with their peers in the writing process.

Conclusions

During the past 50 years, educational language policies for MLLs in both Canada and Sweden have remained predominantly assimilationist in nature despite some government funding for the teaching of heritage languages. In both countries, during the 1970s, programmes to support the teaching of heritage languages were implemented, first within schools in the Swedish case and predominantly outside of regular school programming in the Canadian case. However, there has been minimal support for bilingual programmes involving languages other than the dominant societal languages.

In Sweden, bilingual programmes for Finnish students have declined significantly since the 1980s and in Canada only the province of Alberta (and to a lesser extent Manitoba and Saskatchewan) has implemented genuine bilingual programmes designed to promote literacy in students' first languages throughout their schooling. The multilingual reality of the student body in many urban centres has not translated into coherent school-based policies to encourage and enable students to maintain and develop their knowledge of the full scale of their languages. The predominant orientation to students' multilingualism in both countries has been one of 'benign neglect' (Cummins, 2021).

There are some indications that this benign neglect orientation is being challenged by educators in some schools in both countries. For example, in recent years, in both Canada and Sweden, educators in a number of schools have explored ways of enabling MLLs to use their entire multilingual repertoire to carry out academic tasks and activities (for reviews see Cummins, 2021; Juvonen & Källkvist, 2021; Wedin, 2017). Unlike heritage language teaching, which was largely ignored by the mainstream teaching staff in both countries, these recent developments reflect a change in mindset and orientation at the level of the school such that policy and instruction practice are explicitly focused on affirming students' linguistic and cultural identities. It remains to be seen to what extent this orientation will gain a secure foothold in the educational policies of both Sweden and Canada or remain a marginal phenomenon that fails to bring about institutionalised change in the predominantly assimilationist orientation of both educational systems. It also remains to be seen to what extent and how this new mindset will promote the development of all the languages of MLL students.

References

Aitken, A. and Robinson, L. (2020) 'Walking in two worlds' in the plurilingual classroom: learning from the case of an intergenerational project. In S.M.C. Lau and S. Van Viegen (eds) *Plurilingual Pedagogies: Critical and Creative Endeavors for Equitable Language in Education* (pp. 77–96). Cham: Springer Nature.

Alberta Government (1988) *Language Education Policy for Alberta*. Edmonton, AB: Alberta Government.

Avery, H. (2011) Lärares språkbruk i tvåspråkiga klassrum. In Tema: Tvåspråkig undervisning på svenska och arabiska i mångkulturella storstadsskolor. *Educare*, 2011 (3), 145–176.

Axelsson, M. and Magnusson, U. (2012) Forskning om flerspråkighet och kunskapsutveckling under skolåren. In K. Hyltenstam, M. Axelsson and I. Lindberg (eds) *Flerspråkighet – en forskningsöversikt*. Stockholm: Vetenskapsrådet, Vetenskapsrådets Rapportserie 5/2012.

Bajqinca, N. (2019) *Mother Tongue Education – The Interest of a Nation. A Policy Study in Sweden 1957–2017*. Göteborg Studies in Sociology, 68. University of Gothenburg.

Battiste, M. (2013) *Decolonizing Education: Nourishing the Learning Spirit*. Saskatoon: Purich Publishing.

Belančić, K. (2020) Language policy and Sámi education in Sweden: Ideological and implementational spaces for Sámi language use. Dissertation, Umeå University.

Boyd, S. and Huss, L. (2001) Introduction. In S. Boyd and L. Huss (eds) *Managing Multilingualism in a European Nation-state: Challenges for Sweden* (pp. 1–12). Clevedon: Multilingual Matters.

Bratt Paulston, C. (1983) *Forskning och debatt om tvåspråkighet – en kritisk genomgång av svensk forskning och debatt om tvåspråkighet i invandrarundervisningen i Sverige från ett internationellt perspektiv*. Stockholm: Skolöverstyrelsen.

Chambers, N.A. (2014) 'They all talk Okanagan and I know what they are saying.' Language nests in the early years: Insights, challenges, and promising practices. Dissertation, University of British Columbia.

Chow, P. and Cummins, J. (2003) Valuing multilingual and multicultural approaches to learning. In S.R. Schecter and J. Cummins (eds) *Multilingual Education in Practice: Using Diversity as a Resource* (pp. 32–61). Portsmouth, NH: Heinemann.

Cummins, J. (2021) *Rethinking the Education of Multilingual Learners: A Critical Analysis of Theoretical Concepts*. Bristol: Multilingual Matters.

Cummins, J. and Danesi, M. (1990) *Heritage Languages: The Development and Denial of Canada's Linguistic Resources*. Toronto: Our Schools/Our Selves and Garamond Press.

Cummins, J. and Early, M. (eds) (2011) *Identity Texts: The Collaborative Creation of Power in Multilingual Schools*. Stoke-on-Trent: Trentham Books.

Cummins, J., Chen-Bumgardner, B.X., Al-Alawi, M., El-fiki, H., Pasquerella, A., Luo, Y. and Li, J. (2011) *Evaluation of the Greater Essex County District School Board English/Arabic Bilingual Language Transition Program at Begley Public School*. Report submitted to the Greater Essex County District School Board.

Diskrimineringsombudsmannen (undated) *Diskriminering av samer – samers rättigheter ur ett diskrimineringsperspektiv*. Stockholm: The Ombudsman for Ethnic Discrimination.

Ekstrand, L.H. (1978) Bilingual and bicultural adaptation: Studies in assessment of second language learning and of factors related to bicultural adjustment, with special reference to immigrant children. Dissertation, Stockholm University.

Ellyson, C., Andrew, C., Lemoine, H. and Clément, R. (2015) *Multilingualism in Vancouver: LUCIDE City Report*. University of Ottawa: Institut des langues officielles et du bilinguisme (ILOB)/Official Languages and Bilingualism Institute (OLBI). See https://languagescompany.com/wp-content/uploads/14_1229-Vancouver-LUCIDE-Report-V10_HRONLINE.pdf

Fjellgren, P. and Huss, L. (2019) Overcoming silence and sorrow: Sami language revitalization in Sweden. *International Journal of Human Rights Education* 3 (1). See https://repository.usfca.edu/ijhre/vol3/iss1/4

Ganuza, N. and Hedman, C. (2018) Modersmålsundervisning, läsförståelse och betyg – modersmålsundervisningens roll för elevers skolresultat. *Nordand* 13 (1), 4–22.

Ganuza, N. and Hedman, C. (2019) The impact of mother tongue instruction on the development of biliteracy: Evidence from Somali-Swedish bilinguals. *Applied Linguistics* 40 (1), 108–131.

Ganuza, N. and Hyltenstam, K. (2020) Modersmålsundervisningens framväxt och utveckling. In B. Straszer and Å. Wedin (eds) *Modersmål, minoriteter och mångfald: I förskola och skola* (pp. 37–78). Lund: Studentlitteratur.

Giampapa, F. (2010) Multiliteracies, pedagogy and identities: Teacher and student voices from a Toronto elementary school. *Canadian Journal of Education* 33 (2), 407–431.

Giesbrecht, L. (2020) Michif pilot project aims to revitalize language among young students. *Regina Leader-Post*. See https://leaderpost.com/news/saskatchewan/michif-pilot-project-aims-to-revitalize-language-among-young-students

Gomashie, G.A. (2019) Kanien'keha/Mohawk indigenous language revitalisation efforts in Canada. *McGill Journal of Education* 54 (1), 151–171.

Gynne, A. and Bagga Gupta, S. (2015) Languaging in the twenty-first century: Exploring varieties and modalities in literacies inside and outside learning spaces. *Language and Education* 29 (6), 509-526.

Hagerman, M. (2015) *Käraste Herman*. Stockholm: Natur & Kultur.

Haglund, C. (2007) Flerspråkighet, institutionell ordning och sociokulturell förändring i det senmoderna Sverige. *Nordand* 2 (2), 7–23.

Hansegård, N.E. (1968) *Tvåspråkighet eller halvspråkighet?* Stockholm: Aldus.

Hansegård, N.E. (1991) *Den norrbottensfinska språkfrågan. En återblick på halvspråkighetsdebatten*. Uppsala University, Uppsala Multiethnic Papers, 19.

Hill, M. (1996) *Invandrarbarns möjligheter: om hemspråksundervisning och språkutveckling*. Institutionen för pedagogik. University of Gothenburg.

Honderich, H. (2021) Why Canada is mourning the deaths of hundreds of children. See https://www.bbc.com/news/world-us-canada-57325653

Hult, F. (2012) English as a transcultural language in Swedish policy and practice. *TESOL Quarterly* 46, 30–57.

Hyltenstam, K. and Milani, T.M. (2012) Flerspråkighetens sociopolitiska och sociokulturella ramar. In K. Hyltenstam, M. Axelsson and I. Lindberg (eds) *Flerspråkighet – en forskningsöversikt*. Stockholm: Vetenskapsrådet, Vetenskapsrådets Rapportserie 5/2012, 17–152.

Hyltenstam, K. and Stroud, C. (1982) Halvspråkighet – ett förbrukat slagord. *Invandrare & Minoriteter* 3, 10–13.

Hyltenstam, K., Stroud, C. and Svonni, M. (1999) Språkbyte, språkbevarande, revitalisering. Samiskans ställning i svenska Sápmi. In K. Hyltenstam (ed.) *Sveriges sju inhemska språk* (pp. 41–97). Lund: Studentlitteratur.

Immigration, Refugees and Citizenship Canada (2020) *Annual Report to Parliament on Immigration*. See https://www.canada.ca/en/immigration-refugees-citizenship/corporate/publications-manuals/annual-report-parliament-immigration-2020.html#tr programs

Irvine, J.T. and Gal, S. (2000) Language ideology and linguistic differentiation. In P.V. Kroskrity (ed.) *Language Ideologies: Regimes, Polities and Identities* (pp. 35–84). Santa Fe: School of American Research Press.

Janulf, P. (1998) *Kommer finskan i Sverige att fortleva? En studie av språkkunskaper och språkanvändning hos andragenerationens sverigefinnar i Botkyrka och hos finlandssvenskar i Åbo*. Stockholm: Almqvist & Wiksell.

Juvonen, P. and Källkvist, M. (eds) (2021) *Pedagogical Translanguaging: Theoretical, Methodological and Empirical Perspectives*. Bristol: Multilingual Matters.

Koh, P.W., Xi Chen, X., Cummins, J. and Li, J. (2017) Literacy outcomes of a Chinese-English bilingual program in Ontario. *Canadian Modern Language Review* 73 (3), 343–367.

Kolu, J. (2017) 'Me ollaan mukana tässä experimentissä'. *Lingvistiska resurser och språkpraktiker i tvåspråkiga ungdomssamtal i Haparanda, Stockholm och Helsingfors*. University of Jyväskylä, Jyväskylä Studies in Humanities, 317.

Lainio, J. (2001) The protection and rejection of minority and majority languages in the Swedish school system. In S. Boyd and L. Huss (eds) *Managing Multilingualism in a European Nation-State: Challenges for Sweden* (pp. 32–50). Clevedon: Multilingual Matters.

Lainio, J. (2015) The art of societal ambivalence: A retrospective view on Swedish language policies for Finnish in Sweden. In M. Halonen, P. Ihalainen and T. Saarinen (eds) *Language Policies in Finland and Sweden: Interdisciplinary and Multi-sited Comparisons* (pp. 116–144). Clevedon: Multilingual Matters.

Lainio, J. (2018) The five national minorities of Sweden and their languages – The state of the art and ongoing trends. In N.E. Forsgård and L. Markelin (eds) *Perspectives on Minorities in the Baltic Sea Area*, (pp. 45–76). Helsinki: Magma.

Lainio, J. (2022) When implementation of linguistic human rights does not match legislation – the case of Sweden. In T. Skutnabb-Kangas and R. Phillipson (eds) *Handbook of Linguistic Human Rights, Volume 1*. Hoboken, NJ: Wiley-Blackwell.

Lainio, J. and Pesonen, S. (2021) 'Önskar att jag hade fått hjälp att lära min son finska' – Finskans öden i skenet av 2000-talets utbildnings- och minoritetspolitiska utveckling i Sverige. *Språk och stil* 31 (1), 44–74.

Lag 2009:724 (2009) Om nationella minoriteter och minoritetsspråk. Stockholm: Sveriges Riksdag.

Lam, K., Chen, X. and Cummins, J. (2015) To gain or to lose: Students' English and Chinese literacy achievement in a Mandarin language bilingual program. *Canadian Journal of Applied Linguistics* 18, 96–124.

Language Act (2009) Språklag (2009:600). Stockholm: Sveriges riksdag.

Martin-Jones, M. and Romaine, S. (1986) Semilingualism: A half-baked theory of communicative competence. *Applied Linguistics* 7 (1), 26–38.

Mehlbye, J., Schindler, B.R., Østergaard Larsen, B., Fredriksson, A. and Sjørslev Nielsen, K. (2011) *Tosprogede elevers undervisning i Danmark og Sverige*. Copenhagen: Anvendt Kommunal Forskning.

Milani, T.M. (2007) *Debating Swedish. Language Politics and Ideology in Contemporary Sweden*. Stockholm: Stockholm University.

Mohme, G. (2016) Somali–Swedish girls – The construction of childhood within local and transnational spaces. Dissertation, Department of Child and Youth Studies, Stockholm University.

Municio, I. (1987) *Från lag till bruk*. Stockholm University, Stockholm Studies in Politics, 31.

Municio, I. (1994) Medpart, motpart eller ickepart? In M. Peura and T. Skutnabb-Kangas (eds) *Man kan vara tvåländare också… Sverigefinnarnas väg från tystnad till kamp* (pp. 18-72). Stockholm: Sverigefinländarnas arkiv.

NAE (National Agency of Education) (Skolverket) (2002) *Fler språk – fler möjligheter*. Rapport 228. Stockholm: NAE.

NAE (Skolverket) (2008) *Med annat modersmål – elever i grundskolan och skolans verksamhet*. Rapport 321. Stockholm: NAE

NAE (Skolverket) (2020) *Skolverkets statistik*. https://www.skolverket.se/skolutveckling/statistik (accessed 13 April 2020).

NAE (Skolverket) (2021) *Redovisning av uppdrag om nationell samordning av undervisningen i minoritetsspråk*. Dnr. 7.5.2–2021:451. Stockholm: NAE.

NAE (Skolverket) (2022) *Elever och skolenheter i grundskolan. Läsåret 2021/22*. Stockholm: NAE.

Näkkäläjärvi Utsi, E.S. (2020) *Samisk språkhandbok för förvaltningsmyndigheter*. See https://www.sametinget.se/3986

Regeringens skrivelse (1994) *Finska språkets ställning i Sverige*. Stockholm: Sveriges riksdag.

Reierstam, H. (2020) Assessment in multilingual schools: A comparative mixed method study of teachers' assessment beliefs and practices among language learners – CLIL and migrant students. Dissertation, Stockholm University.

Runfors, A. (2009) Modersmålssvenskar och vi andra. Ungas språk och identifikationer i ljuset av nynationalism. *Utbildning & Demokrati* 18 (2), 105–126.

Salö, L., Ganuza, N., Hedman, C. and Karrebæk, M.S. (2018) Mother tongue instruction in Sweden and Denmark. *Language Policy* 17 (4), 591–610.
Sametingslagen 1992:1433. Stockholm: Sveriges riksdag.
Sami School Board (2020) *Sameskolstyrelsen, Årsredovisning 2020*. Jokkmokk: Sami School Board.
Sampson, S. (2019) Filipino bilingual program in Seven Oaks division on pause due to low enrolment. See https://www.cbc.ca/news/canada/manitoba/filipino-bilingual-program-winnipeg-seven-oaks-1.5162427
Sayers, D. and Lawson, R. (2016) Where we're going, we don't need roads: The past, present, and future of impact. In R. Lawson and D. Sayers (eds) *Sociolinguistic Research: Application and Impact* (pp. 7–22). Abingdon: Routledge.
Schecter, S. and Cummins, J. (eds) (2003) *Multilingual Education in Practice: Using Diversity as a Resource*. Portsmouth, NH: Heinemann.
Schools Inspectorate (Skolinspektionen) (2012) *I marginalen – En granskning av modersmålsundervisning och tvåspråkig undervisning i de nationella minoritetsspråken*. Kvalitetsgranskning Rapport 2012: 2. Stockholm: Schools Inspectorate.
Schools Inspectorate (Skolinspektionen) (2020) *Rätten till modersmålsundervisning i nationella minoritetsspråk i årskurserna 7-9 – en tematisk tillsyn*. Stockholm: Schools Inspectorate.
SFS 2014: 458 Lag om ändring i skollagen (2010: 800). Stockholm: Sveriges riksdag.
SFS 2017: 620 Lag om ändring i skollagen (2010: 800). Stockholm: Sveriges riksdag.
SFS 2020: 605 Lag om ändring i skollagen (2010: 800). Stockholm: Sveriges riksdag.
Skollag 2010: 800 (2010) Stockholm: Sveriges riksdag.
Skutnabb-Kangas, T. (1981) *Bilingualism or Not: The Education of Minorities*. Clevedon: Multilingual Matters.
Snoddon, K. and Weber, J. (eds) (2021) *Critical Perspectives on Plurilingualism in Deaf Education*. Bristol: Multilingual Matters.
SOU 1974: 69 (1974) Invandrarutredningen. Stockholm: Arbetsmarknadsdepartementet.
SOU 1997: 192 (1997) Steg mot en minoritetspolitik – Europarådets konvention om historiska minoritetsspråk. Stockholm: Jordbruksdepartementet.
SOU 1997: 193 (1997) Steg mot en minoritetspolitik – Europarådets konvention för skydd av nationella minoriteter. Stockholm: Jordbruksdepartementet.
SOU 2017: 91 (2017) Nationella minoritetsspråk i skolan – förbättrade förutsättningar till undervisning och revitalisering. Stockholm: Utbildningsdepartementet.
SOU 2019: 18 (2019) För flerspråkighet, kunskapsutveckling och inkludering. Modersmålsundervisning och studiehandledning på modersmål. Betänkande av Utredningen om modersmål och studiehandledning på modersmål i grundskolan och motsvarande skolformer. Stockholm: Utbildningsdepartementet.
Spetz, J. (2012) *Debatterad och marginaliserad: Perspektiv på modersmålsundervisningen*. Rapporter från Språkrådet 6. Uppsala: Institutet för språk och folkminnen.
Spetz, J. (2019) *Språklagen och medborgaren: En undersökning av medborgarmejl*. Uppsala: Institutet för språk och folkminnen.
Statistics Canada (2011) The educational attainment of Aboriginal peoples in Canada. Catalogue no. 99-012-X2011003. See https://www12.statcan.gc.ca/nhs-enm/2011/as-sa/99-012-x/99-012-x2011003_3-eng.pdf
Toth, J. (2018) English-medium instruction for young learners in Sweden: A longitudinal case study of a primary school class in a bilingual English-Swedish school. Dissertation, Stockholm University.
Truth and Reconciliation Commission of Canada (2015) *Canada's Residential Schools: The History, Part 1: Origins to 1939. The Final Report of the Truth and Reconciliation Commission of Canada, Volume 1*. See http://nctr.ca/assets/reports/Final%20Reports/Volume_1_History_Part_1_English_Web.pdf

Tuomela, V. (2001) Tvåspråkig utveckling i skolåldern: en jämförelse av sverigefinska elever i tre undervisningsmodeller. Dissertation, Stockholm University.
Usborne, E., Caouette, J., Qumaaluk, Q. and Taylor, D.M. (2009) Bilingual education in an Aboriginal context: Examining the transfer of language skills from Inuktitut to English or French. *International Journal of Bilingual Education and Bilingualism* 12 (6), 667–684.
Vuorsola, L. (2019) Societal support for the educational provisions of Finnish in the Swedish school system in theory and practice. *Language Policy* 18, 363–385.
Walton, F. and O'Leary, D. (2015) *Siviumut: Towards the Future Together. Inuit Women Education Leaders in Nunavut and Nunavik.* Toronto, ON: Women's Press and Canadian Scholars Press.
Wande, E. (1996) Tornedalen. In J. Lainio (ed.) *Finnarnas historia i Sverige*, del 3. Tiden efter 1945 (pp. 229–254). Helsingfors & Stockholm: Finska Historiska Samfundet and Nordiska Museet.
Wedin, Å. (ed.) (2017) *Språklig mångfald i klassrummet.* Stockholm: Lärarförlaget.
Wickström, M. (2015) Making the case for the mother tongue: Ethnic activism and the emergence of a new policy discourse on the teaching of non-Swedish mother tongues in Sweden in the 1960s and 1970s. In M. Halonen, P. Ihalainen and T. Saarinen (eds) *Language Policies in Finland and Sweden: Interdisciplinary and Multi-sited Comparisons* (pp. 171–195). Bristol: Multilingual Matters.
Wingstedt, M. (1998) Language ideologies and minority language policies in Sweden. Historical and contemporary perspectives. Dissertation, Stockholm University.
Yoxsimer Paulsrud, B. (2014) English-medium instruction in Sweden. Perspectives and practices in two upper secondary schools. Dissertation, Stockholm University.

2 National Curriculum Reforms and Their Impact on Indigenous and Minority Languages: The Sami in Norway and Welsh in Wales in Comparative Perspective

Kamil Özerk and Colin H. Williams

A comparative perspective on the manner in which national curriculum reform has impacted on both the Sami language and the Welsh language reveals some fundamental similarities regarding the role of parental pressure, national ideology, political empowerment, infrastructure development and legislation. Notwithstanding the significant differences in scale, context, demography and institutionalisation, both case studies point to the centrality of formal education and curriculum reform in stimulating language revitalisation efforts. However, questions are raised as to the implication such reforms have on the preponderance of L1 and/or L2 students with indigenous/minority background within the systems and on the degree to which minority languages are used within various socio-economic domains.

Introduction

The aim of this chapter is to compare two contrasting approaches to curriculum reform in favour of promoting indigenous languages in Norway and Wales. In the case of Sami, we will discuss the impact of five national curriculum reforms in Norway on the role played by the Sami in education since the 1930s, together with significant pieces of legislation that have changed the status of Sami speakers. In the case of Welsh, we will track the successive means by which both curriculum developments and wider sociolegal reforms have given a more prominent role to the acquisition of Welsh language skills, but we also query to what extent such skills are being used within national life.

If we confine our attention to indigenous minority languages in northwest Europe, the Sami and Welsh represent opposite ends of a continuum in terms of revitalisation efforts. While the Norwegian state was relatively slow in recognising the needs of the Sami people in the late 1980s (Keskitalo, 1997), the UK allowed the establishment of Welsh-medium primary schools in the 1950s, together with a handful of secondary schools in the 1960s. While the Sami people had a rich and vibrant oral culture, the Welsh have had a written tradition of poetry and religious writing since the 7th century AD. In addition, the Sami were few in number but occupied a vast area covering northern Norway, Sweden, Finland and Russia, while the Welsh were relatively numerous occupying a distinct historically defined territory in the west of Britain. While the Sami's existence and economy comprised reindeer and sheep herding, coastal fishing and fur trapping (Karlstad, 1997), with little inward migration, the Welsh were among the first in the world to experience industrialisation, with consequent huge developments in iron and steel making, coal production, slate quarrying, ship building, tinplate working and port development. Allied to this was a substantial increase in the migration of workers and their families from the rest of the UK and Europe, particularly during the period 1851–1911. This had a real impact on the linguistic, religious and sociocultural character of the increasingly anglicised Welsh population. Social and physical communication networks tied the Welsh inexorably into the burgeoning British state and beyond, while the Sami remained relatively marginal to political developments in Nordic countries.

It is evident then that the scale, context and the conditions of possibility for language revitalisation were very different in Norway and Wales. The intriguing question is: are there any similarities in the impact of curriculum reform and educational development on the vitality of both languages? This would entail interpreting the relative impact of first language (L1) and second language (L2) speakers on the total mass of speakers and evaluating the net contribution of bilingual education to the process of language acquisition in both contexts.

Underlying both case studies is a conscious parental and political edge to developments in education, including the establishment of units, schools, curriculum development, the production of teaching resources in the target language and teacher training more generally. Undoubtedly the most significant pressure for reform has stemmed from parental demands and the lobbying of local and national political representatives by social actors and professional bodies, as analysed by Jones (2013) and Thomas and Williams (2013).

In Norway, all the Sami political parties and Sami associations have consistently advocated for stronger language rights and comprehensive educational reforms. The most notable actor is the Norwegian Sami Association, also known as NSR, founded in 1968. Since its establishment in 1989, the Sami Parliament has also played a leading role and currently has the majority of seats. In Wales, both ideological and pragmatic arguments for the promotion of education as a means of sustaining threatened languages have been propounded by protest groups and nationalist political movements and parties, namely the Welsh Language Society (Philips, 1988) and Plaid Cymru (McAllister, 2001). While we do not detail these parental and political actions, we do acknowledge their salience in prompting the state or local states to make some provision for the education of the respective student populations. Indeed, next to the family and local community, statutory education is the major instrument by which language transmission is achieved and, in the medium-term future, may become the single most important element in language revitalisation.

Consequently, it is hugely significant not only to track developments in this domain but also to ask searching questions as to how effective formal education is in achieving the aims and goals of policy planners and social actors alike.

National Curriculum Reforms and Their Impact on the Availability of Indigenous Sami Teaching for 6–16-Year-Old Students

In relation to compulsory education and the expansion of Sami people's educational rights, Norway has experienced five periods of curriculum reform in the past 80 years. They are summarised in Table 2.1 and we will comment in turn on the impact that each of these reforms has had as revealed by an examination of national curriculum documents.

Table 2.1 The development of Norwegian national curriculum reform[a]

National curriculum document	Main apparent and subtle ideologies and aims
National curriculum of 1939 (NC-39)	Monocultural, monolingual, nationalist and hard assimilation. Subtractive bilingualism
National curriculum of 1974 (NC-74)	Quasi-multicultural, multilingual and soft assimilation
National curriculum of 1987 (NC-87) (some chapters were translated into Sami)	Half-heartedly approving and promoting reconciliation. Additive bilingualism and functional bilingualism
National curriculum of 1997 (NC-97) Sami national curriculum (NC-97-S)	Multicultural, multilingual and partially recognising indigenous rights. Additive bilingualism and functional bilingualism
National curriculum of 2006 (NC-06) Sami national curriculum (NC-06-S)	Multicultural, multilingual, equity and indigenous rights. Additive bilingualism and functional bilingualism

[a]Gjerpe (2017); Özerk (2006a)

The national curriculum of 1939 (NC-39)

In 1922, Norway introduced a 7-year programme of comprehensive elementary schooling free of charge for all 7–14-year-old children. In the absence of a national curriculum, the educational principles and priorities were determined by central educational authorities who communicated their policies through a variety of statutory obligations, laws, directives and regulations.

A new national curriculum (NC-39) was introduced in 1939. NC-39 presented two principles. The first was about establishing national minimum standards in main school subjects. This specified the minimum standards laid down for the skills and subject knowledge that all children in different grades should achieve. In addition to this conventional educational approach, NC-39 also presented a progressive approach to teaching and learning under the name of *'arbeidsskoleprinsippet'* – the 'principle of learning through working/doing' – was inspired both by the German educationist Kerchesteiner and the American educationist John Dewey (Özerk, 2006b: 41).

Underlying the introduction of these educational principles and the interest in building a contemporary educational system, there was a commitment to nation building, seen as a core agenda of the central political authorities. The nation building ideology gave little thought, let alone prominence, to the Sami people and their languages in NC-39. In fact, NC-39 was a major plank of the nationalistic, monocultural and monolingual Norwegian-oriented assimilatory policy toward its indigenous people. With regard to the language of the Sami children, NC-39 functioned as an instrument for inducing subtractive bilingualism (Lambert, 1995; Özerk, 2016).

This policy of subtractive bilingualism formulated NC-39 in such a way that there was no place for mother tongue instruction in Sami as L1. The practice of exposing children to L2 schooling only, without any corresponding allowance for instruction in and through the mother tongue, normally results in sealing the hegemony of the indigenous peoples' L2 as the dominant language of the host society replaces the L1 (Özerk, 2016).

NC-39 and its policy toward the education of Sami children continued until the 1960s and 1970s. After some structural changes in the educational system, a nine-year compulsory education programme was introduced in 1969. This required a review of the national curriculum which, after 35 years of operation, saw the introduction of a new national curriculum in 1974 (Özerk, 2016).

In NC-74, the central authorities modified their monolingual and assimilatory policy and gave Sami children an opportunity to receive a few hours teaching of Sami language each week. However, the pedagogic aims did not change, as subtractive bilingualism remained the dominant ideological and methodological *modus vivendi* (Özerk, 2016).

Changing conditions in the world and in the country necessitated a new curriculum reform in the second half of the 1980s. Thus, 1987 saw the introduction of NC-87, after 13 years of implementing a curriculum that had outrun its course and was now facing fresh challenges and developments in the infrastructural capacity of the Sami people and organisations with their cultural values and awareness (Gaski, 1997). Chief of these was the establishment, in 1973–1975, of the Nordic Sami Institute (NSI) in Guovdegeaidnu, the largest municipality in the core area of Sápmi (Karlstad, 1997).

The NSI has become a thriving research institute with its principal focus on the Sami together with investigations into the social, economic and cultural aspects of Sami indigenous life. The NSI is financed by the Nordic Council together with the governments of Norway, Sweden and Finland. During the early 1970s, several amendments were made to school legislation and Sami parents were given the right to demand language teaching in Sami for their children – regardless of whether or not they used their own language in daily life. This milestone empowered Sami parents and initiated a sustained period of articulating educational, social and political demands in a wider sociolegal context (Özerk, 2016).

The event had a tremendous impact on the NC-87 reform and drew strength from the so-called 'Sami movement' and the 'Alta affair'. In 1980, the Norwegian Government decided to construct a hydroelectric power station on the Alta-Kautokeino watercourse in the core area where the majority of the Sami people live, known as Sápmi. It was feared that construction of the planned hydroelectric power station would damage a beautiful natural setting and affect the livelihood and way of life of many reindeer holders. The Sami people organised huge anti-construction action. Physical attempts at stopping commencement of the construction works were supported by many more Sami activists. Several groups organised hunger strikes and mass demonstrations. This organised act of collective resistance by the Sami people, known as the 'Alta affair', had a significant impact on Norwegian popular opinion, their representatives and on the political establishment in general. While the Sami people failed in their attempt to stop construction of the power station, they did succeed in putting Sami issues firmly on the Norwegian social agenda. The action managed to generate formidable attention in and from mass media (Solbakk, 1997; Özerk, 2009).

Following the Alta affair in 1980, the state authorities started to cooperate with representatives of the Sami people. They initiated some serious committee initiatives with the aim of defining the status and rights of the Sami people. At the same time, Norwegian officials initiated attempts that sought to displace the dominant assimilation policy in different sectors in society by a more sympathetic ideology and framework that could be defended in a democratic and morally just manner (Özerk, 2016).

As a result of these societal and political reorientations, for the first time in Norwegian history, a committee composed of only Sami educational representatives was appointed by the central authorities to work out NC-87. Four chapters in NC-87 were devoted to the education of Sami children. A considerable part of NC-87 was also translated into Sami. Two of the chapters were devoted to the development of a subject curriculum for the teaching of Sami as a first language and the introduction of a subject curriculum for the teaching of Norwegian as a second language for Sami children. In addition to these chapters and new perspectives, NC-87 presented 'functional bilingualism' as the main aim for the language development of Sami children.

The impact of NC-87 on revitalisation of the Sami language

All these changes signalled that the Norwegian authorities were altering their assimilatory and subtractive bilingualism policy. Equality, equity, language revitalisation and additive bilingualism were now the main pillars for the education of Sami children. Additive bilingualism describes a form of language development in which second language learning does not happen at the expense of the first language (Huss, 1999; Lambert, 1995; Özerk, 2016).

Amendments in the Norwegian constitution and the establishment of the Sami Parliament

During the implementation of NC-87, several significant changes improved the status of the Sami people. A more positive approach by the Norwegian authorities in the 1980s and in the beginning of 1990s culminated in Norway's ratification of ILO Convention No. 169 on Indigenous and Tribal Peoples in 1991, which recognised the Sami people as an indigenous people in Norway. This was actioned through Sami Law No. 56, passed by the Norwegian Parliament in 1987. The law established the *Samediggi* (the Sami Parliament), composed of 39 seats elected by all the Sami people throughout the country. A year later, the Norwegian Parliament amended the constitution by adding 'the Sami paragraph', which states 'It is the State's responsibility to provide the conditions necessary for the Sami people to be able to safeguard and develop their language, culture and livelihood' (Ministry of Justice and Public Security, 2020: §108, translation by Özerk).

In 1989, the first Sami Parliament was elected as a consultative parliament considering Sami-related issues. The Norwegian Parliament passed the Sami Language Act in 1990, which had the practical effect of establishing both Norwegian and Sami as official languages. Further developments occurred on 1 January 1992, when several municipalities were defined as part of the 'Sami language administration area' (SLAA). Sami children who live in these municipalities and have Sami as their first language/mother tongue (L1) receive compulsory L1 Sami teaching.

Also in 1989, Sami University of Applied Sciences was established in one of the core areas of Sápmi, in the municipality of Guovdegeaidnu/Kautokeino. Training Sami teachers for kindergartens and schools was given priority in the first period and the university later expanded its programmes (Keskitalo, 1997).

The national curriculum reform of 1997 (NC-97 and NC-97-S)

The Norwegian Government initiated a new curriculum reform in 1997 (NC-97). With increased devolution of power and responsibility, it was now the Sami Parliament, in consultation with its electorate, who would fashion the new curriculum in close collaboration with the central authorities. Accordingly, a 10-year programme of compulsory education for 6–16-year-old students was instituted and two curriculum documents of equal value were introduced: the national curriculum of 1997 (NC-97) and the national curriculum document for Sami education (NC-97-S).

These two official curriculum documents established an additive bilingual strategy as the guiding principle of a new multicultural and indigenous-rights-oriented language policy in education. The NC-97 reform upheld the principle of 'functional bilingualism' as the aim of Sami children's language development (Özerk, 2016).

In the period when NC-97-S was applied (from school years 1997/1998 to 2005/2006), the number of children who enrolled in Sami L1, Sami L2 and Sami Language and Culture classes increased from 1955 to 3055 (Sami allaskuvla, 2011; Statistisk Sentralbyrå, 2008; Todal, 2011). These numbers show that the NC-97 reform, together with its associated NC-97 and NC-97-S documents, had a significant impact on the interest for and recruitment to Sami teaching. NC-97 curriculum documents were used until the school year 2006/2007.

The curriculum documents of 2006 (NC-06 and NC-06-S)

In 2004, the Norwegian Government initiated a broad process to introduce a new curriculum reform under the name 'Knowledge Promotion'. Again, the Sami people were empowered to draft their own curriculum document 'Sami Knowledge Promotion (NC-06-S)'. Several experienced Sami teachers and educationalists were appointed and participated in the curriculum making process, which took 2 years. For the first time in Norwegian history, a national curriculum now covered both basic education and secondary schools, ranging over a 13-year period of schooling (covering pupils aged 6–19 years). NC-06 and NC-06-S were introduced in the school year 2006/2007. This was a multicultural, multilingual, equity and indigenous-rights-oriented reform (Gjerpe, 2017;

Özerk, 2016). At the same time, the new curriculum reform continued to stress the importance of developing functional bilingualism among children from a Sami background. NC-06-S kept:

(1) Sami as first language and
(2) Sami as second language.

However, the 2006 curriculum document abolished the subject Sami Language and Culture. As a result of the disappearance of this subject in NC-06-S, the number of children who enrolled in Sami classes decreased from 3055 in the school year 2005/2006 to 2116 in the school year 2014/2015. In other words, during this period, 939 fewer children received Sami teaching (Sami allaskuvla, 2016; Todal, 2011, 2013).

Individual rights to receive Sami teaching and distance education

Starting from the school year 2006/2007, neither of the two curriculum documents (NC-06 and NC-06-S) contained the school subject Sami Language and Culture. The decline in the number of children receiving any teaching of Sami was mainly the result of abolishing this subject. However, there were also two other causes that partially explain the decline.

Firstly, several Sami families moved out of the SLAA and into other municipalities where there was a shortage of Sami teachers. The right to receive L1 or L2 Sami teaching thus could not be met. Secondly, in 1992, Sami children gained the right to receive Sami teaching as L1 or L2 outside the SLAA. However, due to a lack of Sami teachers, distance education was implemented as a solution. However, the distance education interventions used different technologies (TV, different portals etc.) and its full implementation was not given enough priority. It was an underperforming educational alternative for many years (Özerk, 2016).

The significant decrease in the number of children receiving Sami L1 or L2 teaching made it necessary for the national educational authorities, in collaboration with Sami educational authorities, to highlight the distance education of Sami children as a priority in 2015/2016. The result was the improvement of this provision and a campaign to heighten awareness by informing local educational authorities and Sami families about the alternative possibilities they had for receiving teaching of Sami as L1 or L2 if they lived outside the SLAA.

This initiative and improvement in distance education resulted in an increased number of Sami children able to receive the teaching of Sami as L1 or L2 via Teams, Zoom etc., overseen by qualified Sami teachers employed by schools within the SLAA. In 2021, the SLAA comprised 13 municipalities out of the country's total of 356 municipalities. In other words, this distance education has a huge geographical area to serve. Figure 2.1 shows the number of students enrolled in Sami classes during the period 1990–2020 and the effects of the different curricular reforms in

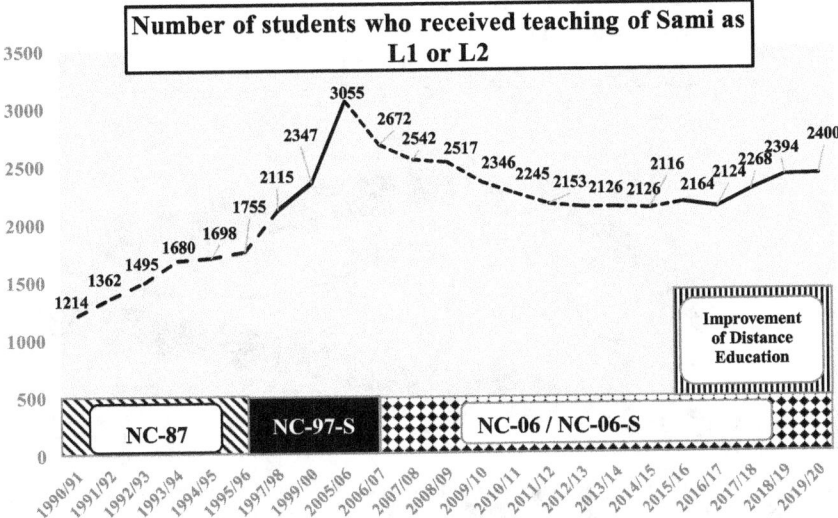

Figure 2.1 Number of students enrolled in Sami classes during the period 1990–2020 and the effects of the different curricular reforms in 1987, 1997 and 2006 and improvement in distance education

1987, 1997 and 2006 and the improvements in distance learning in 2016. It is evident from Figure 2.1 that the improvement in distance education had a positive impact on Sami teaching: the number of Sami students rose by 284, from 2116 in 2016 to 2400 in 2020.

Curriculum reforms and why curriculum documents matter

The increasing and decreasing trends in the number of children who enrolled in Sami language classes in Norway, either as L1 teaching or L2 teaching, during the 30-year period from 1990 to 2020 (Figure 2.1) reveal that the curriculum reforms and the related curriculum documents certainly had an impact. Figure 2.2 shows the overall increase and decrease in the number of Sami children who received Sami language teaching during the 30-year period from 1990 to 2020.

It is evident from Figure 2.2 that NC-87 and NC-97-S had the greatest positive impact on the number of Sami children who received Sami teaching as L1, L2 or Sami Language and Culture. This increasing trend lasted from 1990 to 2006. As already noted, starting from the school year 2006/2007, the new curriculum did not contain the subject Sami Language and Culture. This marked the beginning of a declining trend in the numbers of children receiving Sami teaching. Although the improvement in distance education in 2016 had some positive impact on the number of children who received Sami teaching as L1 or L2, the national curriculum documents of 2006 (NC-06 and NC-06-S) failed to have the same positive

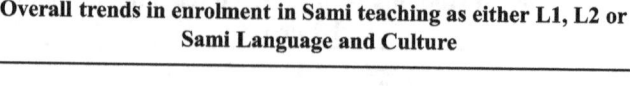

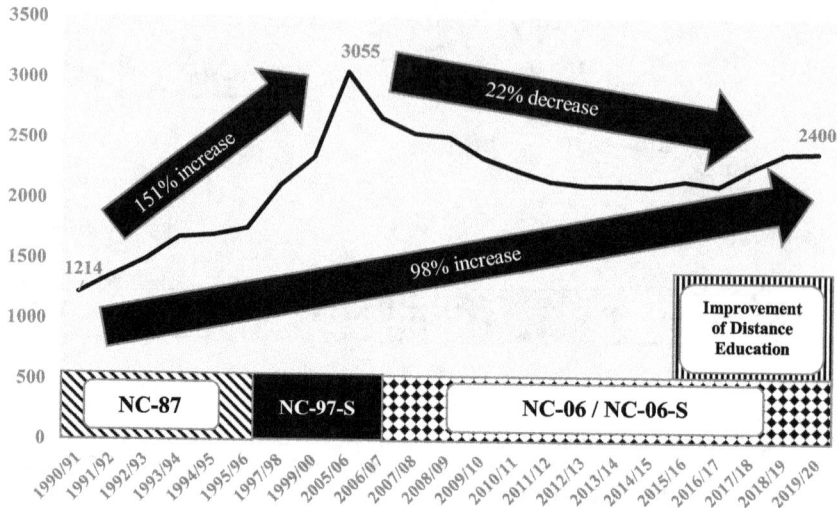

Figure 2.2 Periodic and overall effects of curriculum documents from 1990 to 2020

impact on the number of overall enrolments of Sami children in Sami teaching. During the NC-06 and NC-06-S period, the number of Sami students who received Sami L1 or L2 teaching decreased by 22% compared with the NC-97-S period. However, overall, despite a downward trend since 2006, the number of Sami children with access to any kind of Sami teaching increased by 98% during the period 1990–2020. This can be attributed to the offering of Sami as a separate school subject with its own curriculum and a specified number of teaching hours per week as part of Sami students' comprehensive/compulsory/basic education.

As shown in Figure 2.1, 2400 students were enrolled in Sami teaching in the school year 2019/2020, of which 954 (40%) participated in Sami as L1 classes and 1446 (60%) in Sami as L2 classes (Sami allaskuvla, 2020).

Some of those with Sami as their second language (L2 students) are from Sami–Norwegian bilingual families; the majority are from families in which one or both parents have a Sami background with some skills in Sami. Enrolling in Sami as first language classes (L1 classes) or Sami as second language classes (L2 classes) in compulsory school (ages 6–16) gives children the right to continue to receive L1 or L2 Sami teaching in secondary school. In secondary school, pupils are assessed in Sami as L1 or Sami as L2 and the mark they gain counts when they apply to universities. Both groups are particularly at an advantage if they apply to the Sami University of Applied Sciences, where the medium of instruction is Sami. Another advantage they have is in the job market, particularly in the SLAA where there is huge employment demand for Norwegian–Sami speaking bilinguals. We turn now to some comparative observations from a Welsh perspective.

The Welsh Language in Education: Curriculum Reform and National Strategies

National curriculum reform is a once in a generation phenomenon. That it happens at all within the Welsh-medium education system is a sign of its maturity. The initial start of the system was characterised by slow growth and even slower acceptance and institutionalisation. In the 1950s, there was a limited number of Welsh-medium primary schools, with most located in Anglicised (predominantly English-speaking) areas. There was a limited number of Welsh-medium high schools in the 1960s, all in Anglicised areas. These schools were established as a result of parental pressure and a sympathetic reaction by some in power within local authorities (Thomas & Williams, 2013). Both primary and secondary levels were characterised by strong forms of bilingual education/immersion, but it would become increasingly difficult to define precisely a profile of a Welsh-medium school that was both generic and universally accepted (Williams, 2014).

Having been pioneered by a select number of local authorities, Welsh-medium education was transformed by a major reform that followed the UK's Education Act of 1988. This introduced a national curriculum and changed the relationship between the Department of Education and Science and the local education authorities in England and Wales. In a period of increased centralisation, which saw a diminution in local authorities' discretion to set policy, the establishment of a national curriculum in England and a similar (if separate) one in Wales was a radical departure from previous practice. The one exception in Wales was making a certain amount of Welsh instruction mandatory for all pupils by making it a core subject in the Welsh national curriculum.

Prior to the 1988 reforms, Welsh-medium schools were predominantly an opt-in choice for parents as the default education system was predominantly unilingual English. Within this system, many students were taught a limited amount of Welsh, but 45% of pupils did not receive regular lessons in Welsh (they were pupils in Church schools, both Anglican and Catholic, and those who resided within the Welsh–English border local authority schools) until Welsh was made one of five core subjects in the national curriculum introduced under the Education Reform Act of 1988. This had significant implications for the governance of schools, the preparation of in-service teacher training, the production of appropriate learning resources across a range of school subjects and – most critical of all – a new narrative that sought to convince parents and guardians of both the relevance and the quality of Welsh-medium instruction their children would experience. Thereafter, there was a significant growth in L2 acquisition of Welsh.

The Education Act of 1988

The Education Act of 1988, as applied to Wales, had three significant sociopolitical impacts. Firstly, for the first time in its modern history, the education system introduced a specified amount of Welsh language instruction to all students within the statutory age range. This had the effect of giving – at the very least – an awareness and patina of understanding, if not necessarily fluency to all students, so that the language could be claimed as a public good rather than a minority concern. Secondly, for some students in English-medium education, they could opt to supplement their capacity and interest in Welsh by taking more advanced, demanding qualifications. Thirdly, when such students matriculated and in time became parents, there was a significant increase in the number of children registered in Welsh-medium education coming from mixed-language or predominantly English-speaking households. This accelerated an already long-established pattern of parental choice, which is represented by the lobby group Rhieni Dros Addysg Gymraeg (RhAG, Parents for Welsh-medium Education). RhAG informs, pressurises and evaluates the educational plans of target local authorities so that the needs of Welsh-medium pupils are factored into local and national decision making and policy formulation.

The next 30 years saw a growth in the number of opportunities available to use Welsh within the statutory education system. This was accompanied by a small but incremental growth in the role of Welsh for higher and further education, culminating in the successful Coleg Cymraeg Cenedlaethol (Welsh National College), which works with universities and colleges across Wales to develop Welsh language opportunities. Through this arrangement, the Welsh Government initiative funds Welsh-medium lecturers and offers undergraduate and postgraduate scholarships for students to study higher education courses through the medium of Welsh. In turn, this has accelerated the development of professional cohorts in fields as diverse as science and engineering, health care, pharmacy, optometry, the legal profession and commerce.

Within statutory education, once the new curriculum had been bedded in, a number of concerns were raised about the relative role of Welsh both as a subject and as a medium of instruction. Williams (2010) argued that, despite having a distinct Welsh model of bilingual education, the system was not producing the levels of fluency trumpeted by the national reforms and, in particular, there was a danger of developing a linguistic underclass. The necessary supportive link between the language of home, school, community, media and society was not as robust as anticipated. Policy reforms in both education and official language strategies were in danger of overburdening the education system to deliver and solve linguistic issues (Williams, 2004). More worryingly for policy reformers there was a discrepancy between the institutional perspective and the 'street' perspective on the rights, behaviour and achievements of populations targeted by Welsh language initiatives.

Challenges in developing a bilingual education system

In strict linguistic terms, the increasing diversity of the school cohort background was reflected in issues surrounding linguistic competence and an inconsistent set of skills, especially in writing and the production of material. A more general characteristic was linguistic interference from English in terms of the Welsh 'verb, subject, object' pattern and grammatical rules. Code-switching and the generic capacity to function as equal bilinguals in employment was also an issue because, although spoken Welsh was generally of a good standard, that of written Welsh was less acceptable.

Williams (1995) argued that while current policies were aimed at increasing exposure to various amounts of bilingual education, the anticipated growth in numbers had not automatically translated into the anticipated increased usage of the language. In 1988, Williams raised a conundrum in the title of an inaugural lecture to open the Canolfan Iaith/ Welsh Centre at Bangor University, titled 'Bilingual education in Wales or education for a bilingual Wales?' (Williams, 1988). He argued that it was desirable that the whole education system should be involved in some degree of Welsh-medium instruction if the political goal of forging a bilingual nation was to be advanced. More recently this has become a reality as, in seeking to broaden access to some degree of Welsh language instruction, more and more non-designated bilingual schools have adopted an admixture of teaching both the Welsh language and some subjects through the medium of Welsh, to varying degrees of success (Williams, 2014).

Williams (1988, 2010) also asked that if alternative forms of bilingual education were to be introduced along a continuum, as an admixture of forms of instruction, immersion and exposure to Welsh, could that threaten the integrity of both Welsh-medium schools and Welsh as a first language of instruction? The underlying concerns were twofold. Firstly, in some predominantly rural areas, for reasons of financial pressure, designated Welsh-medium schools might be encouraged to 'merge' or share a site with well-established English-medium schools and, in partial compensation for this rationalisation, the practice of bilingual teaching might be spread more widely in the resultant combined school structure. A second scenario was that, in some areas that did not contain a designated bilingual school, the introduction of a greater amount of Welsh-medium instruction in hitherto English-medium schools, either as streamed classes or through an increased use of translanguaging, might satisfy the requirements of both parents and local authority educational plans. In both scenarios, the spread effect of Welsh would be increased but there was no guarantee that the primacy of Welsh as a first language of instruction would be maintained.

Beyond the nuances of school planning there lies the issue of skill development and the categorisation of whole schools and pupils according to linguistic criteria. The performance of, and division between, L1 and L2 learners has been an abiding concern of practitioners and commentators for some time, so much so that the government announced significant reviews of both the education system writ large and of the role of Welsh within it. An important contribution was 'One language for all: Review of Welsh second language at Key Stages 3 and 4' (Welsh Government, 2013a). The report highlighted a number of issues in Welsh second language provision as follows.

(1) Pupils do not continue to develop their Welsh skills well enough on transition to Key Stages 2 and 3.
(2) The time allocated to teaching the subject is not sufficient; in some schools the allocation is as little as one hour a fortnight.
(3) Many teachers in primary schools lack confidence and ability to teach Welsh as a second language.
(4) Too many pupils who follow the General Certificate of Secondary Education (GCSE) Welsh second language short course are entered for the foundation tier even though they are capable of gaining A*– B grades, which cannot be achieved in the foundation tier.

The report's judgement was that in most schools there are not enough opportunities for pupils to hear and practise using the language beyond formal Welsh lessons and in too many secondary schools the subject is taught by non-specialist teachers who lack a thorough understanding of second language teaching methodology (Welsh Government, 2013a).

The report made a number of recommendations, including the following.

(1) Ensure that Welsh second language continues to be a statutory subject within the national curriculum and continues to be a compulsory subject for all pupils in Wales until the end of Key Stage 4.
(2) The need to embed processes for planning Welsh-medium provision: strengthening strategic planning processes for all phases of education and training should continue to be a priority.
(3) The need for improved workforce planning and support for practitioners: ensuring a sufficient workforce for Welsh-medium education and training is vital.
(4) The need to ensure that young people have the confidence to use their Welsh language skills in all walks of life: education and training alone cannot guarantee that speakers become fluent in Welsh or choose to use the language in their everyday lives.

Welsh was considered within the broader educational framework and was influenced by the Welsh Government's decision to recast its curriculum design following the recommendations of the Donaldson report (Welsh Government, 2015d), which argued that all children and young people will be:

(1) ambitious, capable learners, ready to learn throughout their lives;
(2) enterprising, creative contributors, ready to play a full part in life and work;

(3) ethical, informed citizens of Wales and the world;
(4) healthy, confident individuals, ready to lead fulfilling lives as valued members of society.

It was evident that if the numbers receiving some or all of their education through the medium of Welsh increased, these additional numbers would come from predominantly non-Welsh speaking households and would presumably become new speakers of Welsh. In some European contexts the term 'new speakers' has been adopted as a descriptor for those who are not mother tongue speakers, but who learn and use a language either as a result of formal schooling or as adults. For many, the concept of new speakers is more neutral and less discriminatory than L2, but this is not universally accepted and only a few jurisdictions (e.g. the Basque Autonomous Community, Navarre and Scotland) have made reference to the category within their official documentation (Williams, 2023).

Dilemmas in language education

The structure and nuances of the teaching of Welsh within a variety of educational sectors was revealed by a number of government reports that gave a good overview of the challenges faced by promoting Welsh-medium education. A plethora of reports was published, focusing on Welsh for adults (Welsh Government, 2013b), teacher education (Welsh Government 2014a), Welsh-medium further education (Welsh Government 2014b) and on the teaching of Welsh as a second language (Welsh Government, 2014c). The latter report drew attention to the weaknesses in the manner in which Welsh was taught and advocated abolition of the curriculum and qualification divide between first and second language learners. Drawing on these reports, the Welsh Government announced far-reaching changes to the manner in which Welsh and other languages were to be taught within the statutory education sector as part of a new curriculum for Wales. Education and Skills Minister Kirsty Williams declared:

> We want all our learners to be citizens of both Wales and the world and that means ensuring that all young people from all backgrounds have an opportunity to develop their language skills – whether that's in Welsh, English or international languages. (WalesOnline, 2019)

Consequently, the government devised a new national curriculum launched in two stages: September 2022 for Year 6 and some of Year 7 and September 2023 for Years 7 and 8, which will be rolled out year on year until it includes Year 11 by 2026. In the new curriculum, Welsh will be compulsory for all learners aged 3 to 16 – alongside English – but will be no longer separated into first and second language programmes of study.

All learners will follow the same curriculum and there will be more of an emphasis on improving their skills and use of the language.

> While it would be up to schools to decide how they approach this, they would need to think about opportunities for learners to listen, read, speak and write in Welsh – this might be through use in different parts of the curriculum or outside the classroom. (Welsh Government, 2019)

Four regional school improvement consortia across Wales are currently planning ways to ensure teachers can deliver the agreed changes through professional learning, including the augmentation of a sabbatical scheme of intensive Welsh language training to teachers and teaching assistants. So, a continuum, a sliding scale of performance and assessment and a recasting of the primacy of teaching Welsh as a first language are the elements of the new approach to promoting Welsh within the statutory education system. This reform has sparked some controversy by both supporters and detractors of Welsh, as now discussed.

The reform raises the question as to what descriptor will be used for those significant many who do not become 'full new speakers' of Welsh despite increased exposure to formal instruction in and through the language. Are they to be referred to as Welsh speakers, L2 students or advanced learners? These are important questions, not only for teachers and school managers, but also for curriculum designers, assessors, students and their families. It is probable that this category of student will grow as a proportion of all students and speakers because the conventional L1 category appears not to be growing within a fairly stable system. Recent data suggest that the numbers of Welsh-medium schools and pupils has not grown substantially and indeed, within several local authorities, there are certain schools that have considerable empty additional places despite the careful planning outlined in the statutory Welsh in Education Strategic Plans (WESPs) framework. The School Standards and Organisation (Wales) Act 2013 placed a duty on all local authorities in Wales to consult on, produce and review plans that provide the strategic direction for the planning and delivery of Welsh-medium and Welsh language education in their locality. While this obligation has made the responsibilities, provision and direction of local education policy more transparent and consistent, it has also called into question the episodic and epiphenomenal pattern of Welsh-medium demand. A particular difficulty is succession: as Table 2.2 reveals, there remains a structural difficulty with succession as twice as many pupils are registered in primary schools than in secondary schools (Stats Wales, 2021). Were this succession rate to be improved significantly then the investment in skills and confidence imparted by the primary school experience would strengthen the progressive development of more students and could, in adulthood, lead to a greater use of Welsh in socioeconomic domains.

Table 2.2 Schools where Welsh is the sole or main medium of instruction 2020/2021[b]

School level	Number of schools	Number of pupils
Primary	404	60,770
Middle	8	7,905
High	47	22,715
Total	459	89,390

[b]Stats Wales (2021)

Different categories of bilingual schools

As a category, bilingual schools may be divided into four sub-divisions according to the percentage of subjects taught through the medium of Welsh and whether there is parallel provision in English.

(1) In Type A schools, at least 80% of subjects (apart from Welsh and English) are taught only through the medium of Welsh to all pupils. One or two subjects are taught to some pupils in English or in both languages.
(2) In Type B schools, at least 80% of subjects (excluding Welsh and English) are taught through the medium of Welsh and are also taught through the medium of English.
(3) In Type C schools, 50–79% of subjects (excluding Welsh and English) are taught through the medium of Welsh and also through the medium of English.
(4) In Type D schools, all subjects (except Welsh and English) are taught to all pupils using both languages.

Clearly, with such a variety in actual practice, there is a need for a more robust definition of what counts as a Welsh-medium school or a bilingual school and the government is seeking to generalise or standardise the type of education received within this broad sectoral category.

Currently there is an ongoing debate on the adequacy of curriculum development, the sufficiency of teacher training, the role of Welsh as a subject and Welsh as a medium of teaching. In broader terms there is debate on the whole issue of second language acquisition and a separate, but equally pressing, issue regarding the attitude of some who demonstrate resistance to bilingualism and express fears and suspicions of the bilingual agenda. Part of this has to do with identity politics and part with a perception that too much attention has been focused on the Welsh language of late, which threatens to increase the distinctiveness of Wales within the UK. This is a long-standing issue, as evidenced in other jurisdictions such as Ireland and the Basque Country, and has little to do with the recent Brexit divisions in the UK.

Both government spokespeople and specialists acknowledge that, despite spectacular growth, as evidenced by Thomas and Williams (2013), there are weaknesses in bilingual education provision. The most salient are:

(1) the inconsistency in the nature of the educational experience provided;
(2) the confusion elicited by the four identifiable 'types' of bilingual schools;
(3) the poor succession rates at each stage in education, primary (26%) secondary (17%) tertiary (4%);
(4) the general perception that there is too much fragmentation in the sector.

It may be asked that, if these are generally well-understood structural weaknesses, why have they not been addressed until now?

Part of the answer pertains to the issue of where power lies in the system. The Department for Education and Skills and the Minister have a crucial role to play, but the relationship with local authorities is often tense when it comes to sanctioning or disallowing the establishment of Welsh-medium schools. There have been struggles surrounding school reorganisation in several areas of Wales in the recent past, such as in Cardiff (Morgan, 2013) Caerphilly, Carmarthenshire and Sandfields in Neath[CW5] Port Talbot. Until its abolition in 2012, the Welsh Language Board had a statutory duty to provide strategic oversight of this sector, but in truth it had little real power to direct. Direct oversight now rests with the Welsh Government, which has devised a system of Welsh in Education Strategic Plans (WESPs) to regulate provision and has made important contributions to improvements within the sector. In April 2010, the Welsh-medium Education Strategy (WMES) (Welsh Government, 2010) was made a duty under the School Standards and Organisation (Wales) Act 2013. The strategy sets out six strategic aims and a number of objectives within them.

(1) To improve the planning of Welsh-medium provision in the pre-statutory and statutory phases of education, based on informed parental demand.
(2) To improve the planning of Welsh-medium provision in the post-14 phases of education and training, taking account of linguistic progression and continuing development of skills.
(3) To ensure that all learners develop their Welsh language skills to their full potential, and encourage sound linguistic progression from one phase of education and training to the next.
(4) To ensure a Welsh-medium education workforce that provides sufficient numbers of practitioners for all phases of education and training, with high-quality Welsh language skills and competence in teaching methodologies.
(5) To improve the central support mechanisms for Welsh-medium education and training.
(6) To contribute to the acquisition and reinforcement of Welsh language skills in families and in the community.

The current policy details of the government's aims for this sector are set out in the Welsh in Education Action Plan, 2017–2021 (Welsh Government, 2017a), which states the following:

(1) It is the Welsh Government's policy that all pupils should study Welsh from ages 3–16, either first or second language.
(2) Approximately 16% of pupils attend Welsh-medium schools and study Welsh as a first language. A further 10% attend bilingual, dual-medium or English with significant Welsh provision.
(3) Welsh Government statistics show that, in 2014, 22.2% of 7-year-old learners were assessed through the medium of Welsh first language and 17.1% of 14-year-olds were assessed in Welsh first language.

Several specific educational reforms, when combined with other significant legislative acts, will doubtless help shape the role and expectations of Welsh within national life. The six significant policy innovations are:

(1) A Curriculum for Wales: A Curriculum for Life 2015 (Welsh Government, 2015a).
(2) New Deal for Education Workforce, 2015 (Welsh Government, 2015b).
(3) Welsh-medium Education Strategy, 2016 (Welsh Government, 2016c).
(4) Future Generations Well Being Act, 2015 (Welsh Government, 2015c).
(5) Successful Futures, 2016 (Welsh Government, 2016d).
(6) Cymraeg 2050: A Million Welsh Speakers (Welsh Government, 2016e).

In addition, innovative strategies and acts, when combined, have offered a more robust framework for the promotion and regulation of Welsh, namely:

(1) Taking Wales Forward 2016–2021, 2016 (Welsh Government, 2016f).
(2) A living language: a language for living – Welsh Language Strategy 2012–17, 2012 (Welsh Government, 2012).
(3) A living language: a language for living – Moving forward, 2014 (Welsh Government, 2014e).
(4) Welsh Language (Wales) Measure, 2011 (Welsh Government, 2011).
(5) Welsh-medium Education Strategy (Welsh Government, 2010).

Of these, the Future Generations Well Being Act 2015 and Cymraeg 2050: A Million Welsh Speakers are hugely significant as they set the strategic framework and are sufficiently flexible to enable future policy reforms to be dovetailed into a strong, mainstreamed approach to shaping the contours of society with all the resonance that promoting Welsh within an increasingly multicultural context can sustain.

A further difficulty in implementing the goals of official language strategies such as *Iaith Pawb* (Everyone's Language) (Welsh Government, 2003, 2005) and *Iaith Fyw: Iaith Byw* (A Living Language: A Language for Living) (Welsh Government, 2012) was that these strategies depended heavily on the full mobilisation of the education system to deliver their aims. Difficulties in implementation were predictable. Both language and education strategies ran in parallel, but the Welsh language oversight agency could not necessarily influence the Government's Education Department to dovetail its priorities and resources so as to achieve the goals of the language strategies. The lesson, of course, is that appeals to holistic and integrated planning are fine in the abstract, but often fall foul of the realpolitik of inter-departmental power struggles and the competitive nature of the allocation of public resources.

The new curriculum for Wales

In general, the education system places a great deal of emphasis on formal assessment and some, such as Sinnema *et al.* (2020), aver that this has an impact on pedagogy. A new curriculum for Wales was unveiled in 2021, to be inaugurated in September 2022. It is the first complete reform of the statutory education system in 30 years. Six areas of learning and experience have been identified, namely (1) expressive arts, (2) humanities, (3) health and wellbeing, (4) science and technology, (5) maths and numeracy, (6) languages, literacy and communication. A late addition to the details was the insistence that lifesaving skills and first aid be taught. The broad outline is as follows (The School Run, 2022).

(1) Expressive arts, incorporating art, dance, drama, film and digital media, and music. It will encourage creativity and critical thinking and include performance.
(2) Humanities, incorporating geography, history, religious education, business studies and social studies. It will be based on human experiences and will also cover Welsh culture.
(3) Health and wellbeing, covering the physical, psychological, emotional and social aspects of life, helping students make informed decisions about their health and wellbeing and learn how to manage social influences. It will include physical education.
(4) Science and technology, incorporating biology, chemistry, physics, computer science, and design and technology.
(5) Mathematics and numeracy: in the early years, this will involve learning through play. In later stages, it will include working both independently and collaboratively with others.
(6) Languages, literacy and communication: this will include Welsh and English, literature and international languages. Welsh language teaching will still be compulsory (as an additional language for children who don't use Welsh as their first language).

In addition, literacy, numeracy and digital skills will be embedded throughout all curriculum areas.

Given growing concerns with economic and racial disparities in the UK, made more acute by heightened awareness of the issue of slavery and exploitation during British imperialism and the reaction of various groups to the Covid-19 pandemic, it will be mandatory for the histories of Black, Asian and other Minority Ethnic communities to be taught. For non-curriculum areas, thematic topics will also be addressed in relation to relationships and sexuality education together with religious education. Accordingly, the curriculum aims to produce individuals who are (a) ambitious, capable learners, (b) healthy, confident individuals, (c) enterprising, creative contributors and (d) ethical, informed citizens.

On 14 October 2021 it was announced that English language and English Literature GCSEs would be combined into one qualification, while new GCSEs in Engineering and Manufacturing and Film and Digital Media will be taught from 2025 (BBC Wales News, 2021a). However, such was the uncertainty surrounding the Welsh language qualification that a final decision was postponed. One of the controversial issues was the proposal to abolish the distinction between Welsh L1 and L2 levels and create a single standard of attainment, a continuum reflecting varying skills. Critics have argued that this would weaken the salience of Welsh as a mother tongue qualification and lead to a dumbing down of the language standards. Lest this seem like an attack on Welsh, it should be noted that, from 2025, physics, chemistry and biology will no longer be offered as individual subjects. Rather, pupils will study for one integrated science award that combines the three subjects and will be worth two GCSEs – a decision that has also led to fears of dumbing down (BBC Wales News, 2021b).

The limited evidence we have to date suggests that there is a disconnect between Welsh L2 instruction and its use in normal life outside the classroom setting.

A recent detailed investigation (Rhys & Smith, 2022) has suggested that, despite L2 students asserting that their Welsh language acquisition was a benefit in both cultural and socioeconomic terms, there is some disquiet surrounding the recurring theme of the compulsory status of Welsh within the curriculum, the lack of speaking opportunities within classroom lessons and, most poignantly of all, teaching for a test. As one respondent remarked 'There's no point to take Welsh lesson to just pass exams. Having a GCSE in Welsh might help me get a job, but it won't help me speak Welsh while doing it' (Rhys & Smith, 2022: 18). This student is merely reflecting what formal assessments by Estyn (the education and training inspectorate for Wales) have reported (Estyn, 2018) in that not enough students use the language in their lessons and this has an impact on the number of students entered for formal GCSE examination in that subject. The key to improving this situation, according to Rhys and Smith (2022), is to improve the teaching methods on L2 learning so that not only are current students taught more effectively but that future generations will be able to benefit from an improved teacher training regime and resource development so as to contribute to the government's strategy of making Welsh a more vibrant language, spoken by at least a million by 2050.

The implication of abolishing the formal distinction between L1 and L2 learners is likely to create a space (read vacuum) for a new descriptor of non-native speakers and it is thus likely that a set of descriptors analogous to the new speaker's paradigm will be coined for this phenomenon. But in truth, how sustainable is the idea of a continuum and with what effect for the teaching of Welsh as a first language? Some critics argue that the reforms leave much to be desired and Brooks (2019) has pointed to the fact that:

> A 'language continuum' will destroy the principle of Welsh-medium education, replacing it with an emphasis on 'bilingual' schools. English of course will remain a proper language, taught not on a continuum but as a first language. Welsh instead becomes a second language for all. It a nonsense that children who cannot hold a conversation in a language be on a continuum with those who speak Welsh as a first language all day, every day. This is a damaging idea which will harm the education of children all over Wales.

Recently, the new speaker paradigm has promised a way of easing this tension and providing a new social category of competent speakers who are not mother tongue Welsh, but rather have learned the language either through the education system or as a result of social immersion (O'Rourke & Pujolar, 2019). The difficulty is that there is no universal definition of who qualifies as a new speaker and as a consequence it is that much harder for decision makers to target their needs in a structured manner. Accordingly, there is no certainty among policy makers how this new speaker concept will be operationalised.

Cymraeg 2050: A million Welsh speakers

Clearly the statutory education system is the single most important instrument for Welsh language reproduction. It is anticipated that the new curriculum will go a long way towards fulfilling the flagship government policy of securing a million Welsh speakers by 2050, up from a total of 575,000 out of a total population of 3.168 million in 2016 when the strategy was announced (Welsh Government, 2016b).

Section 78(1) of the Government of Wales Act 2006 requires Welsh Ministers to adopt a strategy stating how they propose to promote and facilitate the use of the Welsh language. Section 78(4) requires Welsh Ministers to keep the strategy under review and enables them to adopt a new strategy. The Welsh Government's policy community was preparing a new strategy to replace *Iaith Fyw: Iaith Byw*, which ended in March 2017. Relying on the background research and evidence-based policy reports that had been fed into the language production and reproduction targets, commentators presumed that the total population of Welsh speakers would reach about 750,000 within two generations.

However, on 1 August 2016, at the National Eisteddfod, the First Minister, Carwyn Jones, declared that the ambition of the new policy would be the creation of a million speakers by 2050 (BBC News, 2016). This changed the whole dynamic of the situation and required policy formulators to rethink their strategy to deliver this declared aim. An executive summary for the revised strategy was prepared for public consultation during the Autumn of 2016. It declared that, in order to reach the target there was a need for:

> ... more children in Welsh-medium education, better planning in relation to how people learn the language, more easy-to-access opportunities for people to use the language, a stronger infrastructure and a revolution to improve digital provision in Welsh, and a sea change in the way we speak about it. (Welsh Government, 2016b)

Six key areas for action were identified, namely:

(1) planning and language policy;
(2) normalisation;
(3) education;
(4) language transmission in the family and workplace;
(5) a supportive infrastructure and improved legislation;
(6) stronger language rights.

The government proposals offer clear objectives for each of these action areas and are supplemented by detailed short-, medium- and long-term recommendations. The key requirement is how best to mainstream the language and Williams (2017) argued that, in order for Welsh to be an integral part of strategic planning at every level, a more robust discourse and consistent time-series data collection and analysis were needed. The creation of new speakers is best achieved through the education system; consequently, investment in a proficient workforce means planning to support the training of teachers and learning assistants, expanding sabbatical schemes and significantly increasing the number and proficiency of workers in the childcare and early years sectors. The fundamental new reality acknowledged in government discourse here is the recognition that the tendency of language attrition within the education system needs to be replaced by a guaranteed linguistic progression and is supplemented by a commitment to maintain a continuum of access and skills development for the workplace.

Following consultation and reflection, the revised strategy reduced the six priority areas to three strategic themes: (1) increasing the number of Welsh speakers; (2) increasing the use of Welsh; (3) creating favourable conditions (infrastructure and context). The underlying message of the

Cymraeg 2050 strategy is to normalise the use of Welsh and the strategic document is replete with well-articulated interventions and proposed actions together with a description on how the success of these reforms is to be measured (Welsh Government, 2017b, 2017c).

Williams (2017) reviewed this policy and argued that the target and its implementation programme are best seen as the latest initiatives that – if they gather momentum and attract the necessary resources – could well bolster the vitality of Welsh. Williams focused on how feasible was the target of achieving 1 million Welsh speakers by 2050 and what challenges were being laid before the door of the education system at large to produce these new speakers. Williams suggested that to realise these policy goals, the education system would need to invest in the required number of new Welsh-medium teachers, open new bilingual or Welsh-medium schools, establish a greater number of dual language schools, embed more effective Welsh-medium teaching in hitherto English schools and support the work of further education and higher education institutions in staff skills development and in curricula design so as to create the effective bilingual workforce lauded in the strategy.

It is anticipated that the new curriculum will contribute to a growth in numbers and the conditions to generate a larger proportion of new speakers who will go on to use Welsh on a regular basis.

Clearly, it is too early to tell whether or not investment will be forthcoming to support the necessary infrastructure developments. However, two early features are promising. The first is the general reaction of agencies and organisations to the broad parameters of the 2050 strategy. They have bought in to the reforms, for both ideological and self-interested reasons, as they are largely dependent on government financial and political support for their legitimacy and maintenance. The second is that, at the heart of the government's Welsh Language Unit, there is now a dedicated team of language policy experts whose evidence-based reforms and adoption of hitherto underemphasised features (such as IT, nudge theory and behavioural language planning) auger well for the implementation of the strategy. Above all, it is the discourse surrounding future Welsh vitality that has engendered a far more positive approach to a holistic language policy and its implementation – at least within official circles.

Conclusion

The case of the Sami demonstrates the impact of curriculum reform on language vitalisation and revitalisation. Radical changes in the emphases and priorities of curriculum reforms and formal curriculum documents have made a significant difference to the official standing of Sami education within the country as curriculum documents now have legal status in the Norwegian system. Local educational authorities must operationalise them as it is a statutory requirement. Accordingly, national curriculum documents have a significant influence on the availability of Sami teaching and the recruitment of indigenous children to receive teaching in and through Sami, either as L1, L2 or in Sami Language and Culture classes. However, we recognise that the abolition of Sami Language and Culture as a school subject in the 2006 reforms had a significant negative impact on the number of children receiving Sami teaching.

In the case of Wales, the two curriculum reforms of the 1980s and that of 2022/2023 reflect not only pedagogical advances, but also social concerns regarding features such as preparing for a more deeply entrenched digital economy, a consideration of the relationship between language revitalisation and socio economic development (Welsh Government 2014d), a greater awareness of multicultural heritage and the lived reality of the nation, and a concern for revitalising the Welsh language by teaching it, at varying levels, to the entire school-age population.

Three things may be gleaned from this comparative analysis.

First, it is parents who are the driving force of mother tongue or L2 demands within an evolving school system that for too long has ignored or undervalued the richness of indigenous languages.

Second, once the state or the local state has recognised the permanent needs and interests of a minority, serving those interests becomes a matter of national responsibility. It follows from this that government policies, the allocation of public monies and the development of an alternative educational experience within the same state-wide educational framework change the relationship between the citizen and the host state. This is best seen when the state gradually transfers some responsibilities for decision making to the indigenous resident population or its representatives. Empowering teachers and educational specialists to engage with curriculum design and reform is an important step, but the larger questions of teacher training, capacity building, infrastructure support, material and resource development, AI and IT developments are matters of 'national' political decision making and the allocation of expenditure to serve the minority's educational sector. Consequently, the establishment of the Welsh Senedd and the Sami Parliament both represent major constitutional developments in the democratisation of minority education, its legitimisation and the allocation of resources to fund it.

Third is the ideological basis of the supportive narrative for minority language education. Justifications for maintenance and arguments on behalf of minority language issues have moved gradually from a concern with unique restitution-type discourses to those that now emphasise the inclusive, multicultural element of mainstreaming such issues as a matter of national, not sectoral, responsibility. Not only does this invoke a majoritarian involvement and co-responsibility, it also redefines resource development and expenditure as a matter of public good.

We have seen that, for both Sami and Welsh, national curriculum reforms have gradually eroded the monolingual monopoly of state education and allowed some degree of divergence; although it does not go far enough, it is an improvement on previous dispensations. Clearly there will remain a profound political element of debate and dissent, as is to be expected in advanced democracies, but many language minorities are now characterised as permanent, not epiphenomenal, policy concerns in the national agenda and consequently share a more equitable basis for future planning, innovation and intervention than was true in times past.

Recognising that Sami and Welsh speakers are at opposite ends of a minority language spectrum, notwithstanding some similar elements identified herein, we argue that they both reflect a common struggle to defend, promote and develop a variant of the theme of a common humanity, involving mutual respect and dignity. The professionalisation of the various issues subsumed within national curriculum reforms should not detract from the basic truth that it is community pressure which animates the drive for indigenous and minority language survival. Yet this drive needs to be articulated through realisable aims that seek to engage the majority and the state in constructing the conditions of possibility for incremental reform, else the energy becomes dissipated and the ambition is dashed – an all-too-common experience for supplicant peoples rather than empowered citizens.

References

BBC News (2016) Welsh language target of one million speakers by 2050. See https://www.bbc.co.uk/news/uk-wales-politics-36924562

BBC Wales News (2021a) GCSEs: New subjects launched as part of overhaul in Wales. See https://www.bbc.co.uk/news/uk-wales-58898196

BBC Wales News (2021b) Wales curriculum: New science GCSE prompts dumbing down fears. See https://www.bbc.co.uk/news/uk-wales-58967630

Brooks, S. (2019) Twitter feed @Seimonbrooks (accessed 4/2/2019).

Estyn (2018) *The Annual Report of Her Majesty's Chief Inspector of Education and Training in Wales, 2017–2018*. Cardiff: Estyn, Welsh Government.

Gaski, H. (1997) Introduction. In H. Gaski (ed.) *Sami Culture in a New Era* (pp. 9–28). Karasjok: Davvi Girji OS.

Gjerpe, K.K. (2017) Samisk læreplanverk – en symbolsk forpliktelse? En begrepsanalyse av det samiske innholdet i Læreplanverket Kunnskapsløftet og Kunnskapsløftet Samisk. *Nordic Studies in Education* 37, 150–165.

Huss, L. (1999) *Reversing Language Shift in the Far North*. Uppsala: Acta Universitatis Upsaliensis. Studia Uralica Upsaliensia.

Jones, M.L.N. (2013) Parental power. In H.S. Thomas and C.H. Williams (eds) *Parents, Personalities and Power* (pp. 209–229). Cardiff: University of Wales Press.

Karlstad, J.K.H. (1997) Aspects of managing renewable resources in Sami areas in Norway. In H. Gaski (ed.) *Sami Culture in a New Era* (pp. 109–126). Karasjohka: Davvi Girji OS.

Keskitalo, J.H. (1997) Sami post-secondary education – Ideals and realities. In H. Gaski (ed.) *Sami Culture in a New Era* (pp. 155–171). Karasjohka: Davvi Girji OS.

Lambert, W.E. (1995) Measurement of the linguistic dominance of bilinguals. *Journal of Abnormal Psychology* 50 (2), 197–200.

McAllister, L. (2001) *Plaid Cymru: The Emergence of a Political Party*. Bridgend: Seren.

Ministry of Justice and Public Security (2020) *The Constitution of the Kingdom of Norway (2020)*. Oslo: Ministry of Justice and Public Security.
Morgan, Rh. (2013) School reorganisation: A lesson in how not to do it. The case of Canton, Cardiff West. In H.S. Thomas and C.H. Williams (eds) *Parents, Personalities and Power* (pp. 242–252). Cardiff: University of Wales Press.
O'Rourke, B. and Pujolar, J. (eds) (2019) From new speaker to speaker. Castell Newydd Emlyn: IAITH. See https://www.nspk.org.uk/images/iaith_digital.pdf
Philips, D. (1998) *Trwy Ddulliau Chwyldro: Hanes Cymdeithas yr Iaith, 1962–92*. Llandysul: Gwasg Gomer.
Rhys, M. and Smith, K. (2022) 'Everything we do revolves around the exam': What are secondary school students' perceptions and experiences of learning Welsh as a second language in Wales? *Wales Journal of Education* 24 (1), 3–30.
Sami allaskuvla (2011) *Samisk Statistikk*. Kautokeino: Sami allaskuvla.
Sami allaskuvla (2016) *Samisk Statistikk*. Kautokeino: Sami allaskuvla.
Sami allaskuvla (2020) *Samiske tall forteller*. Kautokeino: Sami allaskuvla.
Sinnema, C., Nieveen, N. and Priestley, M. (2020) Successful futures, successful curriculum: What can Wales learn from international curriculum reforms? *The Curriculum Journal* 31 (2), 181–201.
Solbakk, J.T. (1997) Sami mass media – Their role in a minority society. In H. Gaski (ed.) *Sami Culture in a New Era* (pp. 172–198). Karasjohka: Davvi Girji OS.
Statistisk Sentralbyrå (2008) *Samisk Statistikk*. Oslo: SBB.
Stats Wales (2021) *Schools by Local Authority, Region and Welsh Medium Type*. Cardiff: Welsh Government.
The School Run (2022) The curriculum for Wales 2022: What parents need to know. See https://www.theschoolrun.com/curriculum-for-wales
Thomas, H.S. and Williams, C.H. (2013) (eds) *Parents, Personalities and Power*. Cardiff: University of Wales Press.
Todal, J. (2011) Alvorleg nedgang for faget samisk som andrespråk. In *Samiske tall forteller 4. Kommentert statistikk 2011*. Kautokeino: Samisk høgskole.
Todal, J. (2013) Kvantitative endringar i den samiske språksituasjonen i Noreg. In *Samiske tall forteller 6*. Kautokeino: Sámi allaskuvla.
WalesOnline (2019) *The subject of second-language Welsh is being abolished in schools in Wales*. See https://www.walesonline.co.uk/news/education/subject-second-language-welsh-being-15693728
Welsh Government (2003) *Iaith Pawb: A national action plan for a bilingual Wales*. Cardiff: Welsh Government. See http://gov.wales/depc/publications/welshlanguage/iaithpawb/iaithpawbe.pdf?lang=en
Welsh Government (2005) *Iaith Pawb and Welsh language scheme annual report 2004–05*. Cardiff: Welsh Government. See http://gov.wales/topics/welshlanguage/publications/iaithpawb/?lang=en
Welsh Government (2010) *The Welsh-medium Education Strategy (WMES)*. Cardiff: Welsh Government.
Welsh Government (2011) *Welsh Language (Wales) Measure 2011*. Cardiff: Welsh Government.
Welsh Government (2012) *Iaith Fyw: Iaith Byw. A living language: A language for living*. Cardiff: Welsh Government. See http://gov.wales/docs/dcells/publications/122902wls201217en.pdf
Welsh Government (2013a) *One language for all: Review of Welsh second language at Key Stages 3 and 4*. Cardiff: Welsh Government. See http://gov.wales/docs/dcells/publications/130926-review-of-welsh-second-lan-en.pdf
Welsh Government (2013b) *Raising our sights: Review of Welsh for adults*. Cardiff: Welsh Government. See http://dera.ioe.ac.uk/18053/1/130712-review-welsh-for-adults-en.pdf

Welsh Government (2014a) *Teaching Tomorrow's Teachers: Final Report Prepared by Prof. J. Furlong*. Cardiff: Welsh Government.
Welsh Government (2014b) *Evaluation of the Welsh-medium education strategy: A study of the work of the bilingual champions in further education*. Cardiff: Welsh Government. See http://gov.wales/docs/caecd/research/2014/140925-welsh-medium-education-strategy-bilingual-champions-en.pdf
Welsh Government (2014c) *Review of Welsh second language at Key Stages 3 and 4: final report of task group chaired by Prof. S. Davies*. Cardiff: Welsh Government. See https://beta.gov.wales/review-welsh-second-language-key-stages-3-and-4-final-report
Welsh Government (2014d) *Welsh language and economic development task and Finish group*. Cardiff: Welsh Government. See http://gov.wales/docs/det/publications/140130-wled-report-en.pdf
Welsh Government (2014e) *A Living Language: A Language for Living – Moving Forward*. Cardiff: Welsh Government).
Welsh Government (2015a) *A Curriculum for Wales: A Curriculum for Life 2015*. Cardiff: Welsh Government.
Welsh Government (2015b) *New Deal for Education Workforce, 2015*. Cardiff: Welsh Government.
Welsh Government (2015c) *Future Generations Well Being Act, 2015*; Cardiff: Welsh Government.
Welsh Government (2015d) *Successful Futures. The Donaldson Report*. Cardiff: Welsh Government.
Welsh Government (2016a) *Consultation on a Welsh Government draft strategy: A million Welsh speakers by 2050*. Cardiff: Welsh Government. See https://consultations.gov.wales/sites/default/files/consultation_doc_files/160729-consultation-doc-en.pdf
Welsh Government (2016b) *Cymraeg 2050: A million Welsh speakers*. Cardiff: Welsh Government. See http://www.assembly.wales/laid%20documents/gen-ld11108/gen-ld11108-e.pdf
Welsh Government (2016c) *Welsh-medium Education Strategy*. Cardiff: Welsh Government.
Welsh Government (2016d) *Successful Futures, 2016*. Cardiff: Welsh Government.
Welsh Government (2016e) *Cymraeg 2050: A Million Welsh Speakers*. Cardiff: Welsh Government.
Welsh Government (2016f) *Taking Wales Forward 2016–2021*. Cardiff: Welsh Government.
Welsh Government (2017a) *Welsh in education action plan, 2017–2021*. Cardiff: Welsh Government. See https://beta.gov.wales/welsh-education-action-plan-2017-2021
Welsh Government (2017b) *Preparing for a Welsh Language Bill, Written Statement by the Welsh Government, 31 January*. Cardiff: Welsh Government.
Welsh Government (2017c) *Cymraeg 2050: A million Welsh speakers*. Cardiff: Welsh Government. See https://gov.wales/sites/default/files/publications/2018-12/cymraeg-2050-welsh-language-strategy.pdf
Welsh Government (2019) *Learners to experience new languages at an earlier age – Kirsty Williams*. Cardiff: Welsh Government. See https://gov.wales/learners-experience-new-languages-earlier-age-kirsty-williams
Williams, C.H. (1988) Addysg Ddwyieithog yng Nghymru Ynteu Addysg ar Gyfer Cymru Ddwyieithog? Bilingual education in Wales or education for a bilingual Wales? *Canolfan Astudiaethau Iaith* 1, 1–28.
Williams, C.H. (1995) Questions concerning the development of bilingual Wales. In R. Morris Jones and P.A.S. Ghuman (eds) *Bilingualism, Education and Identity. Festschrift for Jac L. Williams* (pp. 47–78). Cardiff: The University of Wales Press.
Williams, C.H. (2004) Iaith Pawb: The doctrine of plenary inclusion. *Contemporary Wales* 17, 1–27.

Williams, C.H. (2010) From act to action in Wales. In D. Morris (ed.) *Welsh in the Twenty-First Century* (pp. 36–60). Cardiff: University of Wales Press.

Williams, C.H. (2014) The lightening veil: Language revitalization in Wales. *AREA, Review of Education* 38 (1), 242–272.

Williams, C.H. (2017) Wake me up in 2050. The formulation of language policy in Wales. *Journal of Languages Society and Policy*, 1–7.

Williams, C.H. (2023) *Language Policy and the New Speaker Challenge*. Cambridge: Cambridge University Press.

Özerk, K. (2006a) *Tospråklig opplæring – Utdanningspolitiske og pedagogiske perspektiver*. Vallset: Oplandske Bokforlag.

Özerk, K. (2006b) *Opplæringsteori og læreplanforståelse*. Vallset: Oplandske Bokforlag.

Özerk, K. (2009) The revitalisation of a threatened indigenous language. The case of the Sami people in Norway. In P.A. Danaher, M. Kenny and J.R. Leder (eds) *Traveller, Nomadic and Migrant Education* (pp. 132–144). New York: Routledge.

Özerk, K. (2016) *Tospråklig Oppvekst og Læring*. Oslo: Cappelen Damm Akademisk.

3 Languaging and Language Policies among Multilingual Children and Youth Groups in Finland and Denmark

Anna Slotte, Janus Spindler Møller and Tuuli From

This chapter looks at pupils' languaging and negotiation of language policies in the context of institutional education in Finland and Denmark. The school system in Finland is divided into two monolingual strands as per the two national languages, Finnish and Swedish, whereas Denmark has a monolingual policy promoting standard Danish in schools. Our theoretical perspective is informed by Spolsky's (2004) notion of language policies consisting of the interrelated dimensions of macro-level language management, language ideologies and micro-level language practices. We analyse interviews with pupils in a Finnish-medium school and a Swedish-medium school, video recordings from bilingual workshops in Finland and group conversations with pupils with diverse linguistic backgrounds in Denmark. The results show how the language management policies and monolingual normativity ascribe language-based identities to pupils, shape their ideas of appropriate language practices and determine the value of bilingualism in both contexts.

Introduction

The aim of this chapter is to contribute to the understanding of language policies in institutional education from the perspective of children and youth, informed by Spolsky's (2004) popular classification of language policies consisting of language management, ideologies and practices. Finland is a bilingual country with two official national languages, Finnish and Swedish. Of the whole population, 87.3% have registered Finnish as their first language, whereas 5.2% have registered Swedish (Statistics Finland, 2020). The official language statistics in Finland do not recognise individual multilingualism. To provide equal rights for speakers of both national languages, comprehensive education is organised separately in two monolingual Finnish- and Swedish-medium strands (Basic Education Act 628/1998, 1998). Encounters between Finnish and Swedish speakers in institutional education are thus limited because schools for both language groups (later referred to as bilingual schools) do not exist and only a small proportion of Finnish- and Swedish-medium schools are located in shared facilities, which can be understood as a way to safeguard the right to education in both national languages (e.g. From & Sahlström, 2017; Sahlström *et al.*, 2013).

Different to Finland, Denmark only has one official language, Danish, meaning that Danish is dominant in public sectors. The educational system favours a monolingual regime of (standard) Danish (Karrebæk, 2013) and, in line with this, the use of Danish in the school system is treated as a truism in the national curriculum at the expense of linguistic diversity (Kristjánsdóttir, 2018; Salö *et al.*, 2018). However, a large proportion of the population in Denmark does not have Danish as their first language. As a result of waves of migration from the 1960s onwards, 14% of the population constitute immigrants and their descendants (Danmarks Statistik, 2020).

We pose the following research question: how do children and youth negotiate language policies in multilingual contexts in the frame of institutional language ideologies in the national education systems?

Theoretical Framework

In studying the intersections between formal language policies and everyday language use in local communities, a broad understanding of language policy as multisited and multidimensional has become established. This enables a focus on the interrelations between macro-level language policies and micro-level language practices – in other words, how formal language policies are carried out and negotiated in daily encounters (Bonacina-Pugh, 2012; McCarty, 2015). A focus on children's and youth's everyday realities increases the understanding of language policies as multidimensional constructs and might, for instance, highlight the role of bilingual or multilingual children and youth in reshaping official policies in education (Bergroth & Palviainen, 2017; Boyd & Huss, 2017; Slotte-Lüttge, 2007).

Spolsky (2004) presents language policies as consisting of three interrelated components: language practices, language ideologies and language management. Language practices can be framed as the conventions and patterns of language use in everyday interactions. Shohamy (2006) points out that observation of these practices enables tracing covert and implicit language policies. Language ideologies refer to general beliefs about language, their value and appropriate language use in a particular community. According to Spolsky (2004), there is a two-way connection between language ideologies and language practices; they both derive from and influence each other. Language management refers to formal documents, proclamations of official policies or other interventions that aim to influence language practices in a specific context.

In this chapter, the most essential underlying formal policy representing language management in Finland is the separation of the national languages in basic education into two monolingual Swedish- and Finnish-medium strands. In Denmark, the essential part is the naturalisation of the Danish language as the language that counts academically in the official curriculum.

We especially deal with language policies in relation to languages (e.g. Finnish, Swedish, Danish, Arabic). We stress that, rather than viewing languages as naturally given entities, we view them as ideological constructions resulting from sociohistoric processes (Heller, 2007; Jørgensen et al., 2011). Sets of linguistic features become named languages because groups of people, for whatever reasons, claim and enforce the right to categorise them as such. So-called 'national' languages are the outcome of processes that, over time, have established a bond between a way of speaking and an ethnic identity (Blommaert et al., 2012). A good example is the ideologically constructed yet almost inseparable bond between being a Dane and speaking Danish. On the level of language management, such constructions may lead to the implementation of monolingual normativity on a national level and to the implementation of 'correct' ways of speaking the national language (i.e. ideologies of purism) (Edwards, 2009).

However, as documented in numerous sociolinguistic studies, communication does not necessarily mean speaking one language at a time (e.g. Pennycook & Otsuji, 2015; Rampton, 2006). Furthermore, the simplistic idea of the Western subject as monolingual and monocultural has been challenged by the linguistic and cultural complexity in contemporary urban environments in the Nordic countries inhabited by speakers with different linguistic backgrounds (e.g. Madsen, 2013; Milani & Jonsson, 2012). In the light of such findings, Jørgensen (2008) suggests that a perspective on languages is replaced with a perspective of languaging (see also García & Li, 2014). Languaging denotes people's use of any linguistic resources they have access to that works to achieve their communicative goals. This covers anything that speakers may produce verbally, whether it contains language resources associated with several languages or not. Speakers with access to more than one language can then orient to a monolingualism norm dictating the use of only one language at a time (see e.g. Slotte-Lüttge, 2005, 2007). They may also orient to a polylingualism norm where they use whatever resources they have access to and estimate that the interlocutors have the potential to comprehend even if some speakers view these resources as not belonging together (Møller, 2019).

Data and Methods

The data used consist of interviews and video recordings of conversations that, to a high degree, have a metalinguistic focus.

The Finnish part of the data was derived from a research project with an interest in locally multilingual education (DIDIA, 2021). The project followed six workshops where two classes with children aged 9–10 years met over 10 months during 2019. One of the classes was from a Swedish-medium school (nine pupils participating) and the other was from a Finnish-medium school (eight pupils participating). The schools are situated in a rural area of a bilingual municipality. Most of the students lived in monolingual homes, but there were also many students from multilingual homes, mostly Finnish and Swedish, but also Finnish or Swedish and another language. When the project began, all the pupils had studied the other language as a subject for some months.

The workshops, which aimed to enhance language-crossing activities and multilingual practices, were organised in collaboration with a school development project and took place in the local community. The workshop leaders, adults of different professions, were asked to use both Finnish and Swedish in eligible ways and to create opportunities for the children to work in language-mixed smaller groups. After the first meeting in the school, the actual three-hour workshops were organised in a bakery, museum, market-garden, greengrocer and restaurant.

The workshops were video recorded with two cameras (one of them with only one) that followed different student groups. For each of the cameras, one wireless microphone was connected and placed on a pupil. The microphones recorded sounds from a long distance and were changed to different pupils during the workshops. The recordings (total 18 hours) were coded with qualitative data analysis software (NVivo) in relation to situations where language was topicalised by the participating children: discussing language, language practices and negotiating how to use language. Afterwards, the coded parts were transcribed with a transcribing programme (InqScribe).

We conducted focus group interviews with three or four pupils ($n = 17$) in both schools before the collaboration between the schools started and after the last workshop. The interviews were organised in the school during the normal school day and were led by one of the authors together with a research assistant. In the interviews, the following themes were discussed: everyday language practices and language attitudes, particularly towards Finnish, Swedish and English, and the workshops. One part of the interview was accomplished using a set of formulated statements about language presented by the interviewer. As comments to the statement, the children were asked to choose a green, orange or red card. The green cards meant that they agreed with the statements, with the red cards they showed disagreement. Afterwards, the interviewer often initiated a small discussion. The interview that was conducted after the workshops contained a situation where the interviewer showed a video clip from the workshop and asked questions about the language use (see Excerpt 8).

The interviews were audio recorded (total 5 hours 45 minutes) and transcribed in full. As a guideline for the coding, we drew on Spolsky's (2004) distinction between three components of language policy. We paid specific attention to the negotiation about appropriate language practices in different contexts, particularly in relation to the school institution, which we consider as having a significant role in shaping language ideologies and framing the premises for language management.

For the analyses presented in this chapter, we chose sequences from the coded material (almost 6 hours of interviews and 18 hours of video recordings) that particularly contribute to understanding language policies.

The Danish part of the data was from the Everyday Languaging project (Madsen et al., 2016), which was based in a public school situated in a heterogeneous area of Copenhagen. The overall aim of the project was to investigate processes of enregisterment (Agha, 2007) among the participating pupils; that is, how ways of speaking in their daily lives interrelated with interpersonal conduct, social stereotypes, norms for situated use and sociolinguistic classification and how this developed over time. The participating pupils represented many different linguistic backgrounds. In the class, around two-thirds of the pupils had at least one parent who did not have Danish as their first language. This group was followed from their school start in 2010 until 2020. A number of different data types were collected, including ethnographic observation, video and sound recordings, social media interaction and recordings of arranged group conversations. The data used in this chapter were recorded in spring 2018 when the participants were 13–14 years old and came from arranged group conversations. In advance, the project team had written six open-ended questions on pieces of cardboard, such as 'How do you speak in school/at home/with friends?' In two of the groups, all participants had linguistic minority backgrounds; in both of these groups, practices and ideologies concerning multilingualism were brought up by the participants, which is the reason why we have chosen to work with examples from these conversations. A fieldworker instructed the groups to discuss the questions one by one and they were given a large piece of paper to write down keywords. Then they were left alone to do the task. After approximately 30 minutes, the fieldworkers returned to the room and discussed whatever the participants had written down. Methodologically, the idea was to facilitate a 'space for reflection and dialogue' (Heller et al., 2018: 92) where the participants shared and discussed experiences and general views. The discussions in some cases enabled us to get an understanding of opposite views. In other cases, participants posed new questions spontaneously, such as about 'being bilingual'.

Table 3.1 Transcription key

Key	Meaning
(.)	Short pause (less than 0.2 seconds)
(1.0)	Pause (in seconds)
[	Indicates where an overlap starts
]	Indicates where an overlap ends
text-	Sudden break
((text))	Clarifying comments
(text)	Transcription uncertain
(x)	Inaudible

The interviews were also coded based on Spolsky's notions of language practice, ideology and management and the excerpts presented in this chapter represent the coding results. The transcription key used in the excerpts is provided in Table 3.1

In the following, we discuss nine sequences from the Finnish material followed by five from the Danish data. Then we discuss how the insights gained from the two field sites complement each other and to what degree different types of experiences concerning the regimentation of linguistic diversity may lead to different types of metasociolinguistic positioning.

Reconstructing the Parallel School System: The Finnish Case

Following Spolsky's (2004) thought, the separation of the national languages in Finnish educational legislation can be considered as language management with direct aims to influence language practices in schools. In addition to safeguarding the right to education in both national languages (Finnish and Swedish), the parallel school system has an influence on pupils' language ideologies, identity construction and what kinds of language practices are considered thinkable (see e.g. From, 2020; Slotte-Lüttge, 2005, 2007).

The impact of the parallel school system on pupils' language ideologies and practices comes up both in the interview data and the workshop video recordings. The first video excerpt is from the fifth workshop, where the two classes meet in a local food manufacturer. The workshop leader uses both Swedish and Finnish with the students, switching from one language to another, without repeating everything in the other language. Just before the excerpt begins, the workshop leader (Mia) has given instructions to a group of four students from the Finnish school, primarily addressed to Sebastian who comes from a bilingual home. In this situation, Kira sits close to Sebastian and follows Mia while she is talking. The instructions are given in Swedish and the students topicalise their Swedish knowledge.

Excerpt 1. I just spoke

1	Venla:	emmäkää puhu (.) tai no kyl mä puhun sillee niinku-
		neither do I speak (.) or well actually I speak like-
2	Sebastian:	se on ollu ruotsinkielises päiväkodis
		she has been in a Swedish-speaking childcare
3	Kasper:	onko (.) mä [on ollu a-
		has she (.) I [have been a-
4	Venla:	[silloin mä puhuin kotonaki
		[at that time I even spoke at home
		vähäsen (.) kun mä olin siellä-
		a little (.) when I was there-
5	Kira:	miks
		why
6	Venla:	[koska
		[because
7	Sebastian:	[Kasper
		[Kasper
8	Venla:	siks ei sitä voi (.) emmä tiiä (1.0) mä vaa puhuin
		because one can't (.) I don't know (1.0) I just spoke

The topicalisation of language leads to a comment by Venla that she does not speak Swedish either, shortly followed by adding that she actually does (speak some). Before she continues, Sebastian interrupts her and declares to the group that Venla has attended a Swedish-medium childcare, a comment that is interesting for Kasper who reacts by sharing his own experience. Venla comments that when she was in the Swedish-medium childcare, she spoke some Swedish at home too but does not explain the reason further. Seen through Spolsky's lens, we may observe how the explicit policy of monolingual institutions appears in the children's negotiations of languaging. Sebastian's explanation of Venla's Swedish knowledge relating to childcare makes the Swedish-medium childcare a backdrop for Venla's knowledge and use of Swedish, which is further strengthened by Venla's comment where she connects her earlier practice of sometimes speaking Swedish at home to the time when she was in the childcare.

In a recording from another bilingual workshop, the pupils are given the instruction to pair up with someone who is not in the same class in order to 'mix up as much as possible', as the workshop leader said. Later, she repeats the instruction by reminding the pupils to avoid taking a seat next to their own classmates to get 'fully mixed'. Thus, according to the workshop leader, the classes are mentioned as a basis for the seating.

Having found their seats, some pupils from the Finnish-medium school are sitting by the table, with some empty seats between them. As their classmate Venla enters the room, Kira, Ella and Luna start passing on the instruction they were given.

Excerpt 2. Because between us there is supposed to be a Swede

1 Kira: ((talks to Venla and gestures to another table))
tulepa tähän (1.0) koska meijän välissä pitää olla yks ruotsalainen
come here (1.0) because between us there is supposed to be one Swede
2 Ella: [nii (.) mäkää mä ja Kirakaan ei saada olla vierekkäin
[yeah (.) even Kira and I can't be next to each other
3 Luna: [nii
[yeah
4 Kira: nii me ollaa sit vastapäätä
so we are then opposite

Kira instructs Venla not to sit in one of the empty chairs because 'between us there is supposed to be a Swede' (line 1). Unlike the instruction given by the workshop leader, in this organising practice the pupil from the other school is categorised by Kira in accordance with their school language. Moreover, the pupils from the Swedish-medium school get labelled as Swedes instead of Swedish-speaking (see From & Sahlström, 2017). The situation ends with an argument on how this instruction should be interpreted and seems to imply that the pupils would primarily favour sitting next to their own classmates.

During the same workshop, Ella from the Finnish-medium school and Vera from the Swedish-medium school sit side by side, as instructed. However, they do not talk to each other but turn in opposite directions to talk to their classmates. Ella has difficulties fitting her chair by the table because of Vera's mispositioned chair, but instead of turning to Vera to solve the issue, she discusses the problem in Finnish with her classmates sitting in the other direction. Vera grasps the problem and moves her chair without asking. Ella responds by thanking Vera in Swedish. This seems to imply that, despite the non-committal stance towards the cooperation, there is a tentative will to show interest towards the bilingual practices.

As noted earlier, the monolingual norm was particularly distinct in school-related discussions with the pupils. The separation of Finnish and Swedish in the school system appears as a form of language management, which has a strong influence on pupils' language ideologies (see Spolsky, 2004). Even if many of the pupils mentioned have come across multilingual practices in their spare time and at home, in school-related topics they primarily categorised their peers as monolingual in relation to their school language.

In the following two excerpts, from interviews after the workshop cooperations, the interviewer opens the discussion by presenting a statement about bilingual schools. The pupils are asked to show a green, orange or red card, whereafter the interviewer asks them to comment on their stance. The first excerpt is from the Swedish-medium school.

Excerpt 3. It takes a very long time

1	Interviewer:	ja tycker att svenska å finska barn borde gå i samma skola
		I think that Swedish-speaking and Finnish-speaking children should go to the same school
		((Otto, Rasmus, Vera and Albin show cards))
2	Interviewer:	nån som vill kommentera?
		does anyone want to comment?
3	Otto:	jag jag
		I I
4	Rasmus:	ja e så hä
		I'm like this
5	Otto:	för då om man frå- gör en matteuppgift
		because then if one is ask- doing a maths exercise
		å säger så här gör man (.) så
		and says that this is how it is done (.) so
		förstår- om man säger de på svenska så
		understands- if it is said in Swedish so
		förstår int finska barnen de
		the Finnish children do not understand it
6	Interviewer:	mm
		mm
7	Otto:	så måst man [säga de (.) två gånger
		and one must [say it (.) twice
8	Rasmus:	[så måst man tala två] språk hela
		[then two languages must be] spoken all
		tiden [liksom
		the time [like
9	Interviewer:	[mm
		[mm
10	Rasmus:	å [sen tar de jättelång tid
		and [then it takes a very long time
11	Otto:	[de blir irriterande
		[and it gets irritating
12	Rasmus:	tills man kan börja med uppgiften
		before one can start with the task

For Otto, who presented a red card to show opposition to the idea of Swedish- and Finnish-speaking children sharing schools, potential problems occur with Finnish-speakers' ability to understand instructions given in Swedish. In this case, all content would need to be delivered in both languages, which Rasmus finds time-consuming and irritating. From this point of view, it appears understandable that the pupils do not necessarily see the value in bilingual groups. This might imply that these pupils are aware of Finnish-speakers' often limited proficiency in Swedish. However, we also need to acknowledge that the formulation of the statement presented to the pupils conforms to the idea of two separate language groups and might influence their thinking accordingly.

Interestingly, the monolingual norm seemed to emerge regardless of the pupils' attitudes towards bilingual practices. The pupils in the Finnish-medium school were generally more approving of the idea of bilingual schools but nevertheless had a similar assumption of monolingual individuals as the linguistic norm.

In the following excerpt, Max, a pupil in the Finnish-medium school, ponders the benefits of a bilingual school. This example also begins with the interviewer presenting a statement followed by the children's comments supported by the coloured cards.

Excerpt 4. If, for example, you are friends

1	Interviewer:	minusta suomenkieliset ja ruotsinkieliset
		I think Finnish-speaking and Swedish-speaking
		lapset tulisivat käydä samaa koulua
		children should attend the same school
		((Sebastian shows the green card))
2	Interviewer:	okei (.) mitä ä m (.) mmm kerro lisää siitä
		okay (.) what e m (.) mmm tell more about it
3	Sebastian:	mun mielest se ois hyvä koska (.) sit jos
		I think it would be good because (.) then if
		vaikka sä oot ruotsinkielisen kaveri
		for example, you are friends with a Swedish-speaking
		ja sit ite puhut su- suomee (.) niin sit sä
		and then you speak Fi- Finnish (.) so then you
		saatat oppii siltä (.) ruotsia paljon
		could learn from them (.) a lot of Swedish
4	Lauri:	[nii]
		[yeah]
5	Sebastian:	[ja] se saattaa oppii sulta suomea
		[and] they might learn Finnish from you
6	Interviewer:	mm
		mm
7	Sebastian:	sit osaatte puhuu molemmat molempii kielii
		then you both can speak both languages

In Excerpt 4, Sebastian endorses the idea of a bilingual school because of the potential for mutual language learning. Interestingly, Sebastian presents the other national language as primarily learned through friendship instead of school instruction. This implies the persistence of the monolingual norm of the school institution, particularly regarding curricula and classrooms. In the current educational context, the pupils might intuitively associate the interview question of 'attending the same school' with a co-located school (see e.g. From, 2020; Sahlström *et al.*, 2013). Alternatively, Sebastian's stance underlines an ideology of language as a means of communication and might be influenced by the multilingual practices emerging in the pupils' everyday lives outside school.

In their ideologies and practices, the pupils seemed to rely on a typical view of languages as separate entities (Makoni & Pennycook, 2007), which shows, for example, in their perceptions of multilingual practices emerging in the interviews and workshops. In our data, mixing languages was typically considered peculiar, inconvenient and time-consuming. It can be assumed that, in addition to the general ideological monolingualism in education, the separate school system for Finnish and Swedish speakers has some influence on how children consider bilingual practices in Finland. Almér (2017) found that even children in early childhood education show awareness of the fact that Finnish and Swedish are to be separated in some situations. However, according to previous studies, schoolchildren find ways to challenge the monolingual norm through their ideologies and practices (From, 2020; Slotte-Lüttge, 2007).

In Excerpt 5, from a group interview with pupils in the Swedish-medium school, the interviewer asks the pupils to reflect on the idea of speaking two languages at the same time. This interview took place prior to the workshops.

Excerpt 5. Says the next word in Finnish

1	Interviewer:	mm (1.0) kan man prata två språk samtidit
		mm (1.0) can one speak two languages simultaneously
		tror ni
		do you think
2	Teo:	[jåå]
		[yes]
3	Melina:	[jåå]
		[yes]
4	Oskar:	jå
		yeah
5	Interviewer:	hu gör man då
		how is it done
6	Teo:	nå man ta (.) m ta (.) a si säg (.) säger någo ord å
		well one ta (.) m ta (.) a si sa (.) says some word and
		sen säger man nästa ord på finska å så
		then says the next word in Finnish and so
7	Interviewer:	mm (2.0) t hjåå (.) vem brukar prata så
		mm (2.0) t hyeah (.) who usually speaks like that
8	Melina:	ingen
		no-one
9	Teo:	ingen
		no-one

In the discussion, Teo, Melina and Oskar agree that it is possible to speak two languages at the same time. According to Teo, such a bilingual practice would consist of alternately combining words from both languages. However, when the interviewer asks them to name a person who tends to speak like this, both Melina and Teo reply that no-one does (see Almér, 2017). Thus, a bilingual practice or translanguaging in the form of simultaneous use of two languages by one person appears more as an abstract idea than a considerable practice against the backdrop of a monolingual norm. Furthermore, when asked to speculate about why some people mix languages, the pupils in the Finnish-medium school came up with ideas related to communication and language proficiency, as shown in Excerpt 6.

Excerpt 6. I must say it in Finnish

1	Interviewer:	ööm (2.0) miksi luulette et jotkut sekottaa kieliä? (2.0) Ella
		umm (2.0) why do you think that some mix languages? (2.0) Ella
2	Ella:	no jos on kuuntelijoina suomenkielisiä ruotsinkiel- tai iha minkä tahansa (.) öö niinku vaikka kakskielisiäki (.)ni ö ni sit (.) et ne my- ymmärtää (.) ne ymmärtää molemmat et (.) jos on vaikka suomenkielisiä ja ruotsinkielisiä (.) sekotettuina (.) niin sitten ne senhän pitää puhuu suomeks sekä ruotsiks että ne molemmat ymmärtäis
		well if the listeners are Finnish-speaking Swedish- speaking- or really anything (.) uh like say even bilingual (.) so uh so then (.) so then that they als - understand (.)understand both that (.) if there is, for example, Finnish-speaking and Swedish-speaking mixed (.) so then they should speak both Finnish and Swedish so that they both would understand
3	Interviewer:	okei (.) Sebastian
		okay (.) Sebastian
4	Sebastian:	että (1.0) mä välillä (.) ää puhun erillain jos mä en tiedä sitä sanaa ruotsiks (.) ja sit mä s aluks puhun vaikka ruotsiks (.) ni sit mun on pakko sanoo se suomeks koska mä en tiiä miten se on ruotsiks
		so (1.0) I sometimes (.) speak differently if I don't know that word in Swedish (.) and then I first speak for example, in Swedish (.) so then I must say it in Finnish because I don't know how it is in Swedish

While Ella suggests that a person's motive for mixing languages might have to do with including the audience with varying language proficiencies (with the assumption that Swedish and Finnish speakers do not understand each other's languages), Sebastian, who comes from a bilingual home, suggests that lacking a particular word in Swedish forces one to replace it with a Finnish word – he then speaks 'differently'. Thus, the motive for a bilingual practice may be to compensate for 'incomplete' proficiency in a particular language. Both views represent a monolingual ideology, where individuals are primarily Swedish or Finnish speakers, and even when having proficiency in both languages, like Sebastian, one should aim to stick to a single language to keep up with a coherent language practice.

A similar monolingual stance among the pupils appears in the following excerpt, where the workshop leader, Mia, has given instructions in Swedish to Kira, a pupil in the Finnish-medium school.

Excerpt 7. Soon she talks

1 Sebastian: se on Kira (.) se ei puhu ruotsii
               that's Kira (.) she doesn't speak Swedish
               (9.0)
2 Kasper: Mia (.) Kira ei sit puhu ruotsii
               Mia (.) Kira doesn't speak Swedish
3 Mia: no (.) koht puhuu
               well (.) soon she talks
4 Kasper: koht puhuu
               soon she talks ((laughing))

The instructions are given in Swedish, which leads to a reaction by Sebastian, followed by a repetition by Kasper, who both want to inform Mia that Kira does not speak Swedish. Mia's answer, 'well soon she talks' (line 3), is repeated by Kasper with a laugh. The laugh can be understood as distancing from Mia's reaction, which in turn can be seen as an expression about the possibility to mix languages, where it is not self-evident to keep to a one person–one language format.

The following excerpt is from the interview after the workshops. First, the interviewer showed the students a video clip from one of the workshops, where the workshop leader gave instructions by mixing Swedish and Finnish, switching between the languages, without saying everything in both languages. The interviewer then gave the statement 'I think it has been difficult when the workshop instructors have said some parts in Swedish and some in Finnish' – the pupils were once again supposed to express their opinion of this statement by showing a green, yellow or red card.

Excerpt 8. Most in Finnish and not everything in Swedish

1 Interviewer: [om du tycker att de ha varit jobbigt
                [*if you think that it has been tough/difficult*
                så sätter du upp gröna kortet] (.)
                then you show the green card] (.)
2 Otto: [om man om man tycker jätte (.) jättejobbit (.) jäh]
                [*if you find it very (.) very tough (.) eh*]

3	Interviewer:	om du håller med de här påståendet
		if you agree with this claim
4	Otto:	jättejobbit
		very tough/difficult
5	Interviewer:	mm okej
		mm okay
6	Otto:	jobbigast när hon säger mest finska å int
		most annoying when she says most in Finnish and not
		allt på svenska
		everything in Swedish
7	Interviewer:	okej (.) jå (.) vaför e det jobbit?
		okay (.) yes (.) why is it annoying?
8	Otto:	för att hon säger hh (.) öm saker på finska å sen int
		because she says (.) eh- things in Finnish and then not
		alla saker som hon sa på finska på finska på svenska
		all things that she says in Finnish also in Swedish

In Excerpt 8, inconsistency and imbalance between Finnish and Swedish are presented as making bilingual practices tough, difficult and confusing. Otto expresses difficulties in being able to understand the other language properly. Thus, even if reflecting a monolingual norm, this seems to be not only an ideological stance but also a practical question. In light of our data, the pupils seem to think that, to be included, one must be able to speak and fully understand both languages that are being used in the conversation (see Almér, 2017). Otherwise, they consider bilingual practices reasonable only when the delivered content is identical in both languages.

The next excerpt is from the third workshop. The children sit at tables and the workshop leader, Anni, gives instructions on how to fold paper flowers. While she gives the instructions orally, she does the folding herself in front of the children, meaning that the activity did not depend only on language. Earlier, Anni told the children not to worry if they did not understand, saying 'you'll get to know everything that is important in both languages'. The main parts of the first instructions about folding were presented in Finnish. When Anni was ready, Otto calls to her.

Excerpt 9. Can you say it in Swedish?

1	Anni:	jå Otto
		yes Otto
2	Otto:	kan du säga de på svenska va man sku göra
		can you say it in Swedish what we were supposed to do?
3	Anni:	jå-å
		ye-es
4	Ella:	hhmh
		hhmh
5	Luna:	mä en tajunnu edes (miten teemme)
		I did not even understand (how we will do it)

6 Anni: noo ei [se mitää (.) tää on semmonen]
well no [problem (.) this is something]
7 Ella: [ku sä selitit vaan ruotsiks]
[because you explained it only in Swedish]
8 Anni: tää on semmonen juttu mikä lähtee kokeilemalla (.) nyt
this is something that will work out by trying (.) now
se on outoo jos (.) ruotsinkieliset sanoo voitsä
it is weird if (.) Swedish speakers say can you
selittää myös ruotsiksi ja suomenkieliset et sä
also explain in Swedish and Finnish speakers that you
selitit vaan nytte ruotsiks (.) mut (.) se johtuu ehkä
explained it only in Swedish (.) but (.) it might be
siitä et mä en ollu kauheen hyvä selittämään ku mä
because I was not very good at explaining when I
huomasin et mä ehkä ookkaan niin kauheen hyvä
noticed that I might not after all be very good
tekemään näitä mut mä istun teidän kanssa niin
at making these, but I will sit with you so we can
harjotellaan yhdessä
practice together

The folding activity seems to be demanding for many of the children and some ask for additional help. After Otto's question to Anni to explain in Swedish, Luna (from the Finnish-medium school) continues by saying that she did not understand what they are supposed to do. She does not mention the language, but Ella, also from the Finnish-medium school, follows up on her comment by mentioning the language 'because you only explained it in Swedish'. Both Otto and Ella topicalise a need for instruction in their language. This can be understood as if the rationality of bilingual practices is judged within a monolingual normativity or from the perspective of someone who only masters one of the languages used in the discussion. Interestingly, the leader does not go into the children's motives of language as the reason for the problems but provides her weak competence in folding as the reason for the unclarity. In the children's interviews, a dominant idea seems to be that participating in bilingual practices requires bilingual proficiency to start with (see Almér, 2017).

To Fit or Not to Fit within a Monolingual Regime: The Danish Case

The first excerpt from the Danish study is from Group 1, consisting of girls Lina, Aida, Aisha and Gül. Gül is not talking in this excerpt but is referred to by Aisha. All the participants have parents who speak a first language other than Danish. The excerpt is from right after the fieldworkers left the participants to discuss the questions. The one they start out with is 'Which ways of speaking do you know?'

Excerpt 10. Like others say Quran

1	Lina:	hvilke måder at tale på kender I? - what?
		which ways of speaking do you know? – what?
2	Aida:	hvilke måder at tale på kender I
		which ways of speaking do you know?
3	Lina:	ja
		yes
4	Aida:	okay øh
		okay eh
5	Aisha:	øh
		eh
6	Aida:	hvad mener de med det?
		what do they mean by that?
7	Aisha:	jeg kender godt en måde at tale på Gül hun er meget
		I know a way of speaking, Gül is very
		grim hun ligner mit røvhul
		ugly she looks like my asshole
		((deltagerne griner))
		((the participants laugh))
8	Aida:	må må jeg lige læse det hurtigt
		may may I just quickly read it
9	Aisha:	(x)
10	Lina:	det er forskellige måder ligesom andre siger koran
		its different ways like others say quran
		jeg sværger jeg ved ikke hvad
		I swear I don't know what
11	Aisha:	eller mig det der slang ew jeg sværger jeg topper dig
		or me that slang hey I swear I top you
		din fucking hund
		you fucking dog
12	Aida:	jeg kender ikke så meget for jeg taler på en meget
		I don't know that much because I speak in a very
		normal måde så er der nogen som der siger tyve
		normal way then there are some people who say twenty
		((twenty pronounced with palatalised t))
		eller sådan noget
		or something like that
13	Lina:	nej kom til Tåstrup abi
		no come to Tåstrup brother
		((to and Tåstrup pronounced with palatalised t))

After a phase of clarifying what the fieldworkers mean by the question (lines 2–9) and joking around (line 8), the participants discuss a way of speaking that Aisha categorises as slang in line 11. In connection to this, the participants describe or exemplify a number of features they associate with this way of speaking: Lexically, they point to '*abi*' (brother in Turkish), '*ew*' (hey or similar in Kurdish), '*Koran*' (Quran in Danish), '*jeg sværger*' (I swear in Danish), '*jeg topper dig*' (I top you in Danish, here with the meaning I beat you up) and 'fucking'. Furthermore, they enhance the phonetic feature of t-palatalisation ([t] pronounced as [tj]). An important point in connection to our argument is that this way of speaking involves language resources associated with Danish alongside a range of other languages – in this excerpt, Turkish, Kurdish and English. Thereby, the example displays that the participants are familiar with alternatives to monolingual normativity.

In connection to the participants' description, it is interesting that two of them actually distance themselves from this way of speaking (Lina in line 10 and Aida in line 12). Seen through Spolsky's theoretical framework, this underlines how the levels of practice and ideology interplay. The participants can describe and mimic a practice in detail and distance themselves from it on the level of ideology at the same time. We know from our fieldwork in general that this way of speaking is well known by our participants and associated with toughness and masculinity as well as a migration background (Hyttel-Sørensen, 2017; Madsen, 2013) and this may be part of the reason why this distancing occurs.

The next excerpt is from the beginning of the discussion in the other group. The questions they read in the excerpt translate into 'How do you speak with your friends?' and 'How do you speak in school?'

Excerpt 11. They view it as gang

1	Mehmet:	hvordan taler I med jeres venner? vi taler slang you
		how do you speak with your friends, we speak slang you
		know slang (.) tror jeg det hedder hedder det
		know slang (.) I think it is called isn't it
		ikke slang
		called slang
2	Isaam:	det hedder slang
		it's called slang
3	Mehmet:	vi taler altså dejligt og vi
		we speak you know lovely, and we
		hygger og ((fnisen)) ((laver sin stemme om))
		are having a good time and ((giggles)) ((changes his voice))
4	Isaam:	øh rigsdansk
		eh standard Danish
5	Mehmet:	vi taler høfligt og (x) kom fuck det Alexei her
		we speak polite and (x) come fuck it Alexei
		tag et spørgsmål
		take a question
6	Isaam:	nej altså vi snakker slang ah
		no you know we speak slang right
7	Alexei:	hvordan taler i i skolen?
		how do you speak in school?
8	Isaam:	samme måde
		same way

9	Mehmet:	neej (.) foran lærerne taler vi sådan -
		noo (.) in front of the teachers we speak like
10	Alexei:	foran lærerne snakker vi ikke sådan der
		in front of the teachers we do not speak like this
11	Mehmet:	ja [de ser det som] bande
		yeh [they view it as] a gang
12	Isaam:	[der snakker vi]
		[there we speak]
13	Mehmet:	der snakker vi høfligt og pænt og vi siger
		there we speak polite and nice, and we say
		godmorgen
		((changes his voice)) good morning

In lines 1 and 2, Mehmet and Isaam establish that the way of speaking they associate with communication with friends is 'slang'. We know from fieldwork more generally that this way of speaking corresponds to what the girl group also categorised as slang in Excerpt 10. In line 3, Mehmet mimics another way of speaking. He changes to a more standard-like prosody, a higher pitch and uses the phrase '*vi hygger*', where the expression '*hygge*' (cosiness) is emblematic for (the majority of) Danish culture. Isaam reacts by categorising this as '*rigsdansk*' (standard Danish) in line 4. In this way, the participants summarise a system of two ways of speaking (slang and standard Danish), identify with the first and distance themselves from the other by means of parodic stylisation (Rampton, 2009). Mehmet continues the parody in line 5 but interrupts himself and says 'fuck it', which can be interpreted as a contextualisation cue (Gumperz, 1982) signalling that the parodic performance is over. He then urges Alexei to read out the next question.

From line 8 onwards, the participants interpret the question 'How do you speak in school?' as how they speak in front of the teachers. Alexei and Mehmet both state that they do not use 'slang' in these situations and Mehmet comments that the reason is that the teachers associate this way of speaking with gang activities (line 11). Then Mehmet performs a new parody (line 13), which resembles the way of speaking introduced in line 3 by using a similar prosodic pattern and higher pitch. Again, he mentions speaking '*høfligt*' (polite). In this way, the boys describe how the teachers expect to hear standard Danish and how they cope with this expectation to avoid being labelled derogatively as, for example, gang members. Viewing the example through Spolsky's terminology, they assign the role of language managers with the power to enforce the monolingual ideology of standard Danish to the teachers.

Returning to the girls' group, the next excerpt is a description of a teacher's explicit language management. This excerpt is from when the fieldworkers re-entered the room and discussed the task with the participants. The fieldworker addresses the question 'How do you speak in school?'

Excerpt 12. Then he throws himself on the floor

1	Thomas:	hvordan taler I i skolen? det var det sidste
		how do you speak in school? that was the last
2	Aisha:	pænt
		nice
3	Thomas:	pænt ja
		nice yes
4	Gül:	nej
		no
5	Thomas:	nej
		no ((questioning intonation))
6	Gül:	vi taler grimt i skolen
		we speak in an ugly manner in school
7	Thomas:	også i timerne
		also during lessons
8	Gül:	når Poul han er der ikke også så siger jeg sådan for
		when Poul he is there, you know then I say like for
		eksempel hvis jeg siger hold kæft så gør Poul sådan
		example if I say shut up then Poul does like
		her
		this ((Gül puts her hands to her heart))
		og så kaster han sig ned på
		and then he throws himself on ((turns her eyes up))
		gulvet og så siger jeg bare rolig Poul du er gammel du
		the floor and then I say relax Poul you are old you
		skal passe på hjertet
		need to take care of your heart

Gül states in line 6 that she sometimes speaks 'ugly' while in school and then turns to describe how a named teacher (here called Poul) reacts if he hears her say '*hold kæft*' (shut up). Poul is the class teacher, so he also has responsibility for the wellbeing of the pupils. Furthermore, he is the teacher who spends most weekly hours with the class. Gül describes how Poul performs a reaction of physical shock through gestures, eyesight and simulated fainting when hearing foul language. She hints that the reaction is excessive by jokingly describing how she urges the teacher to relax and watch his heart. Poul's reaction can be seen as language managing. Based on an ideology prescribing the correct way of speaking in the classroom, he intervenes when he experiences Gül transgressing this norm. In this way, Gül's narrative personifies Poul in the role of language manager of the language ideology of the school.

In fact, Poul is often referred to by the pupils as a key representative for a linguistic norm representing standard Danish. The next excerpt shows how the participants feel that this position may lead to an insufficient view on bilingualism. Noteworthy, the question posed by Aida in line 1 was not formulated by the fieldworkers in advance but put forward on their own initiative when the group had finished discussing the questions prepared by the researchers.

Excerpt 13. A bit Poul-ish

1	Aida:	det her lyder måske sådan lidt Poul-agtigt hvordan er
		this perhaps sounds a bit Poul-ish what is
		det at være tosproget? (.) øh (0.3) egentlig som
		it like to be bilingual? (.) eh (0.3) really as a
		person hvordan synes I det er at være tosproget?
		person how do you think it is to be bilingual?
2	Aisha:	altså jeg [synes det er meget godt]
		well I [I think it is fine]
3	Lina:	[jeg synes det er nemt]
		[I think it is easy]
4	Gül:	[jeg synes også det er fint]
		[I also think it is fine]
		(short discussion about where Poul comes from in Denmark is left out)
5	Lina:	han tror tosproget at være tosproget det er svært
		he thinks bilingual to be bilingual it is tough
		det er det sgu [ikke
		it is bloody [not
6	Aisha:	[nej
		[no
7	Gül:	han skal altid gøre det som om det er en dårlig ting
		he always has to make it like it is a bad thing
		når han siger det
		when he says it
8	Aisha:	og Poul han skal altid tale om Tyrkiet mand
		and Poul he always has to talk about Turkey man
		er vi enige
		do you agree?
9	Lina:	ja jeg får psykose
		yeah, I get psychosis
10	Aisha:	og det værste der er kun en tyrker
		and the worst thing is there is only one Turk, the
		resten er kurdere
		rest are Kurds

In the first line, Aida frames her question as 'a bit Poul-ish' (the teacher referred to in Excerpt 12) and then asks the other participants how it is to be bilingual. The question points to a language ideology that divides speakers into monolinguals and bilinguals. First, the other three participants describe it as 'fine' and 'easy' (lines 2–4). Then they turn to discuss where Poul's view on bilinguals comes from and how it affects them. In line 9, Lina summarises the discussion by claiming that Poul (wrongly) thinks it is difficult to be bilingual and Gül adds that Poul's actions show his insufficient view on bilingualism. In terms of language ideology, the description of Poul's view and actions can be said to reconstruct an understanding of monolingualism (in the shape of standard Danish) as the normal and privileged in the school. Remembering the descriptions of Poul's reactions to cursing (Excerpt 12), the participants describe a central representative for the school's institutional language ideology, which represents the correct, normal Danish language and, at the same time, assumes that bilingualism must be a difficult challenge for pupils. This position makes sense in an educational system where the 'normal' (or normalised) pupil is constructed as monolingual and monocultural.

However, the participants object being constructed as different and disadvantaged and challenges the teacher's acts. Aisha accuses Poul of always wanting to talk about Turkey and describe how he overlooks that a range of pupils identify as Kurds (and not as Turks). On the one hand, this description works in the situation to destabilise Poul's assumptions in general. On the other, it points to an important paradox: Poul's role in the class is to promote monolingualism and monoculturalism and to make sure that all pupils are included. Aisha's description points to a strategy where Poul handles this paradox by including phenomena related to countries he believes the pupils have connections to in his lessons. However, according to Aisha, this does not create the effect of inclusion because it is based on the oversimplified assumption that a person's ethnicity can be simply deduced from the nation their families migrated from – what Irvine and Gal (2000) describe as an ideological act of erasure.

We wish to underline that the purpose here is not to critique the teacher. In fact, he is, in our experience, generally well-liked and respected by the pupils. The problem illustrated by the participants should rather be seen as an example of what can happen when teachers are asked to make a regime of monolingualism and monoculturalism work in classes where the pupils have a range of different language backgrounds, national affiliations and migration histories.

In the last excerpt from Denmark, the group of boys explain to the fieldworkers what they talked about in connection to the question 'How do you speak at home?'

Excerpt 14. Mix between kebab and chicken

1 **Isaam:** og så hvad vi taler derhjemme det er du ved
and then what do we speak at home it is you know
nogen de snakker jeg ved ikke halv dansk halv
somebody they talk I don't know half Danish, half
tyrkisk vil jeg tro
Turkish I believe

2 **Mehmet:** (x) man laver den der man siger tre ord på det
(x) you do that thing you say three words
tyrkisk så kommer lige et ord på dansk og så er
in Turkish then a word in Danish just comes in
sådan der (.) man laver lige et mix
it's like that (.) you just make a mix

3	Isaam:	jeg snakker
		I talk
4	Mehmet:	ligesom når man er sulten og spiser shawarma
		like when you are hungry and eat shawarma
5	Isaam:	jeg snakker bare [dansk]
		I just speak [Danish]
6	Mehmet:	[mix] mellem kebab og kylling
		[mix] between kebab and chicken
7	Isaam:	jeg snakker bare dansk og du snakker halv halv ikke
		I just speak Danish and you speak half-half, right

In line 1, Isaam reports from the pupils' earlier discussion that some claimed that they used 'half Danish, half Turkish' at home. Mehmet elaborates on this in lines 2, 4 and 6, comparing the language use to mixing different types of meat when eating shawarma. Both Mehmet's use of *'lige'* (just) in line 2 and his use of the shawarma metaphor construct the use of Danish and Turkish juxtaposed as a mundane routine activity. An interesting question here is why Mehmet chooses to include the comparison to shawarma at this point of the conversation. The activity of 'mixing languages' was not spelled out when the participants were by themselves. In this light, a likely explanation is that Mehmet assumes this way of using language is new to the two (majority Danish) fieldworkers, and they therefore need a pedagogical introduction. In this way, Mehmet's description displays the knowledge that linguistic features associated with different languages may be routinely combined in interaction and that this may come as a surprise to speakers he believes to represent a Danish monolingual standard ideology. Members of the research group were very careful to never take a normative linguistic stance, but the participants still occasionally ascribed the role of linguistic authorities to them.

Apart from reporting what the other students said earlier, Isaam states that he only speaks Danish at home. In line 7, he sums his and Mehmet's different positions up as 'speaking Danish' and 'half-half'. In other words, he describes how some may orient to a monolingual norm at home, while others orient to a polylingual norm. The two norms are not described as competing or in a hierarchy but simply as two different possibilities for linguistic behaviour.

Discussion

The following discussion derives from the research question: How do children and youth negotiate language policies in multilingual contexts in the frame of institutional language ideologies in the national education systems?

We begin with summarised discussions of the analyses from both contexts separately, after which we proceed to consider how the insights gained from the two field sites may complement each other. In line with Spolsky (2004), we understand language policies as interactions in highly complex dynamic contexts, where the three interrelated components (language practices, language ideologies and language management) are constantly dependent on each other and a modification of any part may have correlated effects and causes on any other part. This means that more formal macro-level language policies, established ideologies and practical micro-level language practices are carried out and negotiated in daily encounters (Bonacina-Pugh, 2012; McCarty, 2015).

The most significant result from the Finnish case is that the separation of the national languages in school institutions is a backdrop for language ideologies and bilingual practices. They explain pupils' knowledge and use of a language during childcare experiences and explain why pupils interpret the workshop leader's comment of mixing classes as mixing languages and react when a workshop leader does not keep to a one person–one language format – they even comment on the leader's choice to use the 'other' language with a pupil. The school thus becomes a language-managing institution, with an impact on language practices and language ideologies. This monolingual ideology is reflected in the pupils' discourse of appropriate language practices: when the students are asked about their view of a bilingual school, their answers reflect the persistence of the monolingual norm in the classroom, indicating that bilingualism would mean two parallel language ideologies and language use where everybody can take part in teaching in their own language.

Translanguaging in the form of the simultaneous use of two languages by one person appears to be an abstract idea more than a considerable practice against the backdrop of a monolingual norm. A bilingual school would thus create possibilities for language learning in meetings between two monolingual persons. This expressed emphasis of monolingual practice reflects another central aspect that lies near the importance of schools as linguistic lighthouses. Moreover, the children have a pragmatic view of language as a medium of communication in everyday encounters. Bilingual practices are considered time-consuming and irritating, based on a perception that all content should be provided in both languages. This, in turn, is connected to the assumption of the monolingual individual who neither speaks nor understands the 'other' language. The potential to participate to the best of one's ability and learn along the way is not often raised (see Almér, 2017). There are situations in the video excerpts where a translanguaging practice – children using parts from their language repertoire to get understood – potentially could have been a functioning method. Instead, the children mostly keep to one language and thus keep the languages separate.

Summing up the Danish case, we can identify three sets of language ideologies as described by the participants. First, the pupils describe a way of speaking referred to as 'nice', 'polite' and 'standard Danish', that is closely linked to the linguistic regime enforced by their schoolteachers. Teachers are described as language managers that react to foul language such as swearing. Second, the pupils describe a way of speaking they call 'slang'. This exists especially among peers with migration backgrounds and one of its characteristics is that Danish is juxtaposed with Arabic, Turkish, Kurdish, English and so on. Third, the pupils describe a way of speaking that involves the simultaneous and juxtaposed use of two languages – what the participant Mehmet described as making 'a mix'. This refers to language practices among family members. In other words, the pupils describe how they experience and manoeuvre between monolingual and polylingual language ideologies. They also display knowledge of when to perform polylingual practices and when to hide them strategically. One group describes how 'slang' is to be avoided in front of teachers because teachers relate it to gang activities. Another group describes how they find the focus on their 'bilingualism' annoying because it becomes associated with problematic and disadvantaged positions in the school system.

In the Finnish data, the parallel school system seems to be at the core of shaping linguistic normativity and the monolingual norm whereas, in the data from Denmark, language management is negotiated in relation to linguistic purism (i.e. the standard language of the school) and ways of speaking that are not legitimised by the school system. The experience of the monolingual language ideology in the Danish school system in rather concrete ways leads to experiences among pupils with a migration background of being viewed as disadvantaged, which may result in the strategic hiding of polylingual practices. Being older than the pupils in the Finnish study, the Danish pupils displayed awareness of the school's role in shaping linguistic normativity. They could recognise and discuss the monolingual language ideology and the dominance of standard Danish, and displayed resistance by making a parody of it.

When it comes to the Finnish excerpts, it is important to see them in the bigger picture. In the bilingual workshops, the language policies that the pupils from the Finnish- and Swedish-medium schools encountered were very different from what the pupils are used to during normal school days, where teachers use one language. As Spolsky (2004: 10) put it: 'pupils quickly discover which language choices (and language items, too) are appropriate and which are discouraged' and they also 'learn that the teacher has the privilege of determining who speaks and when and of judging how appropriate is the form of speech to be used, as well as the permitted topics'. Even though a slow change in attitude and understanding towards a more multilingual approach among teachers has been noticed and the classrooms can be assumed to be more linguistically dynamic than previously (Kimanen *et al.*, 2019; Slotte-Lüttge, 2005, 2007; Tarnanen & Palviainen, 2018), it is fair to describe most of the

Swedish- and Finnish-medium schools as dominated by a strong monolingual language practice.

The Danish case should be understood in light of the political development in Denmark over the last decades, where people with migration backgrounds are increasingly viewed as a cultural and economic problem for the welfare state (Padovan-Özdemir & Moldenhawer, 2016). In line with this (standard), Danish is generally viewed as the key to societal success and what the participants refer to as 'slang' is stigmatised as the opposite (Hyttel-Sørensen, 2017). The pupils describe how they are familiar with this ideology, to the degree where they have developed daily practices of not using certain ways of speaking in front of teachers. Again, this is in line with Spolsky's thoughts on adaptation to teachers' language ideologies, with the important nuance that participants risk being ascribed identities as unruly pupils as well as the 'non-Danish other' when using slang.

Another important insight from the Danish case is that language-based identity ascriptions do not only occur as reactions to situated language use. This becomes clear in the discussion of being referred to as 'bilingual' in Excerpt 13, where being 'bilingual' becomes associated with a disadvantaged position in the Danish school system. The term 'bilingual' does not in itself imply an insufficient view on bilingualism. In fact, the term *'tosproget'* (bilingual) was instigated in a Danish context in the 1990s by researchers who wished to highlight competences in minority languages as a resource rather than a deficit. However, despite good intentions, the term may still be used with negative connotations if the logic behind it is that the school system is tailored for monolingual and monocultural pupils.

The distinction between monolinguals and bilinguals in the Danish case leads to an important point when compared with the Finnish case. A similar stigma does not appear in the discourse of bilingualism in the Finnish data, even though bilingual practices are not necessarily recognised as valuable by the pupils. Moreover, the pupils in our Finnish data conform to the linguistic norm and ideal linguistic subjectivity promoted by the parallel school system and identify with one of the two legitimised language ideologies. None of the pupils treat any of these identities as more attractive than the other, and reported problems in relation to language choice mainly occur if the instructor does not give balanced instructions in both languages, thereby failing to live up to a language policy of double monolingualism. In Denmark, the pupils reacted strongly to being characterised as 'bilinguals'. The point here is that the identities of 'Finns', 'Swedes' and 'bilinguals' are outcomes of the monolingual ideologies of the institutions. When monolingual regimes are enforced in educational systems, they do not only result in language policies and practices but also in categorisations and senses of belonging.

References

Agha, A. (2007) *Language and Social Relations. Studies in the Social and Cultural Foundations of Language*. Cambridge: Cambridge University Press.

Almér, E. (2017) Children's beliefs about bilingualism and language use as expressed in child–adult conversations. *Multilingua* 36 (4), 401–424, https://doi.org/10.1515/multi-2016-0022

Basic Education Act 628/1998 (1998) See https://finlex.fi/fi/laki/ajantasa/1998/19980628 (accessed June 2021).

Bergroth, M. and Palviainen, Å. (2017) Bilingual children as policy agents: Language policy and education policy in minority language medium early childhood education and care. *Multilingua* 36 (4), 375–399.

Blommaert, J., Leppänen, S. and Spotti, M. (2012) Endangering multilingualism. In J. Blommaert, S. Leppänen, P. Pahta and T. Räisänen (eds) *Dangerous Multilingualism. Northern Perspectives on Order, Purity and Normality* (pp. 1–24). Basingstoke: Palgrave Macmillan.

Bonacina-Pugh, F. (2012) Researching 'practiced language policies': Insights from conversation analysis. *Language Policy* 11 (3), 213–234.

Boyd, S. and Huss, L. (2017) Young children as language policy-makers: Studies of interaction in preschools in Finland and Sweden. *Multilingua* 36 (4), 359–373.

Danmarks Statistik (2020) *Indvandrere i Danmark 2020 (Immigrants in Denmark 2020)*. See https://www.dst.dk/da/Statistik/Publikationer/VisPub?cid=29447 (accessed May 2021).

DIDIA (2021) DIDIA – Multilingual didactics and dialogs. Diversity, multilingualism and social justice in education. See https://www2.helsinki.fi/en/researchgroups/diversity-multilingualism-and-social-justice-in-education/projects/didia-multilingual-didactics-and-dialogs (accessed 21 June 2021).

Edwards, J. (2009) *Language and Identity*. Cambridge: Cambridge University Press.

From, T. (2020) 'We are two languages here': The operation of language policies through spatial ideologies and practices in a co-located and a bilingual school. *Multilingua* 39 (6), 663–684.

From, T. and Sahlström, F. (2017) Shared places, separate spaces: Constructing cultural spaces through two national languages in Finland. *Scandinavian Journal of Educational Research* 61 (4), 465–478.

García, O. and Wei, L. (2014) *Translanguaging: Language, Bilingualism and Education*. London: Palgrave Macmillan.

Gumperz, J.J. (1982) *Discourse Strategies*. Cambridge: Cambridge University Press.

Heller, M. (2007) Bilingualism as ideology and practice. In M. Heller (ed.) *Bilingualism: A Social Approach* (pp. 1–22). London: Palgrave Macmillan.

Heller, M., Pietikäinen, S. and Pujolar, J. (2018) *Critical Sociolinguistic Research Methods. Studying Language Issues That Matter*. New York: Routledge

Hyttel-Sørensen, L. (2017) 'Gangster' or 'wannabe'. Experimental and ethnographic approaches to a contemporary urban vernacular in Copenhagen. Dissertation, University of Copenhagen.

Irvine, J.T. and Gal, S. (2000) Language ideology and linguistic differentiation. In P. Kroskrity (ed.) *Regimes of Language* (pp. 35–83). Santa Fe: School of American Research Press.

Jørgensen, J.N. (2008) *Languaging. Nine Years of Poly-lingual Development of Young Turkish–Danish Grade School Students*, vols I and II. Copenhagen: University of Copenhagen.

Jørgensen, J.N., Karrebæk, M.S., Madsen, L.M. and Møller, J.M. (2011) Polylanguaging in superdiversity. *Diversities* 13 (2), 23–37.

Karrebæk, M.S. (2013) 'Don't speak like that to her!' Linguistic minority children's socialization into an ideology of monolingualism. *Journal of Sociolinguistics* 17 (3), 355–375.

Kimanen, A.L., Alisaari, J. and Kallioniemi, A. (2019) In-service and pre-service teachers' orientations to linguistic, cultural and worldview diversity. *Journal of Teacher Education and Educators* 8 (1), 35–54.

Kristjánsdóttir, B. (2018) *Uddannelsespolitik i nationalismens tegn (Educational Policy in the Light of Nationalism)*. Aarhus: Aarhus Universitetsforlag.

Madsen, L.M. (2013) 'High' and 'low' in urban Danish speech styles. *Language in Society* 42 (2), 115–138.

Madsen, L.M., Karrebæk M.S. and Spindler Møller, J. (2016) (eds.) *Everyday Languaging: Collaborative research on the language use of children and youth*. Berlin: Mouton de Gruyter.

Makoni, S. and Pennycook, A. (2007) Disinventing and reconstituting languages. In S. Makoni and A. Pennycook (eds) *Disinventing and Reconstituting Languages* (pp. 1–41). Clevedon: Multilingual Matters.

McCarty, T.L. (2015) Ethnography in language planning and policy research. In F.M. Hult and D.C. Johnson (eds) *Research Methods in Language Policy and Planning* (pp. 81–93). Malden, MA: Wiley.

Milani, T.M. and Jonsson, R. (2012) Who's afraid of Rinkeby Swedish? Stylization, complicity, resistance. *Journal of Linguistic Anthropology* 22 (1), 44–63.

Møller, J.S. (2019) Recognizing languages, practicing languaging. In J. Jaspers and L.M. Madsen (eds) *Critical Perspectives on Linguistic Fixity and Fluidity: Languagised Lives* (pp. 29–52). New York: Routledge.

Padovan-Özdemir, M. and Moldenhawer, B. (2016) Making precarious migrant families and weaving the welfare nation-state fabric 1970–2010. *Race, Ethnicity and Education* 20 (6), 723–736, https://doi.org/10.1080/13613324.2016.1195358

Pennycook, A. and Otsuji, E. (2015) *Metrolingualism: Language in the City*. New York: Routledge.

Rampton, B. (2006) *Language in Late Modernity: Interaction in an Urban School*. Cambridge: Cambridge University Press.

Rampton, B. (2009) Interaction ritual and not just artful performance in crossing and stylization. *Language in Society* 38 (2), 149–176.

Sahlström, F., From, T. and Slotte-Lüttge, A. (2013) Två skolor och två språk under samma tak. In L. Tainio and H. Harju-Luukkainen (eds) *Kaksikielinen koulu – Tulevaisuuden monikielinen Suomi = Tvåspråkig skola - Ett flerspråkigt Finland i framtiden (Bilingual school – Multilingual Finland in the future)* (pp. 319–341). Turku: The Finnish Educational Research Association.

Salö, L., Ganuza, N., Hedman, C. and Karrebæk, M.S. (2018) Mother tongue instruction in Sweden and Denmark. Language policy, cross-fields effects, and linguistic exchange rates. *Language Policy* 17 (4), 591–610.

Shohamy, E. (2006) *Language Policy: Hidden Agendas and New Approaches*. New York: Routledge.

Slotte-Lüttge, A. (2005) Ja vet int va de heter på svenska: Interaktion mellan tvåspråkiga elever och deras lärare i en enspråkig klassrumsdiskurs (*I dunno wha' it is in Swedish: Interaction between bilingual students and their teachers in a monolingual classroom discourse*). Dissertation, Åbo Akademi University.

Slotte-Lüttge, A. (2007) Making use of bilingualism – construction of a monolingual classroom, and its consequences. *International Journal of the Sociology of Language* 2007 (187/188), 103–128.

Spolsky, B. (2004) *Language Policy*. Cambridge: Cambridge University Press.

Statistics Finland (2020) *Population Structure*. Helsinki: Statistics Finland. See http://www.stat.fi/til/vaerak/index_en.html

Tarnanen, M. and Palviainen, Å. (2018) Finnish teachers as policy agents in a changing society. *Language and Education* 32 (5), 428–443.

4 'I Am a Plurilingual Speaker, but Can I Teach Plurilingual Speakers?' Contradictions in Student Teacher Discourses on Plurilingualism in Spain, Slovenia and Finland

Júlia Llompart, Tjaša Dražnik and Mari Bergroth

This chapter investigates student teacher discourses on plurilingualism in four European initial teacher education (ITE) institutions located in Spain (Catalonia), Slovenia and Finland. As part of the European project called Linguistically Sensitive Teaching in All Classrooms, we collected student group thoughts using reflection instruments based on strengths, weaknesses, opportunities and threats (SWOT) analysis. Data from 173 student teachers enrolled in ITE at four universities located in Barcelona, Ljubljana, Vaasa and Jyväskylä were explored using qualitative analysis. By analysing the SWOT characteristics expressed by student teachers, we identified certain contradictions regarding plurilingualism and the use of plurilingual pedagogies. These contradictions relate to the positioning as 'being a plurilingual speaker' and 'becoming a teacher dealing with plurilingualism'. We discuss the similarities and differences between student voices in the light of the wider linguistic landscapes in the three countries and four universities.

Introduction

In Europe, over the last two decades, migration and mobility phenomena have added more diversification to the already existing regional linguistic diversity. Therefore, schools and high schools – especially in urban centres – are now multicultural and multilingual in terms of their composition. In fact, according to the Organisation for Economic Co-operation and Development (OECD), the percentage of students of immigrant background in the countries included in the OECD report increased by 6% between 2003 and 2015 (OECD, 2019a). Second-generation migrant students represented the group that had increased the most. This reality has launched changes and initiatives at different levels to change monolingually framed educational policies, programmes and practices. In fact, according to Conteh and Meier (2014), a desired turn towards multilingualism in education and research has been promoted, especially with the appearance of several concepts, models and didactic proposals, such as plurilingual competence (Coste *et al.*, 2009), language awareness (Cenoz *et al.*, 2017) and pluralistic approaches to languages and cultures (Candelier, 2008) in European policies and discourses. According to Busch (2011), the challenge for education stakeholders in different European regions is to decide which model to follow according to their particular sociolinguistic situation and needs.

Bergroth *et al.* (2021a) state that linguistically sensitive teaching (LST) is 'about acknowledging and understanding the role of languages of schooling, foreign/regional/minority languages taught in school and languages brought to school by the students, staff and the surrounding linguistically diverse society for learning and identity' (2021a: 3). In line with the multilingual turn and considering that teachers are key in promoting and applying LST in classrooms, initial teacher education (ITE) programmes in Europe have included linguistic and cultural diversity as a component in their courses. Although this component remains insufficient and fragmented (European Commission, 2017), research shows that there is implementational space for improvement (Bergroth *et al.*, 2021a). In fact, according to Alisaari *et al.* (2019), this multilingual turn in ITE is crucial to reach the desired change towards LST, which implies teachers' sensitivity towards the language dimension of education (Alisaari *et al.*, 2019; Lucas & Villegas, 2013).

This study took two main challenges, pointed out in previous research (Birello *et al.*, 2021), as points of departure:

(1) on the one hand, multi/plurilingual pedagogies are not fully integrated into teacher education practices (Bergroth *et al.*, 2021a);
(2) on the other, student teachers perceive that they are not being sufficiently trained for the linguistic and cultural diversity of schools (Llompart & Moore, 2020).

Moreover, Birello *et al.* (2021) noted that, although the positive discourse of the 'goodness of plurilingualism' and the recognition that it has to be carried out in schools are generally established, when student teachers position themselves as teachers in practice, their attitude towards plurilingualism is transformed into negative feelings of being under-trained.

In this chapter we focus on the contradictions observed in student teachers' discourses in three European contexts regarding their existing 'being a plurilingual speaker' discourse, their perception of plurilingualism and their 'emerging becoming a professional' discourse as teachers engaged in and promoting multilingualism (at the level of society) and plurilingualism (at the level of individuals). Moreover, we examine and discuss similarities and differences regarding this matter in the four ITE institutions located in three countries where the data were collected. To do this, we analyse the discourse of student teachers on linguistic diversity as they participate in discussion activities. The research questions guiding the study were as follows.

(1) What are student teachers' beliefs about plurilingualism and LST?
(2) What are student teachers' beliefs/feelings when positioning themselves as teachers who have to manage their teaching practice in multilingual environments and with plurilingual students?
(3) What, if any, are the relevant similarities and/or differences among the three contexts?

In the next sections, we first present the three country contexts where the data for this study were collected. Second, we focus on the theoretical framework, including student teachers' discourse, beliefs and ideologies. Third, we present the methodology and the means of analysis followed in this study. Fourth, we then analyse and discuss the data and, finally, offer conclusions and a closing discussion.

Linguistic Diversity in Schools in Spain (Catalonia), Slovenia and Finland

Catalonia is now multicultural and multilingual, with 16.2% of the population of migrant origin (Idescat, 2020). According to Grup de Llengües Amenaçades (2016), more than 300 languages are spoken in the region. As a first language, the population speaks Catalan (31.5% of the population), Spanish (52.7%), both Catalan and Spanish (2.8%), Arabic (2.2%), Romanian (1.1%) and other languages (3%). Several languages are spoken as first language by less than 1% of the population, namely Galician, French, Amazigh, Russian, Portuguese, Italian, Chinese, German and English (Idescat, 2018).

Catalan schools and high schools have been affected and are continuously challenged by the sociolinguistic reality. As a region within the Spanish state, Catalonia is regulated by the Spanish Law of Education (Ley Orgánica 3/2020, 2020), by which the general dispositions for education are established. There is freedom given to each region to create an educational curriculum, which can include the teaching and learning of a co-official language. In Catalonia, Catalan has been established as the vehicular language in education since the 1980s; it is taught with Spanish and at least one other language, usually English or French (Generalitat de Catalunya, 2017a). Historically, the region has managed plurilingualism – especially Catalan and Spanish – but the arrival of students from diverse countries, especially over the last three decades, has resulted in an extra challenge to adapt to increasing linguistic heterogeneity. Several phases of adaptation have been promoted by the Catalan Government (Llompart & Birello, 2020).

First, in 2004, the so-called Linguistic and Social Cohesion Plan (Generalitat de Catalunya, 2004) was created. This plan had the objectives of

(1) promoting the teaching and learning of Catalan following a language immersion approach;
(2) integrating students of migrant origin;
(3) achieving social cohesion and equal opportunities for children and youth.

Second, in 2017, a decree on educational inclusion (Generalitat de Catalunya, 2017b) was passed. This also indicated that the linguistic and cultural diversity of students had to be considered to attain full social cohesion and just and equitable education.

Third, in 2018, in line with the lower numbers of migrants arriving and the consolidation of European recommendations on plurilingual and pluricultural education, a new framework for linguistic diversity in schools was proposed, called the Language Model of the Catalan Education System: Language Learning and Use in a Multilingual and Multicultural Educational Environment (Generalitat de Catalunya, 2018). This document proposes plurilingual and pluricultural education in line with the current diverse backgrounds, family languages and linguistic practices found in educational institutions, and aims to help students prepare for a globalised world. Both the new framework and the decree proposed by the Catalan Government align with the present linguistic and cultural reality of Catalonia.

In the last two decades, to align with the reality in schools and the new demands, there has been adaptation in ITE degree plans, and new subjects have been added in response to the curricula for early childhood, primary and secondary education, other framework documents and the sociolinguistic reality of schools. For instance, in adapting the former ITE programme to transform it into a bachelor's degree (following the Bologna Process), in 2009 the Universitat Autònoma of Barcelona added a subject on School Language Policy and Plurilingualism for all primary school student teachers; in addition, an elective subject on Linguistic Reception in Schools was opened for early childhood and primary student teachers. Despite the enormous diversity among students in schools and high schools, student teachers of migrant backgrounds are still not common in ITE institutions in Catalonia but, as noted by Llompart and Birello (2020), student teachers of migrant backgrounds have begun to enrol in ITE programmes in recent years.

The next context, Slovenia, has always been a heterogeneous area. Its territory was always part of a larger, multinational entity, for example the Habsburg Monarchy and Yugoslavia in its various guises. Up to the 20th century, Slovene had the status of a minority language, used only in the private domain. However, over the last two centuries, the Slovene language was a crucial element in the process of creating the Slovene nation and its development into a nation state (Novak-Lukanovič & Limon, 2012) and, as stipulated in the Constitution of the Republic of Slovenia, it became the country's official language at the independence of Slovenia in 1991.

According to the last population census in 2002 (as quoted in Eurydice, 2021), Slovenian is the native language of 88% of the Slovenian population and 92% of the population uses the Slovenian language at home. In 2002, the total population of Slovenia was almost 2 million, of which 83% declared themselves to be Slovene. At that time, the constitutionally recognised minorities were Hungarians (0.3%), Italians (0.1%) and the Roma (0.2%). The other notable (self-declared) minorities were Serbs (2%), Croats (1.8%), Muslims (including Bosniacs) (1.6%), Albanians (0.1%), Macedonians (0.20%) and Montenegrins (0.1%). A total of 8.9% reported being of unknown ethnic group (Eurydice, 2021). Research in 2017 (Eurydice, 2017) also showed that 7.6% of 15-year-old learners in Slovenia speak a language different from Slovene at home.

The Slovenian language is the general language of instruction, as stipulated by Article 6 of the Basic School Act (1996). In border areas populated by Italian and Hungarian communities, the language of the minority has the status of an official language. Accordingly, members of Italian and Hungarian national communities in linguistically mixed areas have the right to education in their respective language, to radio and television programmes, and to communicate in their language with the authorities (Novak-Lukanovič & Limon, 2012). Two models of bilingual education have been implemented in linguistically mixed areas. In the first model, practised in the Slovene–Italian region, the educational process is conducted in the mother tongue and the second language is a compulsory subject. In the second model, used in the Slovene–Hungarian region, both languages are languages of instruction and school subjects. In the latter bilingual educational model, the concurrent method is applied during each lesson, with language switching (Novak-Lukanovič & Limon, 2012).

Increasingly, Slovenian education policies recognise multilingualism as one of the principles of a modern society and the foundation of tolerance between nations and linguistic communities (Krek & Metljak, 2011). The white paper on education in Slovenia (Krek & Metljak, 2011) recommends that schools offer a wide variety of languages: beyond languages that are part of the curriculum, schools should also suitably include languages that are not part of the curriculum but are present in the learning environment (e.g. students' first languages). One of the goals of the Resolution on the National Programme for Language Policy (Republic of Slovenia, 2021) is the development of multilingual and intercultural awareness to consider linguistic diversity and promote functional multilingualism. To achieve these aims, this resolution on language policy proposes concrete measures, including the promotion of multilingualism and plurilingualism in schools, systematic training of preschool teachers and teachers for establishing a plurilingual educational environment, training of other education staff in the basics of plurilingualism and plurilingual didactics, and language-sensitive teaching for working with immigrant students.

The third context of this study, Finland, is officially bilingual but also multilingual and multicultural, with a history of emigration (especially to the neighbouring country, Sweden) rather than immigration. However, today, immigration exceeds emigration and the only declining languages in Finland are the official national languages – Finnish and Swedish (Karlsson, 2017). According to the latest official statistics (Statistics Finland, 2021), at the end of 2020, 87% of the population resident in Finland had a Finnish-speaking background, 5.2% had a Swedish-speaking background and 7.8% had a foreign language background. When looking closer at foreign language speakers in Finland, the mobility from neighbouring countries is clear. The biggest groups of people with foreign backgrounds are from the neighbouring countries of Russia (or the former Soviet Union) and Estonia, and immigration has intensified since the collapse of the Soviet Union in the 1990s. Persons with former Soviet Union area backgrounds make up one-fifth of the total population of foreign background. Although Russia is a very large neighbouring country, it is not common for Finns to learn Russian as a foreign language in school. As noted by Mustajoki and Protassova (2015: 70) 'it is hard to find another country in the world where learning the language of a big neighbour is so rare'. However, Russian as a home language can be supported in Finland as there are around a dozen bilingual Finnish–Russian preschools and a bilingual state-owned school (Protassova *et al.*, 2022).

Like in Estonia – a country where the national language is closely related to the majority language of Finland (Finnish) – immigration to Finland has mainly been based on work and family relations (Jakobson *et al.*, 2012). Furthermore, the largest proportion of the foreign population in Finland is found in the monolingual Swedish autonomous region Åland (16.7%) but, of this group, 41% come from Sweden and speak the majority language of the region (Statistics Finland, 2021). Therefore, Russian, Estonian and Sweden-Swedish (i.e. Swedish as spoken in Sweden) speakers are not necessarily the first linguistic groups one thinks of when talking about pupils with immigration backgrounds.

Looking more closely at the statistics, they show that, of second-generation people with foreign backgrounds (born in Finland), 22% have

African backgrounds, 28% have Asian backgrounds and 46% have European backgrounds (Statistics Finland, 2021). In 2016, languages such as Arabic, Persian and Vietnamese were the fastest growing languages in Finland in terms of the number of speakers (Karlsson, 2017); these languages are therefore often connected with newly arrived immigrants. According to Eurydice (2019), in general, Finnish (education) language policies are deemed to place a strong emphasis on diversity. Linguistic rights are stated in the Constitution of Finland. Other than the national languages of Finland (Finnish and Swedish), the constitution states that the Sami, as an indigenous people, as well as the Roma and other groups, have the right to maintain and develop their languages and cultures. The language of instruction in Finland is either Finnish or Swedish, as stated in the Basic Education Act (628/1998). According to the act, the language of instruction may also be Sami, Roma or sign language. However, the act also states that teaching may be given partially in another language if this does not risk the pupils' ability to follow teaching, giving teachers the freedom to use languages other than the official language(s) for instruction. However, in the core curriculum for basic education (Finnish National Board of Education, 2016), in a way this freedom to use other languages turns into an obligation.

The view of linguistic and cultural diversity as an asset is identified as one of the core values guiding basic education and it is stated that, among other things, languages should be appreciated and the parallel use of various languages in school daily life should be seen as natural. Languages are identified to be of key importance for learning, interaction and cooperation. According to the curriculum, the role of languages in the building of identities and socialisation needs to be understood in schools. However, despite acknowledgement of linguistic and cultural diversity at policy level, there are still challenges in implementing the policies in practice.

On the one hand, the positive view of linguistic diversity is often related to globally valued languages such as English and French. In fact, English is often taught as a foreign language in schools and high schools, but it has also been implemented as a medium of instruction in ITE specialisations in Spain (Catalonia) and Finland, for instance. The spread of English as a medium of instruction but also as lingua franca has some implications for the study of student teachers' discourses regarding multilingualism and teaching plurilingual students (Dražnik et al., 2022). On the other hand, most ITE institutions include teaching related to diversity in their curriculum, but teacher educators have expressed a need for professional development courses regarding the theme of cultural diversity (Räsänen et al., 2018).

Despite the efforts made in each of the three contexts regarding both official documents and ITE, in 2017 the European Commission reported that student teachers feel unpreparedness to manage and teach students from diverse cultural and linguistic backgrounds (European Commission,

2017). More specifically, in Finland, it has been found that although most teacher education institutions include teaching related to diversity, student teachers struggle to see the connection between LST and teachers' relational competence during their practicums (Haagensen, 2020) and even teacher educators feel the need for continuing education on cultural diversity (Räsänen *et al.*, 2018). In Catalonia, student teachers have reported feeling insecure and lacking in training for managing diversity (Llompart & Moore, 2020). In Slovenia, teachers have stated that they are not well prepared to teach in a multicultural or multilingual setting, with 14% reporting a strong need for professional development in teaching in such settings (OECD, 2019b).

The aforementioned reports and studies were based on surveys and/or discourse analysis of student teachers, which were highly connected to their beliefs and ideologies – as in the present study. In the next section, we present the theoretical framework that allowed us to analyse student teachers' discourse on plurilingualism and their teaching practice in diverse environments.

A Framework to Analyse Student Teachers' Beliefs on Being and Becoming a Linguistically Sensitive Teacher

As already noted, since the turn of the millennium, European promotion of multilingualism and plurilingualism as a necessary, positive and a desirable objective in education has been running in the form of official documents, frameworks and didactic proposals. Indeed, research has shown that the pro-multilingualism European discourse seems to have entered into theory teachers' mindsets (Erling & Moore, 2021; Haukås, 2016). In spite of this, in teaching practice, the monolingual habitus (Gogolin, 2013) still seems to have a significant presence in classrooms. In fact, several studies have pointed to the existing contrast between the positive discourses of teachers and student teachers on plurilingualism as a phenomenon and the negative discourses on their beliefs and feelings regarding teaching in linguistically diverse classrooms (see e.g. Bergroth & Hansell, 2020; Birello *et al.*, 2021; Bredthauer & Engfer, 2016; Llompart & Birello, 2020). This contradiction is emphasised in the title of this chapter – specifically, student teachers are willing to adjust their experience of being a plurilingual speaker in line with European plurilingual discourses (being a plurilingual speaker is a positive feature), but they face challenges in teaching for plurilingualism (becoming a teacher of plurilingual students is a challenge).

According to Young (2014), crucial steps to successfully move towards LST in classrooms involve uncovering and analysing teachers' ideologies regarding language. Inspired by this, we draw on research on linguistic ideologies – which should help connect beliefs and real linguistic social conduct (Schieffelin *et al.*, 1998; Silverstein, 1979) – teacher cognition and, specifically, teachers' beliefs and ideologies in our research. Linguistic ideologies, initially defined by Silverstein (1979) and Irvine (1989), are beliefs about languages related to perceived language structure and use; they thus involve moral and political interests. For Woolard (2020), the term 'linguistic ideology' refers to implicit knowledge about languages and practices, related to a 'repeated social experience' a habitus, as described by Bourdieu (1991) and Woolard (2020: 2), which can be deployed implicitly or explicitly through verbalisations and/or embodied practices. In expanding the work on linguistic ideologies, Kroskrity (2010) proposed analysing them in terms of how they shape professional discourses and thus construct professional competence, as well as determining how professionals in specific fields perform linguistically. In this sense, analysing linguistic ideologies might be key to understanding implications for teachers and teaching practices.

The study of teacher thinking has been ingrained in studies on teacher cognition. Borg's work on teacher cognition (Borg, 2003, 2006, 2019), which he defines as what teachers think, know, believe and do, has been fundamental for understanding the complexity of teachers' thinking. According to Borg, teacher cognition is a dynamic interaction of the triad of cognition, context (whether professional, cultural, social or historical) and personal experience regarding schooling, contextual factors, training and classroom teaching practice (Borg, 2019). What student teachers and teachers believe may influence their present and future pedagogical decisions (Johnson, 1994; Pajares, 1992; Phipps & Borg, 2009). Thus, in the classroom

> teachers produce, affirm and/or disconfirm language policies every day – when they allow or disallow the use of one language or variety rather than another, when they choose to use a particular variety of a language to communicate with their students, when they prefer a certain structure over another in the curriculum, when they show their lack of knowledge about certain languages or varieties, etc. (Farr & Song, 2011: 660)

Despite living in the era of post-monolingualism (Yildiz, 2012) and superdiversities, one of the recurring language ideologies for education and language policy is still that of monolingualism (Farr & Song, 2011; Pulinx *et al.*, 2017). Recent research on teachers' beliefs regarding multilingual education points out a general tendency among teachers to perceive multilingualism as positive, valuable and something to be promoted (Bergroth & Hansell, 2020; Griva & Chostelidou, 2012; Haukås, 2016). In this sense, studies show, for instance, that teachers believe that language knowledge is important to promote intercultural communication (Arocena Egaña *et al.*, 2015) and that students' diverse languages should be encouraged (De Angelis, 2011). However, as indicated by Gkaintartzi *et al.* (2015), teachers' positive understandings of multilingualism are not directly translated into teaching practice. In fact, research shows that there might be a gap between positive beliefs about multilingualism and negative beliefs about linguistic diversity in classrooms and in teaching practice (Haukås, 2016). In this sense, teachers feel overwhelmed by students' multilingualism (Bredthauer & Engfer, 2016) and, as indicated by Birello *et al.* (2021), believe that instruction should be carried out only in one language and translation should be avoided (Cummins, 2014), that languages should be taught separately (Arocena Egaña *et al.*, 2015) to avoid interference and misunderstanding (Fallas Escobar & Dillard-Paltrineri, 2015) and teachers should know a language to allow its use in the classroom (De Angelis, 2011).

Pajares (1992) noted that teachers' beliefs might contradict one another. As recent research on teachers' beliefs about multilingualism shows, there is a gap between general positive beliefs about multilingualism and negative beliefs in teaching in practice (Basturkmen, 2012; Bergroth & Hansell, 2020; Dockrell *et al.*, 2022). As Bredthauer and Engfer indicate (2019: 112) 'The blatant discrepancy between the theoretical approval of multilingual didactics and lack of actual translations into teaching can be explained with regard to the teachers' insecurity and lack of knowledge how to integrate the concepts into their lessons'. Despite what Otwinowska (2014) indicated – that in-service teachers and plurilingual teachers are more aware of linguistic diversity than student teachers and non-plurilingual teachers – studies focusing on student teacher beliefs about multilingualism indicate that the results found regarding some teachers' beliefs can be greatly transferred into those of student teachers (Gkaintartzi *et al.*, 2015). In a recent study conducted by Birello *et al.* (2021), the discourse of student teachers clearly showed the contradiction between general positive beliefs about multilingualism and negative beliefs when imagining themselves in classroom practice. Other studies have pointed out that, among student teachers, feelings of being unprepared to be teachers in diverse environments are common (Llompart & Moore, 2020; Stunell, 2021).

The current study will contribute to the field of future teachers' beliefs – a field that has not been extensively explored (Iversen, 2021) – by offering a multi-sided analysis of student teachers' beliefs about plurilingualism and teaching in linguistically diverse environments. Moreover, it will allow us to observe a general tendency related to ITE in some European contexts and to offer some recommendations.

Methodology

The data for this study were collected within the framework of a European action research project called Linguistically Sensitive Teaching in All Classrooms (Listiac, 2021), which is an Erasmus+ Programme (Key Action 3: Support for Policy Reform). The aim of this three-year project (2019–2022) is to bring forth educational change at multiple levels by developing and experimenting with a theoretically informed reflection tool aimed at making (future) teachers linguistically more sensitive in their beliefs, attitudes and actions in mainstream classrooms. It mainly targets teacher educators, student teachers and in-service teachers. Nine European universities (from Belgium, Finland, France, Lithuania, Portugal, Slovenia and Spain) and three public ministries (from Finland, Portugal and Slovenia) participated in the project. The data for this study were collected in four of the nine higher education institutions, located in Vaasa (Finland), Jyväskylä (Finland), Catalonia (Spain) and Ljubljana (Slovenia), specifically in some groups of their ITE programmes. Details on the number of participants and their courses of study are shown in Table 3.1.

Following an action research methodology (see Bergroth *et al.* (2021b) for more details), the researchers, teacher educators and student teachers worked together to reflect on LST, their training in LST and their preparedness to manage diverse classrooms in their future classes. A Listiac reflection tool based on strengths, weaknesses, opportunities and threats (SWOT) analysis was used to promote discussion. There was an initial discussion based on a video. Then, student teachers carried out an individual SWOT analysis. When this task was finished, the student teachers were divided into groups of five or six and asked to prepare a collective SWOT document, which was discussed by the whole group at the end. The discussions were video and/or audio recorded, transcribed for analysis and translated into English; for space reasons, only translations to English are used in the data analysis section. All of the participants gave informed consent.

The analysis applied followed two main lines. In the first line, the analysis invoked discourse in interaction (Heller, 2005), focusing on student teachers' discourse in the discussion to construct collective SWOT analyses in groups. Doing this allowed us to discover common themes related to student teachers' beliefs and ideologies; at the same time, using SWOT analysis as a methodological tool prompted the student teachers

Table 3.1 Description of data

Location of institution	Course (study year)	Number of participants
Vaasa, Finland	Didactics II (third year) Intercultural education (third/fourth year)	41
Jyväskylä, Finland	Practicum seminar (first year) Language awareness (optional summer course)	45
Catalonia, Spain	School language policy and plurilingual education (third year) Practicum (third/fourth year)	61
Ljubljana, Slovenia	English through primary school curriculum (fourth year) Linguistic and intercultural awareness (fifth year)	26

to focus on strengths and opportunities versus weaknesses and threats. Thus, in the second line, when trying to identify emerging categories from the data, two main categories of beliefs and ideologies were identified:

(1) student teachers as plurilingual speakers: positively charged beliefs and ideologies;
(2) student teachers as future teachers for plurilingualism: negatively charged beliefs and ideologies.

The first category emerged mainly from analysing discourses regarding strengths and opportunities, whereas the second category emerged mainly from analysing discourses regarding weaknesses and threats. At the same time, each category was divided into more detailed sub-categories.

Data Analysis

As already mentioned, the data revealed that student teachers from the three countries participating in the study hold both positive and negative beliefs regarding plurilingualism and teaching in multilingual classrooms. In this section, we analyse student teachers' beliefs and connect them to their identity construction as future teachers for plurilingualism.

The appreciation of being a plurilingual speaker

The student teachers who participated in the study in the four ITE institutions are part of a generation of future teachers who have already been educated either bilingually or plurilingually and who grew up during the era of European promotion of multilingualism. It is thus not strange to observe in the data that these student teachers have a general pro-multilingualism and pro-multiculturalism discourse, as demonstrated in the following excerpts.

Excerpt 1.
As an opportunity, I also put the fact that there is so much cultural diversity in our society is an opportunity (Student teacher, Catalonia, Spain)

Excerpt 2.
What I would emphasise here is that you should portray it as something positive in the sense that you don't perceive it as annoying but as a challenge and a big plus for the others when you're discussing cultures and so on (Student teacher, Slovenia)

Excerpt 3.
In my opinion, language awareness doesn't take up space from the other languages, such as the languages that are usually taught in school – Finnish, English or Swedish – but it enriches every pupil's language use, way of thinking and development (Student teacher, Jyväskylä, Finland)

Excerpt 4.
OK for example, I said that I consider as my strength that I can speak three/four languages and knowing them can also help with including them in class – well, and if I understand them and also speak them, then maybe that helps with the work I've got to put into this (Student teacher 2, Catalonia, Spain)

yes, in fact, I said the same. Being plurilingual makes us know it first hand (Student teacher 1, Catalonia, Spain)

yes (Student teacher 3, Catalonia, Spain)

In these excerpts, both diversity and multilingualism are portrayed as positive: each concept is a 'chance', an 'opportunity', something 'positive', 'enriching', 'a plus' and even a 'strength' for the teaching profession. Our data show that this positiveness regarding multilingualism and diversity can be linked to the construction of a plurilingual speaker and teacher identity from a theoretical perspective. Our data reveal three main categories related to student teachers' positive beliefs, as detailed below.

Plurilingualism related to globalisation, intercultural communication and movement

Excerpt 5.
but I do imagine that as a teacher, you can justify that through... A lot of work today, it's very global and the economy is... It's good to know different languages and to be able to get along with people who have different cultural backgrounds and so on. Well, then this thing that it's... Easier to move outside... Or easier to move about internationally and cooperate with others globally (Student teacher, Vaasa, Finland)

Excerpt 6.
and... I also said that the world is now ruled by globalisation; ultimately, it is way easier to see different languages (Student teacher, Catalonia, Spain)

Excerpt 7.
maybe about the strengths – we have a lot of strengths – but maybe the most important is that we can, these students... is that if we can speak a lot of languages, that is a value, actually (Student teacher, Slovenia)

Student teachers construct an image of the clear need for plurilingualism in today's global, mobile and diverse world. Thus, student teachers' beliefs about plurilingualism are highly positive: being a plurilingual speaker is crucial for success. In spite of this, they seem to refer to an elite plurilingualism/multilingualism (Barakos & Selleck, 2019) – that is, those languages that are 'useful' for economic reasons, for work and to communicate on a global scale. This is related to the commodification of certain languages as capital that allows people to move and to participate in the economy (Heller *et al.*, 2014); this point has already been observed in previous studies (Birello *et al.*, 2021) and we return to it in the next section. Student teachers also consider that language knowledge – although only of certain languages – is a personal asset in terms of consciousness regarding people and cultures, as shown in the next excerpt.

> **Excerpt 8.**
> I like to think that I am a very language aware being. I notice different languages, their forms and cultures in the people and things around me. Also, I have always been eager to learn different languages, which certainly partly affects my language awareness and how it is revealed to others (Student teacher, Jyväskylä, Finland)

Plurilingualism and diversity as a compulsory component

Our data show that the student teachers participating in the study connect plurilingualism and diversity as a component in the policy documents, the laws and/or the curriculum.

> **Excerpt 9.**
> We have that which [name] said – we have the linguistical sensitivity in our policy documents so everyone like knows that it is something they should work towards (Student teacher, Vaasa, Finland)

> **Excerpt 10.**
> Yes, I put the inclusion decree… I wrote that most of the schools go for inclusive education, and so it is part of their educational project (Student teacher, Catalonia, Spain)

The student teachers thus believe that considering LST is not an option but a compulsory task in their profession – whether it comes from the core curriculum, as in the case of Finland, or the decree of inclusion, as in the case of Catalonia. Slovenia differs from the other cases because the data show that student teachers in this context do not seem to be aware of the existing official dispositions in Slovenia regarding how to be a linguistically sensitive teacher.

> **Excerpt 11.**
> I also wrote that the school curriculum or at least the Slovene one is not adapted to pupils who do not speak the official language. I mean, it's not mentioned anywhere [unclear] like coordinated xx so how are you supposed to work with such a student? (Student teacher, Slovenia)

In the three cases, student teachers are aware that LST is either in the policy/official documents (in Finland and Catalonia) or should be (Slovenia). This seems to result in their awareness of what can or cannot be done in classroom practice regarding LST. In this sense, they constructed the idea of a good teacher as the one who knows and follows the rules. We consider their discourse about LST and classroom practice in the next section.

Plurilingualism and classroom practice

Student teachers from the three country contexts analysed seem to have clear beliefs about what is required and what is not required to be a linguistically sensitive teacher in the classroom. We found several beliefs in our data regarding plurilingualism and classroom practice. On the one hand, student teachers believe that it is their duty to adapt to new situations and new ideas in schools (Excerpt 12).

Excerpt 12.
But if you work in a school setting, you need to adapt to new [concepts] (Student teacher, Vaasa, Finland)

On the other, they believe they have to fight common monolingual ideas to value pupils' plurilingualism, as demonstrated in the following excerpts.

Excerpt 13.
I also think I remember that in that course, at least in my group, we discussed this quite a bit, when you have another language than the language of schooling as [your] mother tongue, it's quite common that teachers get this attitude that 'in our school, we speak Swedish'. Because you don't want to, you don't quite understand what the pupils are saying to each other in their mother tongue, and you don't want there to be any bullying or something that you can't notice. But what you're basically saying then is that 'your mother tongue isn't as valuable and you can't speak it here'. That's so wrong (Student teacher, Vaasa, Finland)

Excerpt 14.
And since everyone should have the right to equal education then you have to, it doesn't matter what language. So, that is like our obligation then (Student teacher, Vaasa, Finland)

Excerpt 15.
I think that, uh, this is important because that way people who come from other countries feel less excluded, they have better chances to develop, and if we are open to new cultures, our students will be too as we are their models so that way there would be less stigma – less stereotypes – and therefore, new students would feel more accepted and welcomed (Student teacher, Slovenia)

Excerpt 16.
Under 'opportunities', I wrote that… there is a chance to value cultural identity… to work from the other point of view, to give more visibility to other cultures and to keep on fighting for inclusion (Student teacher, Catalonia, Spain)

As can be observed from these excerpts, the student teachers seem aware that there are still monolingual ideologies that circulate in the school context – such as 'one school, one language' – and the traditional conception that the teacher needs to understand and know everything. They believe that this should be avoided and that they need to value students' home languages. Moreover, this is not only something that *could* be done, but something that s*hould* be done. Student teachers construct the idea of a good teacher for plurilingualism and diversity as someone who must avoid monolingual ideologies and fight against exclusion and stereotypes and for an equal education regarding languages. For them, a good linguistically sensitive teacher should be a welcoming and accepting role model. In addition, student teachers pointed out the whole-school approach that they believe a linguistically sensitive teacher should take (Excerpt 17).

> **Excerpt 17.**
> I think the best is doing it in every subject, or not subject – like, take every opportunity – because that way is like language, it is part of communication and communication is present in every moment or educational opportunity, so if you only do it while teaching languages – well, it is like if here we only spoke about mm… linguistic sensitivity in the plurilingualism subject we are limiting it… to a certain amount of hours (Student teacher, Catalonia, Spain)

Thus, for student teachers, being a linguistically sensitive teacher is a global task that should be done without time and subject limitations.

Overall, analysis of the data from the four ITE institutions in the three contexts displays the construction of the student teachers as plurilingual speakers and linguistically sensitive teachers in a similar fashion. We observed that student teachers accommodate their own identification, on the one hand, as plurilingual speakers for living in today's world – which permeabilises neoliberal ideologies about certain elite languages (Barakos & Selleck, 2019) – and, on the other, as linguistically sensitive teachers. In the second case, the student teachers categorise a good teacher as a professional who knows the rules – or the absence but necessity of them (and thus who knows what the policy documents, laws and/or curriculum indicate regarding LST) – and who is respectful, inclusive and adaptive towards the diversity of languages in the classroom and aware of the need to avoid certain monolingual ideologies and practices that circulate in society. Thus, in the three contexts, when they situated themselves as speakers and as teachers in theory, student teachers' beliefs regarding multilingualism and multiculturalism in the classroom were positive, which is in line with previous studies focusing on in-service teachers (Arocena Egaña *et al.*, 2015; De Angelis, 2011; Griva & Chostelidou, 2012; Haukås, 2016).

In the next section we present data where the student teachers position themselves in the roles of in-service teachers and in teaching practice to observe the continuity or discontinuity of this positiveness.

Moving into practice: What now?

When picturing themselves in diverse/multilingual and multicultural classrooms, the student teachers' current novice teacher status and negatively charged ideas emerged in the discourse. In general, these ideas relate to what the participants describe as weaknesses that they have as future teachers, contributing to a collaborative construction of their identification as teachers for LST.

One finding from the data is that student teachers at the four ITE institutions in the three contexts believe that they are not sufficiently trained to be linguistically sensitive in the classroom, especially to teach students of migrant origin, as demonstrated in the following excerpts.

> Excerpt 18.
> I think that since we're students, we might not have had the opportunity to practice how to face these kinds of situations with several different… with students who have different backgrounds in the field. In theory, we might know how to handle it, but we don't know how to handle it when we're in that situation (Student teacher, Vaasa, Finland)

> Excerpt 19.
> I don't actually have any experience in linguistically sensitive teaching, but I hope to get it during my studies or after graduation (Student teacher, Vaasa, Finland)

> Excerpt 20.
> also, we don't have a lot of experience with such pupils – at least during our studies, we didn't have unless you happened to meet some during practice. So basically, we don't have any experience to be able to say that we've worked for one week with non-native pupils (Student teacher, Slovenia)

> Excerpt 21.
> I mean, at university, they give us some ideas and some things, but once we start working as teachers, we will have very little experience, and we will be very young and maybe eh… We try this thing, which is really well done, but when we actually try it, we see that there are several mistakes or that we really cannot do it because… apart from other difficulties… (Student teacher, Catalonia, Spain)

As can be observed in these excerpts, the student teachers believe that they are theoretically trained professionals but lack practical hands-on experience regarding LST and, consequently, do not have enough practice, resources and strategies to act in the field. Thus, when positioning themselves as teachers in the classroom, the positive ideas on linguistic and cultural diversity and education shift to emphasising their novice status, and negatively charged beliefs appear as they categorise themselves as young, unexperienced, fearful (see Dražnik *et al.*, 2022, for more detail) and doubtful professionals who are not ready for LST. Moreover, this lack of experience and resources is related to the insufficient and/or inadequate training they have received during their ITE so far, as previously observed by Llompart and Moore (2020).

The data also reveal that there is a big shift towards plurilingualism in the classroom being viewed as a problematic aspect that student teachers express as not knowing how to manage.

Excerpt 22.
Yeah, I think that maybe that teachers maybe find it tough to like use their energy to... maybe if there are students with a different mother tongue than they are used to that it takes like a lot of time, surely, and some things might need to be explained like more thoroughly and gone through. And if the teacher isn't, for example, so good at let's say English and has to speak like partly in English with someone, then maybe they find it tough and start avoiding the situation in a sense (Student teacher, Vaasa, Finland)

Excerpt 23.
... and ehm it was quite hard. Then when you realised that there is not really a shared language, that she/he could not speak English at all, or like very badly, and then like how you explain for example in history [class] what a sailing boat is. When you can't say it in English. And I can't speak Turkish, so how do you kind of find that shared language? Then to teach these things so will it then be enjoyable (Student teacher, Vaasa, Finland)

Excerpt 24.
I put down how to even work with such children – that we're scared, then how to find help. I don't know, maybe how to even tackle the problem of not understanding their language. I mean, it's a big burden for us as well, or I mean, it's hard for us [to be in the position of] not [being able] to understand (Student teacher, Slovenia)

Excerpt 25.
... but then once they get back to the class, how do you incorporate someone whose language roots are so different? (Student teacher, Catalonia, Spain)

Notably, student teachers' beliefs towards managing plurilingualism in the classroom are negatively charged and strongly connected to being scared and anxious. Thus, when positioning themselves as teachers in classrooms, the diversity of languages becomes challenging – it is something that requires energy and something a teacher might want to avoid. For them, non-elite plurilingualism – especially when it does not include English – is problematic for communication and for teaching success. As teachers in a diverse classroom, they categorise themselves as professionals who lack strategies to communicate with students with whom they do not share the same language. This reinforces the previous idea that student teachers' positive beliefs regarding multilingualism are connected to their identity as speakers and to some kind of elite multilingualism. However, this could also be connected to a fear that is echoed from society, which is the idea of the need to master all languages in a multilingual classroom to be a competent teacher in a diverse environment. In this sense, a clear need to address these ideas in ITE appears. Moreover, regarding the previously expressed linguistic awareness, once student teachers imagine being faced with diverse languages in class, bringing languages into play and comparing them becomes problematic, as expressed in the following excerpt.

> **Excerpt 26.**
> I think that the difficulty is finding the balance between learning a language and also another one, making them comparable and giving them the same importance – because nowadays, there are a lot of kids who speak Amazigh and we don't give them the space we might have to give them. But then of course, we aren't trained in this aspect, so I think here is the dilemma of it all (Student teacher, Catalonia, Spain)

We thus observed a shift from an accepted and promoted theoretical linguistic and cultural diversity to a problematic one, as imagined in the real teaching practice. Furthermore, the student teachers do not seem to recognise their plurilingualism as a resource for either managing the classroom or having the necessary relational competence with both students and their families.

> **Excerpt 27.**
> 'write things that we are afraid of and need help to tackle' – that is like just that we like get uncomfortable when something differs from what we are used to when there are other cultures that behave [in different ways], that have other norms, etc. We feel uncomfortable, so we get maybe a little scared of the situation (Student teacher, Vaasa, Finland)

> **Excerpt 28.**
> The same for contact with parents, as well, that we might have read about it a bit, but at least in my case, it still feels quite scary. (Student teacher, Vaasa, Finland)

Regarding relational competence, our data show that student teachers assume that their (perceived) ignorance of other cultures and norms might affect their communication with some students and their families. They categorise themselves as teachers who would be uncomfortable and scared of not knowing how to deal with the unknown.

All in all, this section has allowed us to analyse the shift in the student teachers' discourse from categorising themselves as aware and accommodating of modern views of plurilingualism and teachers for LST in theory to insecure, resourceless and unprepared future teachers in classrooms. Although these results are in line with those of previous studies (e.g. Birello *et al.*, 2021; Haukås, 2016), they offer us a multi-contextual observation on what is still to be improved regarding ITE and teacher preparedness for classrooms that are linguistically and culturally diverse.

Discussion

In this chapter, focusing on four ITE institutions in three contexts – Finland, Spain (Catalonia) and Slovenia – and analysing student teachers' SWOT identification regarding plurilingualism and conducting LST, we have been able to answer our three initial research questions.

(1) What are student teachers' beliefs about plurilingualism and LST?
(2) What are student teachers' beliefs/feelings when positioning themselves as teachers who have to manage their teaching practice in multilingual environments and with plurilingual students?
(3) What, if any, are the relevant similarities and/or differences among the three contexts?

Regarding the first question, we observed a positive construction of student teachers as plurilingual speakers and as teachers for plurilingualism – in theory.

In seeking an answer to the second question, we noted a negative construction of their imagined future teacher identification for plurilingualism, which they relate to not having enough practical training, experience or language knowledge, and not being able to rely on their relational competence in linguistically diverse situations. We have thus identified an existing gap between positive beliefs and negatively charged ones. This shift from a positive discourse to a negatively charged one and the reasons for it that teachers and student teachers display regarding plurilingualism have been noted in previous works (Birello *et al.*, 2021; Bredthauer & Engfer, 2019; Haukås, 2016). Our study contributes to this field of enquiry in the sense that we have focused on student teachers and we have offered a multi-context analysis that points to rather similar situations in several ITE institutions in Europe. In fact, a similar pattern was observed in the four ITE institutions in the three contexts, which answers the third initial research question. The general tendency observed might be crucial for the rethinking of some aspects regarding ITE.

We acknowledge that, by using the SWOT tool for later analysis of the student teachers' discourse, we specifically prompted weaknesses and fears as part of the data collection. At the same time, this explicit prompting might be necessary to surpass the surface of matters and help student teachers to go beyond the 'right answers' (as we have observed previously, Bergroth & Hansell, 2020), relating to European, national and regional discourses regarding multilingualism – especially if only scrutinised through the lens of 'elite' languages. Moreover, using the SWOT tool as a means of data collection allowed the student teachers to express anxieties and fears regarding their future teaching practice in diverse environments. We suggest that further research on these fears and anxieties might give clues to better plan courses that support diversity by lowering these anxieties, which might impair future LST in all classrooms (Dražnik *et al.*, 2022).

The results of this research are in line with Young's (2014) postulate regarding the need to listen to student teachers. In this sense, it seems clear that reflection has proven to be a very important tool to face fears regarding LST in ITE training. Our data show that student teachers relate their fears to a lack of practical training, knowledge and experience. We suggest that, to overcome these fears, practical elements should be incorporated in various ITE courses. Based on the data, some of these elements could involve looking up basic terminology in different languages (e.g. the word 'addition' in the most common foreign languages in the country), learning alphabets in different writing systems, using Google Translate to translate authentic messages from teachers in languages not familiar to students and looking at official resources for information about education systems in different languages. These types of 'survival skills' in diverse languages may be useful reminders that teachers do not need to master 'other' languages as experts.

We also conclude that, apart from the need for more practical training, it might also be necessary to include training in critical sociolinguistics within ITE. Self-reflection on beliefs about language and language learning and use, linguistic ideologies, linguistic norms, elite and non-elite languages, and understanding neoliberal discourses will also be important in ITE because student teachers' beliefs and ideologies will be translated into their future teaching practice and actions. Substantial attention has been paid to training regarding how people learn languages – going from a monolingual view to a plurilingual view, competences, constructivism and so on – but we might still need to focus on other societal discourses that circulate and engage in self-reflection. Other scholars have proposed including a critical linguistic awareness component in ITE, in in-service continuing professional training (Taylor *et al.*, 2018; Young, 2014) and in schools (Martín-Rojo, 2019).

Our data show that student teachers expect to rely heavily on the use of English in cases where there is no shared language between the pupil and the (student) teacher. The use of English often helps the teacher but, for the pupil, it may add to the number of languages they need to handle in practical situations because it may replace instructions in one majority language (school language) with yet another majority language (English). Although English-medium instruction is gaining a foothold even in ITE programmes (Dafouz, 2018) and it is often thematically connected with supporting multilingualism (Bergroth *et al.*, 2021a), based on our analysis, we recommend that ITE institutions do not place too much emphasis on the role of English as the only way to prepare teachers to reduce social and linguistic inequities in education. Indeed, our data strongly suggest that, during their studies, student teachers need to meet, react and act in languages that are not in a majority position or taught in schools as national/regional/foreign languages to prepare for their future profession. Providing a 'safe space' for testing out different interactional solutions during teacher training will not necessarily give all the right answers for all the situations/languages that teachers encounter in schools, but it may give teachers much-needed self-confidence and trust in their own capacity to be both plurilingual speakers and to teach plurilingual speakers.

Acknowledgements

The authors thank Listiac project partners Josephine Moate and Pauliina Sopanen for collecting and sharing the data from Jyväskylä, Finland. This work was supported by the EACEA under Grant 606695-EPP-1-2018-2-FI-EPPKA3-PI-POLICY.

References

Alisaari, J., Heikkola, L.M., Commins, N. and Acquah, E. (2019) Monolingual ideologies confronting multilingual realities: Finnish teachers' beliefs about linguistic diversity. *Teaching and Teacher Education* 80, 48–58.

Arocena Egaña, E., Cenoz, J. and Gorter, D. (2015) Teachers' beliefs in multilingual education in the Basque Country and in Friesland. *Journal of Immersion and Content-Based Language Education* 3 (2), 169–193.

Barakos, E. and Selleck, C. (2019) Elite multilingualism: discourses, practices, and debates. *Journal of Multilingual and Multicultural Development* 40 (5), 361–374.

Basic School Act 12/96 (1996) Basic School Act 12/96. *Official Gazette of the Republic of Slovenia (Uradni list RS)* (29 February 1996).

Basturkmen, H. (2012) Review of research into the correspondence between language teachers' stated beliefs and practices. *System* 40, 282–295.

Bergroth, M. and Hansell, K. (2020) Language-aware operational culture – Developing in-service training for Early childhood education and care. *Apples* 14 (1), 85–102. https://apples.journal.fi/article/view/98004

Bergroth, M., Llompart, J., Pepiot, N., van Der Worp, K., Dražnik, T. and Sierens, S. (2021a) Identifying space for mainstreaming multilingual pedagogies in European initial teacher education policies. *European Educational Journal* 21 (5), 801–821. https://doi.org/10.1177/14749041211012500

Bergroth, M., Llompart, J., Pepiot, N., Sierens, S., Dražnik, T. and van Der Worp, K. (2021b) Whose action research is it? Promoting linguistically sensitive teacher education in Europe. *Educational Action Research* 1–20. https://doi.org/10.1080/09650792.2021.1925570

Birello, M., Llompart, J. and Moore, E. (2021) Being plurilingual versus becoming a linguistically sensitive teacher: Tensions in the discourse of initial teacher education students. *International Journal of Multilingualism* 12 (4), 586–600. https://doi.org/10.1080/14790718.2021.1900195

Borg, S. (2003) Teacher cognition in language teaching: A review of research on what teachers think, know, believe, and do. *Language Teaching* 36 (2), 81–109.

Borg, S. (2006) *Teacher Cognition and Language Education: Research and Practice*. London: Bloomsbury Publishing.

Borg, S. (2019) Language teacher cognition: Perspectives and debates. In X. Gao (ed.) *Second Handbook of English Language Teaching*. Cham: Springer.

Bourdieu, P. (1991) *Language and Symbolic Power*. Cambridge: Polity Press.

Bredthauer, S. and Engfer, H. (2016) Multilingualism is great – but is it really my business? Teachers' approaches to multilingual didactics in Austria and Germany. *Sustainable Multilingualism* 9, 104–121.

Busch, B. (2011) Trends and innovative practices in multilingual education in Europe: An overview. *International Review of Education* 57 (5–6), 541–549.

Candelier, M. (2008) Approches plurielles, didactiques du plurilinguisme: Le même et l'autre. Recherches en didactique des langues et des cultures (Pluralistic, didactic approaches to plurilingualism: The same and the other. Research in the teaching of languages and cultures). *Les Cahiers de l'Acedle* 5, 65–90.

Cenoz, J., Gorter, D. and May, S. (eds) (2017) *Language Awareness and Multilingualism*. Cham: Springer.

Conteh, J. and Meier, G. (eds) (2014) *The Multilingual Turn in Languages Education: Opportunities and Challenges*. Bristol: Multilingual Matters.

Coste, D., Moore, D. and Zarate, G. (2009) *Plurilingual and Pluricultural Competence: With a Foreword and Complementary Bibliography*. Strasbourg: Council of Europe.

Cummins, J. (2014) Rethinking pedagogical assumptions in Canadian French immersion programs. *Journal of Immersion and Content-Based Language Education* 2 (1), 3–22.

Dafouz, E. (2018) English-medium instruction and teacher education programmes in higher education: Ideological forces and imagined identities at work. *International Journal of Bilingual Education and Bilingualism* 21 (5), 540–552.

De Angelis, G. (2011) Teachers' beliefs about the role of prior language knowledge in learning and how these influence teaching practices. *International Journal of Multilingualism* 8 (3), 216–234.

Dockrell, J.E., Papadopoulos, T.C., Mifsud, C.L. et al. (2022) Teaching and learning in multilingual Europe: Findings from a cross-European study. *European Journal of Psychology of Education* 37, 293–320.

Dražnik, T., Llompart, J. and Bergroth, M. (2022) Student teachers' expression of 'fear' in handling linguistically diverse classrooms. *Journal of Multilingual and Multicultural Development*, https://doi.org/10.1080/01434632.2022.2086258

Erling, E. and Moore, E. (2021) Socially just plurilingual education in Europe: Shifting subjectivities and practices through research and action. *International Journal of Multilingualism* 18 (4), 523–533. https://doi.org/10.1080/14790718.2021.1913171

European Commission (2017) Preparing teachers for diversity. The role of initial teacher education: Final report – study. See https://publications.europa.eu/en/publication-detail/-/publication/b347bf7d-1db1-11e7aeb3-01aa75ed71a1

Eurydice (2017) *Key Data on Teaching Languages at School in Europe – 2017 Edition*. Eurydice Report. Luxembourg: Publications Office of the European Union.

Eurydice (2019) *Integrating Students from Migrant Backgrounds into Schools in Europe: National Policies and Measures*. Eurydice Report. Luxembourg: Publications Office of the European Union.

Eurydice (2021) Slovenia overview. See http://eacea.ec.europa.eu/national-policies/eurydice/content/slovenia_en

Fallas Escobar, C. and Dillard-Paltrineri, E. (2015) Professors' and students' conflicting beliefs about translanguaging in the EFL classroom: Dismantling the monolingual bias. *Revista de Lenguas Modernas* 23, 301–328.

Farr, M. and Song, J. (2011) Language ideologies and policies: Multilingualism and education. *Language and Linguistics Compass* 5 (9), 650–665.

Finnish National Board of Education (2016) *National Core Curriculum for Basic Education 2014*. Helsinki: Finnish National Board of Education.

Generalitat de Catalunya (2004) Pla per a la llengua i la cohesió social (Language and social cohesion plan). See https://enxarxats.intersindical.org/nee/pla_lleng_cohesocialGC.pdf

Generalitat de Catalunya (2017a) Curriculum d'educació primària (Primary education curriculum). See https://educacio.gencat.cat/web/.content/home/departament/publicacions/colleccions/curriculum/curriculum-ed-primaria.pdf

Generalitat de Catalunya (2017b) Decret 150/2017, de 17 d'octubre, de l'atenció educativa a l'alumnat en el marc d'un sistema educatiu inclusiu (Decree 150/2017, 17 October, for educational attention to students in the frame of an inclusive educational system). *Diari Oficial de la Generalitat de Catalunya.*

Generalitat de Catalunya (2018) The language model of the Catalan education system: Language learning and use in a multilingual and multicultural educational environment. See http://ensenyament.gencat.cat/web/.content/home/departament/publicacions/monografies/model-linguistic/model-linguistic-Catalunya-ENG.pdf

Gkaintartzi, A., Kiliari, A. and Tsokalidou, R. (2015) 'Invisible' bilingualism – 'invisible' language ideologies: Greek teachers' attitudes towards immigrant pupils' heritage languages. *International Journal of Bilingual Education and Bilingualism* 18 (1), 60–72.

Gogolin, I. (2013) The 'monolingual *habitus*' as the common feature in teaching in the language of the majority in different countries. *Per Linguam* 13 (2), 38–49.

Griva, E. and Chostelidou, D. (2012) Monolingual competence development in the Greek education system: FL teachers' beliefs and attitudes. *International Journal of Multilingualism* 9 (3), 257–271.

Grup de Llengües Amenaçades (2016) Les llengües a Catalunya (The languages in Catalonia). See http://www.gela.cat/doku.php?id = llengues

Haagensen, J. (2020) Lärarstuderandes förståelse av språklig mångfald som en del av den relationella kompetensen (Student teachers' understanding of linguistic diversity as a part of the relational competence). In H. Hirsto, M. Enell-Nilsson, H. Kauppinen-Räisänen and N. Keng (eds) *Workplace Communication III* (pp. 88–99). Vaasa: VAKKI Publications. See https://vakki.net/index.php/2020/12/31/workplace-communication-iii/

Haukås, Å. (2016) Teachers' beliefs about multilingualism and a multilingual pedagogical approach. *International Journal of Multilingualism* 13 (1), 1–18.

Heller, M. (2005) Discourse and interaction. In D. Schiffrin, D. Tannen and H.E. Hamilton (eds) *The Handbook of Discourse Analysis* (pp. 250–264). Oxford: Blackwell Publishers.

Heller, M., Pujolar, J. and Duchêne, A. (2014) Linguistic commodification in tourism. *Journal of Sociolinguistics* 18 (4), 539–566.

Idescat (2018) Enquesta d'usos lingüístics de la població. Població segons llengua inicial (Survey of the linguistic uses of the population. Population according to initial language). See https://www.idescat.cat/pub/?id=eulp&n=3163

Idescat (2020) Població a 1 de gener. Total i estrangera (Population on January 1. Total and foreign). See https://www.idescat.cat/poblacioestrangera/?b=0

Irvine, J.T. (1989) When talk isn't cheap: Language and political economy. *American Ethnologist* 16, 248–267.

Iversen, J. (2021) Negotiating language ideologies: Pre-service teachers' perspectives on multilingual practices in mainstream education. *International Journal of Multilingualism* 18 (3), 1–14. https://doi.org/10.1080/14790718.2019.1612903

Jakobson, M.L., Järvinen-Alenius, P., Pitkänen, P., Ruutsoo, R., Keski-Hirvelä, E. and Kalev, L. (2012) The emergence of Estonian–Finnish transnational space. In P. Pitkänen, A. Içduygu and D. Sert (eds) *Migration and Transformation: International Perspectives on Migration*, vol. 3 (pp. 159–206). Dordrecht: Springer.

Johnson, K. (1994) The emerging beliefs and instructional practices of preservice English as a second language teachers. *Teaching and Teacher Education* 10 (4), 439–452.

Karlsson, F. (2017) *The Languages of Finland 1917–2017*. Turku: Lingsoft.

Krek, J. and Metljak, M. (eds) (2011) Bela knjiga o vzgoji in izobraževanju v Republiki Sloveniji (White Paper on Education in Slovenia). Ljubljana: Zavod RS za šolstvo. See http://pefprints.pef.uni-lj.si/1195/1/bela_knjiga_2011.pdf

Kroskrity, P. (2010) Language ideologies: Evolving perspectives. In J. Jaspers, J.O. Östman and J. Verschueren (eds) *Handbook of Pragmatics Highlights 7. Society and Language Use* (pp. 192–211). Amsterdam: John Benjamins.

Ley Orgánica 3/2020 (2020) Ley Orgánica 3/2020 de 29 de diciembre, por la que se modifica la Ley Orgánica 2/2006, de 3 de mayo, de Educación (Organic Law 3/2020, of December 29th, amending the Organic Law 2/2006, of May 3rd, of Education) *Boletín Oficial del Estado, 340*, 30 December 2020, 122868–122953. See https://www.boe.es/eli/es/lo/2020/12/29/3

Listiac (2021) Linguistically sensitive teaching in all classrooms. See https://listiac.org/

Llompart, J. and Birello, M. (2020) Migrant and non-migrant origin pre-service teachers' beliefs about multilingualism and teaching in multilingual classrooms: convergences and divergences. *Sustainable Multilingualism* 44, 112–123. https://doi.org/10.2478/sm-2020-0015

Llompart, J. and Moore, E. (2020) *La reflexión para la didáctica lingüísticamente inclusiva (Reflection for linguistically sensitive teaching). Textos de Didácitca de la Lengua y la Literatura* 88. Barcelona: Graó.

Lucas, T. and Villegas, A.M. (2013) Preparing linguistically responsive teachers: Laying the foundation in preservice teacher education. *Theory Into Practice* 52 (2), 98–109.

Martín-Rojo, L. (2019) El difícil camino de la integración en Madrid (The difficult path towards integration in Madrid). *Archi-letras Científica* 11, 275–292.

Mustajoki, A. and Protassova, E. (2015) The Finnish–Russian relationships: The interplay of economics, history, psychology and language. *Russian Journal of Linguistics* 23 (4), 69–81.

Novak-Lukanovič, S. and Limon, D. (2012) Language policy in Slovenia. *Language, Culture and Curriculum* 25 (1), 27–39.

OECD (2019a) *The Lives of Teachers in Diverse Classrooms*. Education Working Paper No. 198. Paris: OECD Publishing.

OECD (2019b) TALIS 2018 results (volume I): Teachers and school leaders as lifelong learners. Paris: OECD Publishing. See https://read.oecd-ilibrary.org/education/talis-2018-results-volume-i_1d0bc92a-en

Otwinowska, A. (2014) Does multilingualism influence plurilingual awareness of Polish teachers of English? *International Journal of Multilingualism* 11 (1), 97–119.

Pajares, F. (1992) Teachers' beliefs and educational research: Clearing up a messy construct. *Review of Educational Research* 62 (2), 307–332.

Phipps, S. and Borg, S. (2009) Exploring tensions between teachers' grammar teaching beliefs and practice. *System* 37, 380–390.

Protassova, E., Golubeva, A. and Mikelsone, I. (2022) Russian as a home language in early childhood education. In M. Schwartz (ed.) *Handbook of Early Language Education* (pp 373-402). Springer, Cham.

Pulinx, R., Van Avermaet, P. and Agirdag, O. (2017) Silencing linguistic diversity: The extent, the determinants and consequences of the monolingual beliefs of Flemish teachers. *International Journal of Bilingual Education and Bilingualism* 20 (5), 542–556, https://doi.org/10.1080/13670050.2015.1102860

Republic of Slovenia (2021) Resolucija o Nacionalnem programu za jezikovno politiko 2021–2025 (Resolution on the National Programme for Language Policy of the Republic of Slovenia 2021–2025. *Official Gazette of the Republic of Slovenia (Uradni list RS). 94/21*. See http://www.pisrs.si/Pis.web/pregledPredpisa?id = RESO123

Räsänen, R., Jokikokko, K. and Lampinen, J. (2018) Kulttuuriseen moninaisuuteen liittyvää osaaminen perusopetuksessa – Kartoitus tutkimuksesta sekä opetushenkilöstön koulutuksesta ja osaamisen tuesta (Knowhow on cultural diversity in basic education – A survey on research and teaching staff training and need for support). See https://www.oph.fi/sites/default/files/documents/

Schieffelin, B.B., Woolard, K.A. and Kroskrity, P.V. (eds) (1998) *Language Ideologies: Practice and Theory*. Oxford: Oxford University Press.

Silverstein, M. (1979) Language structure and linguistic ideology. In P. Clyne, W.F. Hanks and C.L. Hofbauer (eds) *The Elements: A Parasession on Linguistic Units and Levels* (pp. 193–247). Chicago: Chicago Linguistic Society.

Statistics Finland (2021) Population structure. Annual Review 2020. See http://www.stat.fi/til/vaerak/2020/02/vaerak_2020_02_2021-05-28_tie_001_en.html (accessed September 2021).

Stunell, K. (2021) Supporting student-teachers in the multicultural classroom. *European Journal of Teacher Education* 44 (2), 217–233. https://doi.org/10.1080/02619768.2020.1758660

Taylor, S., Despagne, C. and Faez, F. (2018) Critical language awareness. In J.I. Liontas (ed.) *The TESOL Encyclopedia of English Language Teaching* (pp. 1–15). Hoboken: Wiley.

Woolard, K.A. (2020) Linguistic ideologies. In J.M. Stanlaw (ed.) *The International Encyclopedia of Linguistic Anthropology*. Hoboken: Wiley.

Yildiz, Y. (2012) *Beyond the Mother Tongue: The Postmonolingual Condition*. New York: Fordham University Press.

Young, A.S. (2014) Unpacking teachers' language ideologies: Attitudes, beliefs, and practiced language policies in schools in Alsace, France. *Language Awareness* 23 (1–2), 157–171.

5 In Search of Dominant Language Constellations among Multilingual Young Adults in Cyprus and Finland: The Influence of Multiple Language Use and Practices on Linguistic Identity and Trajectories as Future Teachers

Sviatlana Karpava, Mikaela Björklund and Siv Björklund

This chapter examines multiple language use, practices and language identity of young adults in two multilingual contexts – Cyprus and Finland. The aim of the study is to explore the possibilities of identifying dominant language constellations (DLCs) in elicited answers that focus on language use, practices, mastery and linguistic identity. Data on these thematic issues were collected with the help of questionnaires, group discussions and written assignments. Both contexts are represented by the voices of university students (eight students in Cyprus and six in Finland) who communicate daily in several languages via their university studies, bilingual communities and/or mixed-marriage families, and who all have ambitions for a future profession in education. The analysis is twofold. The first part investigates the relationship between the role of the presence of individual languages in the participants' multiple language contexts and the participants' emic perspective on their linguistic identity. The second part focuses on whether and how the participants' multilingual contexts are mirrored in future trajectories for DLCs and multiple language use as professionals within education.

Introduction

Recent increases in migration, globalisation and glocalisation have changed our linguistic, social and communicative practices and our perception of the reality and the multilingual, multicultural environment (Aronin, 2020; Kirby, 2009) that has been characterised as current multilingualism (Singleton *et al.*, 2013) or the new linguistic dispensation (Aronin, 2017). The language–society interdependence is complex and depends on various factors, such as language status and legitimisation, politics, ideology, education, geographical and social contexts (Aronin, 2015, 2019, 2020). This study focuses on student teachers in two geographically and linguistically different teacher education settings in order to explore the students' multilingual practices (see Aronin, 2020) and current dominant language constellations (DLCs), and how these are interconnected and may affect their linguistic identity and future trajectories as professionals within education. This kind of comparison across different contexts aims to contribute to the body of research on DLCs and multilingual practices, especially within the field of education (see Aronin and Vetter (2021) for recent DLC studies in this field). Inspired by Larissa Aronin's discussion on *longue durée* as a valid perspective in studying DLCs (Aronin, 2020), this chapter tries to uncover DLCs as a useful tool in search of linguistic identities and future trajectories of teaching practices in the classroom.

Multilingualism as a characteristic of individuals, organisations and societies

Multilingualism, as analysed within complexity/dynamic systems theory (Aronin & Jessner, 2015; Jessner, 2008, 2012; Larsen-Freeman, 2012, 2016), takes into consideration individual and societal multilingualism and multilingual practices that are dynamically intertwined with individuals' cognitively based autonomous subsystems, interacting and triggering the emergence of new qualities within the whole system (Aronin, 2020; Capra & Luisi, 2014). Complexity is further associated with diversity (Aronin, 2020; Vertovec, 2007).

Different languages come into contact to create a situation of dynamic multilingualism (Lo Bianco & Aronin, 2020). Geopolitical, historical, sociocultural, political, environmental, ideological and material factors come into play, along with the 'prestige' of one language. Not all languages are used, maintained and transmitted, which can lead to a situation of language attrition and shift. In these dynamic multilingual contexts, self-identity is fluid and flexible; it comprises individual and collective identity, habitus or unconscious identity, agency and reflexivity, which are re-evaluated and adjusted throughout the life trajectory of an individual and is connected to citizenship and solidarity (Lizardo, 2017).

Since global migration, multilingualism and multiculturalism have become the norm (Cenoz & Gorter, 2015), it is important to include critical language awareness as a component in teacher training programmes so that there is a link between theory and practice (Gorter & Arocena, 2020; Young, 2014). Student teachers need to develop a positive attitude towards multilingualism and inclusive teaching, learning and assessment (De Angelis, 2011; Haukås, 2016; Heyder & Schadlich, 2014; Jakisch, 2014; Otwinowska, 2014). In this context, multilingual practices and prevalent DLCs among teachers and in educational institutions become a relevant focal point (e.g. Björklund *et al.*, 2020).

Perspectives on DLCs

DLCs allow us to critically examine multilingual practices as they can reveal the vehicle languages of multilingual speakers – the cluster of languages that helps them operate in society at the current time and place, and which can change throughout their life trajectory (Aronin, 2006, 2016; Singleton *et al.*, 2013; Vertovec, 2014). Thus, DLCs can help describe the current stage, in time and space, of the multilingual practices of an individual, which will undergo certain modifications over a long time period (*longue durée*: Braudel, 1958), and can be predicted by the DLC based on patterns of uniformity and congruity (Aronin, 2020). DLCs can have individual and societal levels of analysis and attention is also paid to new DLCs, multimodal entities, whose key features are connectedness and relationships among linguistic, emotional, cognitive, physiological and material dimensions (Aronin, 2020).

According to Aronin (2020), there are certain conditions that should be fulfilled for languages to be part of a DLC: they all need to have certain common functions and be (reasonably) immediately available for (authentic) communication (cf. Kannangara, 2020). A DLC, as an abstract construct as well as a model for research and a unit of analysis, can help us to represent the multilingual reality in settings under investigation (Aronin, 2020). It is important to pay attention to the emergent quality of the DLC as a unit, which is not exactly the sum of its parts. The focus is on (1) how languages are interrelated and contribute to the configuration of the DLC and (2) presenting this information in visual and tangible forms (Aronin, 2020). A DLC is thus characterised by internal coherence – the integration of languages in one communicative, linguistic, cultural, cognitive and sociological unit – the constituent parts of which are in constant interaction, transformation and configuration (Aronin, 2020).

Based on the qualities associated with DLCs, the concept seems to be a valuable instrument in language learning, teaching and language policy studies (Aronin, 2016; Lo Bianco, 2020). According to Lo Bianco and Aronin (2020), the diffusive spread of English as lingua franca or global language worldwide cannot be ignored in the study of multilingualism, although the presence and use of English in various domains differ from country to country. English is a prominent language in both contexts of this study and it is included as a way of capturing the complex reality of multilingual practices among a sample of student teachers in Cyprus and Finland.

By implementing a DLC framework in this study, our analysis focuses on the dynamic and fluid nature of multilingualism and language pluralism (Lo Bianco, 2020; Slavkov, 2020). We distinguish between the linguistic repertoire, the total number of languages known by the participants and the DLC, which is the vehicle (selected languages for use) and forms the core or the most active part of the linguistic repertoire. As suggested by Banda (2020), the use of a DLC uncovers overlaps of DLCs – effective communicative choices that can be constrained by social changes, agency and subjective needs and motivations (Lo Bianco & Aronin, 2020). To identify the DLCs of our participants, we used both an etic perspective (DLC = carrying out the complete set of functions characteristic of a human language and reasonable immediacy) and an emic perspective (self-identification of linguistic identity), which also served to identify the sample of the student population to be included in the study.

Languages and Language Varieties in the Two Contexts of this Study

Cyprus

Cyprus can be characterised as multilingual. Apart from Greek Cypriot and Turkish Cypriot communities, there are minorities who live in the country (e.g. Armenians, Latins, Maronites), residents of British origin and immigrants from various countries of the EU, non-EU Eastern Europe, Asia and especially the former Soviet Union (Hadjioannou *et al.*, 2011). In addition, Greek Cypriots are considered to be bilectal (Grohmann *et al.*, 2017; Rowe & Grohmann, 2013, 2014) as they use two varieties (Standard Modern Greek and Cypriot Greek), which differ in the domain of use (formal vs. informal, urban vs. rural), status (high vs. low) and in terms of phonetics, morpho-phonology, lexicon and morphosyntax (e.g. Arvaniti, 2010; Chatzikyriakidis, 2012; Newton, 1972; Pappas, 2014; Revithiadou, 2006). Regarding the mainstream secondary educational system, Standard Modern Greek is used at public Greek-speaking schools rather than the pupil's home variety as the latter is associated with an inferior language status, negative stereotypes and the view that it is an obstacle for academic success (Ioannidou, 2009; Ioannidou *et al.*, 2020; Tsiplakou *et al.*, 2018).

Among the foreign language groups, the Russian community is considered to be the largest. The Russian-speaking population living in Cyprus is not homogeneous. They come from Russia and other republics of the former Soviet Union and vary in terms of their socioeconomic status, reasons for coming to and staying in Cyprus and family composition. Mixed-marriage families, with one partner Russian and the other Greek Cypriot, are multilingual, having Greek, English and Russian in their DLCs. Russian immigrant families, with both spouses of Russian origin, are mainly bilingual, using Russian and English in their daily lives (Karpava, 2015, 2020; Karpava *et al.*, 2018). Russian is one of the important languages on the island with regard to the linguistic landscape, business and tourist spheres (Eracleous, 2015; Karpava, 2022).

English is a global language and is widely used all over the island for communication, education and business (Buschfeld, 2013; Schneider, 2003, 2007). Cypriot Greek has a lot of borrowed English words and English–Greek code-switching is a common phenomenon in the country (Papapavlou & Satraki, 2013). According to Karoulla-Vrikkis (2010), there are two ideological positions in Cyprus: Hellenisation and Cypriotisation. The supporters of the first consider English be a threat to 'Greekness', Greek national identity, language, culture and religion, whereas those in favour of the second position try to promote the use of English as it is associated with the modern world and globalisation (Themistocleous, 2019).

Finland

Finland is an officially bilingual country in northern Europe and both national language groups (Finnish-speaking and Swedish-speaking) are judicially guaranteed equal linguistic rights in society. According to Statistics Finland (2021a), of the total population of 5.5 million people, the majority (87.3%) has registered Finnish as their first language (L1), 5.2% have registered Swedish as their L1 and the remaining 7.5% have reported a 'foreign language' as their L1. The number of foreign language speakers has undergone a distinct change during the last 20 years. In 2000, the proportion of 'foreign language' speakers was only 1.9%, increasing to 7.8% in 2020 (Statistics Finland, 2021b). The proportion of the two national languages has remained relatively stable, albeit with a slow decrease for Swedish and a small increase for Sami, 1734 L1 Sami speakers in 2000 compared with 2008 L1 Sami speakers in 2020 (Statistics Finland, 2021b). Since only one language can be registered as L1, the statistics do not reveal the everyday bilingualism encountered by many Swedish speakers in Finland. However, this bilingualism is visible, for example in the fact that education is arranged on Finnish- and Swedish-medium educational paths from early childhood education to higher education (Bergroth & Hansell, 2020).

Only approximately half of the pupils in Swedish-medium primary schools (Grades 1–6) come from monolingual Swedish homes. A substantial proportion (40%) of pupils come from bilingual (Swedish–Finnish) backgrounds and 4% are from monolingual Finnish homes. The available statistics do not account for other types of bi/multilingual homes, but 5% of the pupils in Swedish-medium primary schools are reported to come from homes with another home language altogether (Hellgren et al., 2019). In addition, according to reports from the early 2000s (Oker-Blom et al., 2001), every fifth pupil in Grades 1–6 in Swedish-medium schools is bilectal (standard Swedish and a dialectal vernacular). There are also great local variations regarding the proportion of both bilingual (Finnish–Swedish) and bilectal pupils in Swedish-medium schools. Similar regional variations apply also for languages other than the national ones in both Swedish- and Finnish-medium schools.

When recent comparisons were made between first foreign language (English) and the two second national languages in the Finnish context (Björklund et al., 2020), the second national language is not necessarily a second language in the traditional sense (see Baker & Prys-Jones, 1998; Kachru, 1985): the so-called first foreign language English seems to enjoy a much stronger position in the community than would be expected for a traditional foreign language (cf. Leppänen et al., 2008).

Björklund (2007) pointed out that if the move towards regarding English as a second language in Finland continues, one needs to be aware of the probable effects it will have on the second national languages. If this trend continues, Swedish–Finnish bilinguals and children with immigrant backgrounds are probably the only groups who will become functionally trilingual, whereas initially monolingual students (Finnish or Swedish) will, in practice, become bilingual Finnish–English or Swedish–English. However, as the statistics show, there is also a noticeable increase in ethnical and linguistic variation on the educational scene in several communities in Finland, which has brought about the need for a broadened set of tools related to linguistic and cultural awareness for teachers (see Hellgren et al., 2019). In the national curriculum guidelines for comprehensive education from 2016, policy measures were taken to support this development (Bergroth & Hansell, 2020).

Aims of the Study

The aim of this study was to investigate how different individual and societal multilingual practices contribute to shaping individuals' conceptualisation of their linguistic identity and their future trajectories as professionals in education. By comparing different DLCs in two contexts we sought to uncover cross-contextual multilingual practices that influence the self-identification of linguistic identity of participants enrolled in teacher education that may affect possible DLCs in their future professional life.

The study builds on previous research on individual DLCs in Cyprus (Karpava, 2020) and Finland (Björklund *et al.*, 2020). The Cyprus case was focused on DLCs among Russian-speaking students and adult females, native speakers of Russian, members of mixed-marriage families in Cyprus and mothers of bi/multilingual children. The Finnish case described the DLC Finnish–Swedish–English in national curricula for basic education and among student teachers with either Swedish or Finnish as their first language. Whereas the previous studies were centred on mapping and including multilingual practices for identification of individual DLCs, we now further explore how different factors in DLCs (such as society, language policy, ideology, attitudes, language usage, life trajectories) are mirrored in how student teachers (future English teachers in Cyprus and future class teachers in Finland), during their initial teacher education, define their linguistic identity and indicate their future roles as teachers in language-diverse classes.

Although surrounded by a similar institutional context (in this case university students aiming at the teaching profession), the status of the languages in the DLCs differs in the two contexts.

In Cyprus, a heritage language, used mainly at home and with family, constitutes an essential language for individual DLCs as well as the prominent role of English (due to the post-colonial situation).

In Finland, the two national languages (Finnish and Swedish) interplay with English. This DLC constellation was prominent in a comparison between the DLCs emerging in the national core curriculum from 2004 and 2014 as well as in individual student teacher voices (Björklund *et al.*, 2020). However, the clear pattern of the three languages among the student teachers differed somewhat depending on the linguistic background of the participants of the study, resulting in the balance between English and the second national language (Swedish) being 'specifically delicate and subject to change' (Björklund *et al.*, 2020: 113).

The following research questions are addressed:

(1) How does the perceived language identity of the study participants relate to daily multiple language practices?
(2) What future trajectories as professionals in education do the DLC patterns of the participants of the study indicate?
(3) What similarities and differences in the DLC patterns are there among student teachers in Cyprus and Finland?

Data

The data for this study comprise two sets of student teacher data. Both data sets were derived from data from a larger population of student teachers. Originally, the data from the two contexts were designed for other studies; for this study, similar issues relating to multiple language use and linguistic/cultural identity were chosen for comparison. Although the themes are similar, it should be noted that the questions for initiating the different themes were not identical. However, within both data sets, the student teachers' self-identification of linguistic identity served as the main criterion for inclusion in the study. Variety in self-identification expressed as monolingual, bilingual or multilingual identity was the starting point for further analysis of how well self-identification meets multilingualism as defining characteristics for individual, societal and institutional multilingual practices that are dimensions of the conceptual perspective of DLCs. The label 'student teacher' is used here to refer to the whole data set, but it should be noted that the participants in Cyprus were future English language teachers whereas the participants in Finland were future primary level teachers or special needs education teachers.

In Cyprus, the study participants were eight student teachers and data were collected in 2020–2021 with the help of questionnaires, individual interviews and focus group discussions. In Finland, the participants were six student teachers and data were collected during spring semester 2018 through small group discussions and individual written assignments. All participants in both contexts gave their consent to participate in the research project and for the data to be used for research purposes, in line with ethical considerations.

Method and Analysis

The Cyprus data were collected via written questionnaires and in-depth semi-structured oral individual and focus group interviews, reflecting a qualitative method (Flick, 1998; Hatch & Wisniewski, 1995; Lamnek, 1989). This type of interview, which does not impose the question–response structure, offers a more in-depth participant perspective. It also offers a selection of themes and topics, ordering and wording for the questions, while eliminating the possibility of interviewer influence.

The interview questions were based on the results of a large-scale questionnaire (Karpava *et al.*, 2018, 2019, for more details) with a focus on participants' socioeconomic background, their language and cultural identities, and their immigrant experience in Cyprus, both online and offline. The oral mode allowed the speakers to elaborate more on certain issues and to provide more information, supported by actual examples from their immigrant life experiences and detailed descriptions of actual conditions, which helped to define meaning categories. The interviews lasted for 30–60 minutes, and were carried out in Greek, English or Russian, based on the preference of each student. A snowball sampling technique and a convenience sampling technique were used to access the participants (i.e. selection of an initial group of immigrant/minority students, who then indicated other potential participants who belong to various immigrant/minority communities in Cyprus).

The Finnish data were collected through small group discussions (3–5 students in each group) or individual written reflections with a cohort of student teachers after an introductory academic course on language education for student teachers attending Swedish-medium primary education and special needs education programmes. The participants were asked to reflect upon four different themes related to their own language learning, bi- and multilingualism, language usage and experiences of language and culture in the teaching profession. Each small group had approximately 40 minutes to discuss the four themes. The themes and questions have been piloted in other studies (e.g. Peltoniemi *et al.*, 2020). The language backgrounds of the students varied to some extent, but all had Swedish as their L1 or one of their regularly used languages. For this study, six participants were chosen based on their own language identifications. In our analysis of the data, we implemented the conceptual perspective of the DLC to help us explain both societal and individual multilingual practices among student teachers. The social status of a language is a crucial factor (Lo Bianco & Aronin, 2020) and therefore the two chosen contexts provide a starting point for contrasting individual DLCs within different multilingual societal contexts.

Results

Cyprus

The Cyprus context was represented by eight students (age range 18–26; seven females and one male) with various L1 backgrounds and linguistic repertoires (see Table 5.1). They had a minority or immigrant L1 background and different linguistic identities and perceptions of their monolingual, bilingual or multilingual status.

Not all of the participants were born in Cyprus. Their length of residence in Cyprus ranged from 9–26 years and their age of onset to Greek ranged from 0–12 years. They mainly had a hybrid language identity (see Boland, 2020) and only half of them considered themselves full members of Cyprus society. Due to the bilectal setting in Cyprus, most of the participants mentioned Greek as part of their linguistic identity. Their linguistic repertoires comprised up to five languages, while their DLCs included two to three languages, which were their L1, Greek and English (Figure 5.1).

Linguistic self-identification as a mirror of multilingual practices

The Cyprus participants differed in terms of their linguistic identity (self-identification) – whether they considered themselves monolingual (C2 and C4), bilingual (C3 and C8) or multilingual (C1, C5, C6 and C7).

Table 5.1 Participants in Cyprus

	Gender	L1	Linguistic repertoire	DLC
Student teacher 1 (C1)	Female	Romanian + Greek + English	Romanian, Greek, English	Romanian, Greek, English
Student teacher 2 (C2)	Female	Bulgarian	Bulgarian, Greek, English, Spanish, Russian	Bulgarian, Greek, English
Student teacher 3 (C3)	Female	Lebanese + Greek	Lebanese, Greek, English, French	Lebanese, Greek, English
Student teacher 4 (C4)	Female	Greek	Greek, English, Arabic	Greek, English
Student teacher 5 (C5)	Female	Greek + Russian + English	Greek, Russian, English, Spanish	Greek, Russian, English
Student teacher 6 (C6)	Female	Russian + Ukrainian + Greek + English	Russian, Ukrainian, Greek, English	Russian, Greek, English
Student teacher 7 (C7)	Male	Greek + Russian + English	Greek, Russian, English, Georgian	Greek, Russian, English
Student teacher 8 (C8)	Female	Armenian + Cypriot Greek	Armenian, English, Greek, French, German	Armenian, English, Greek

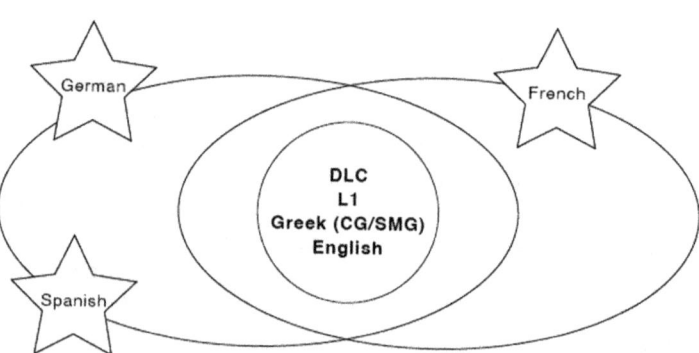

Figure 5.1 DLCs of the participants in Cyprus (CG = Cypriot Greek; SMG = Standard Modern Greek)

As shown in the interview Excerpt 1, C4 stated that she has a monolingual identity even though she knows and speaks other languages. She identifies herself with the dominant languages of society.

Excerpt 1.
As for my language identity it is Greek, but of course I know English and use it a lot [...] Arabic does not play a great role in my everyday life, even though it is my native language. (C4)

The situation seems to be even more complex in the case of C2, as she considers herself multilingual and emphasises the benefits of being multilingual in her everyday life and future career but, at the same time, identifies herself only with one language – Bulgarian – as her L1, her heritage language.

> **Excerpt 2.**
> For me being bilingual/multilingual is something good because I deal with languages, I always wanted to deal with languages as a profession, to become a teacher or to do translation or something similar. I can say that by now except for Bulgarian, Greek and English, I also learn Russian and Spanish, Spanish I can say even at a better level than Russian because in Russian I understand better as it is close to Bulgarian but I cannot speak properly. Yes, I consider myself to be multilingual and this is something good because languages open new horizons and new doors if I can say for the future. As for my language identity I would say that I identify myself with Bulgarian because it is my mother tongue and I feel that I possess it/ know it better than other languages, I feel more comfortable with it. (C2)

Another pattern among the participants was to identify themselves as bilinguals regarding their language identity. C3 identified herself with the majority language (Greek) and minority language (Lebanese), even though she also knows English and French.

> **Excerpt 3.**
> The two languages with which I identify myself are Greek and Arabic (Lebanese), because English and French I consider as extra languages, they are not part of my language identity but of my language competence probably. (C3)

C8 can be characterised as an emergent multilingual, her linguistic identity is bilingual (Armenian and Greek), but she has learned other languages. Her linguistic repertoire has expanded with English, German and French, even though her DLC comprises Armenian, Greek and English and at home she speaks mainly Armenian with her family. It seems that her views regarding linguistic identity are not static, but change throughout her life trajectory.

> **Excerpt 4.**
> I am multilingual, before I would say that I am bilingual, I grew up bilingual, Greek and Armenian and then throughout my life I became multilingual. Ok, I speak Greek and Armenian, my friends are mainly Cypriots and Armenians. The grandfather of my grandmother came to Cyprus. I am probably the fifth or sixth generation of Armenians in Cyprus. We have an Armenian community in Cyprus, primary and secondary schools. At school, I have learned Armenian, Greek and English. At home, my parents and me speak Armenian, but because we live in Cyprus and when we [children] had our first connection with school, we had contact with Greek, from the neighbours as well and with the TV, the internet, so we are influenced by Greek. We code-switch a lot at home, Greek–Armenian, but we speak mainly Armenian at home. (C8)

The other four participants in Cyprus identified themselves with multiple languages, with their L1, Greek, English and maybe other foreign languages. In the case of C1, these languages are Romanian, Greek and English (Excerpt 5). It is noteworthy that the linguistic repertoire, DLC and linguistic identity of C1 fully correspond to each other. C5 has a similar match concerning linguistic identity and DLC, which includes Greek, Russian and English, even though her linguistic repertoire was wider as she was also learning Spanish at the time of the study.

> **Excerpt 5.**
> I will say that my language identity is in three languages because ok, I am from Romania, I was born there, then I came to Cyprus. I have learnt Greek very well, I speak English very well, I read books in English, I have a very good connection with English, so I can say that I identify myself with three languages [...]. (C1)

As regards C6, it seems that her linguistic identity, linguistic repertoire and DLC have undergone changes during her life trajectory, especially after she immigrated to Cyprus. She came to Cyprus with knowledge of her L1 (Ukrainian), L2 (Russian) and some English (L3). Then, she had to learn Greek (L4), which she now considers the most important language for her. There is an overlap between linguistic identity and linguistic repertoire, but her L1 (Ukrainian) is not in her DLC anymore as it is not one of the vehicle languages for her in Cyprus.

> **Excerpt 6.**
> I would say Russian, Greek, English [language identity], but the most important for me now is Greek, not even English, as I am planning to stay in Cyprus. I came to Cyprus when I was 7 years old. I knew some English, but I had to learn Greek... I can say that the status of the Russian language in Cyprus now is high, it depends on political and economic factors. Now I feel much more comfortable to use Russian with my friends in comparison to the situation six years ago. (C6)

C7 considers multilingualism as a great benefit, but thinks that several languages from a young age may be challenging. There is an overlap in terms of his linguistic identity, and DLC: Greek, Georgian and Russian are the vehicle languages, but the level of proficiency and domain of use of these languages differ. It seems that the majority language (Greek) and English (lingua franca on the island and the medium of instruction at his university) were considered to be the most important languages for him at this stage of his life.

> **Excerpt 7.**
> To be a multilingual, when you know more languages it makes you good, but maybe it is difficult for younger children, for example one of our neighbours speaks Greek, English and Bulgarian, when he was younger, he did not know any of the languages properly, there was no balance among the languages [...] I personally did not have any confusion/

mixture among the three languages Russian, Greek and English. As for my language identity, if I have to choose one language then it is Greek, but now that I am at university, I use English a lot, I have classes in English, I have started to think more in English, I know more words in English and the Russian so and so… With my parents I speak some Georgian, but not so often […]. (C7)

Hybrid language identity depends on the amount of time spent in the country and language proficiency in the target language and on the type of family setting (e.g. mixed marriage, bilingual, multilingual). Strong links with the L1 country and culture, history and traditions, cuisine, TV programmes, heritage language use, maintenance and transmission are some of the factors that contribute to the L1 linguistic identity. The linguistic behaviour of both mother and father is of great importance, as is that of the extended family and relatives. Linguistic and cultural identities are affected by customs, material culture and stereotypical rules in the L1 countries, as noted by C5.

> Excerpt 8.
> Cypriot, Greek and Russian, I identify myself with the particular cultures due to matters of origin; my mother is Russian and my father is half-Cypriot and half-Greek. I grew up with relatives from all three countries, being heavily influenced, and having consistent associations with the countries' cuisines, customs, prejudices as well as manners and/or ethics. (C5)

The participants also commented that the majority language speakers, Greek Cypriots, also have a favourable view on multilingualism in Cyprus, although they admit that there is a difference between younger and older generations of the Cypriot Greek population regarding the acceptance/discrimination of 'foreign' influence in Cyprus, with the former tending to be 'more open-minded'. Their attitudes depend on immigrant/minority language(s) status, socioeconomic factors and the level of proficiency in the majority language.

> Excerpt 9.
> My answer is yes and no. Some people are but some are not. When I moved to Cyprus in 2007 there was more racial discrimination but now they are more open minded. Personally, I did not experience discrimination but some people that were from other countries did and I have seen it. The main reason was that they do not speak correctly the language. (C1)

> Excerpt 10.
> Most of the residents accept people who speak other languages than their language, they often ask you something about your culture or even try to learn your language. (C2)

Greek Cypriots could have a negative attitude towards foreigners if they speak their own L1 as they do not understand what they say. Some of them have stereotypical judgments, as shown in the following excerpts.

Excerpt 11.
At primary school because people could not understand my language and that was something annoying to some of them who might think that I was talking against them. (C2)

Excerpt 12.
Sometimes in Cyprus they have some stereotypes such as the word *Αράπης* [Arab], which I find it very offensive. (C4)

Excerpt 13.
There are still people from my country of residence who are bullying and discriminating people from other countries [...] They tell people that speak other languages to go back to their countries. (C7)

Some of the students admitted that they still observe bullying, discrimination or negative attitudes that depend on socioeconomic factors and L1 origin.

Stance towards future teacher pedagogy as a mirror of self-experienced multilingualism

It seems that the students' bi/multilingual background affected their stance towards the teaching of English. They supported the multilingual turn in teaching (Conteh & Meier, 2014; May, 2014, 2019), taking their complex and dynamic life trajectories into consideration, the benefit of bilingualism and multilingualism, communicative needs and contextualisation (Creese & Blackledge, 2010).

Excerpt 14.
For the purposes of teaching English as a foreign or second language, the most practical version of the language to employ is English as lingua franca. This is because it constitutes a more universal form of the language, and has been precisely been modelled in order to facilitate communication between people on a global scale for various purposes. Considering its function, as well as the learners' goals, which are usually along the lines of practical communication, English as a lingua franca can prove more dynamic and inclusive than a native form of English. (Focus group discussion)

In addition, the students prefer to have a combination of cultures in order to promote diversity but at the same time implement contextualisation (Excerpt 15).

Excerpt 15.
As for which culture it is more advisable to be taught in an EFL classroom, a combination of cultures could be the most suitable option. This is because, on the one hand, being able to use English in a global context requires that one familiarises with the Western cultural context, as it is the source culture. On the other hand, however, the teacher may also need to culturally contextualise his/her teaching by focusing on the local culture, in order to make the lessons more relatable to the students, and thus both engage their interest and make the material more

comprehensible. Nevertheless, teaching methods and materials with a global thematic combination could be useful in preventing cultural hegemony, while promoting diversity. (Focus group discussion)

The students also suggest a shift from teacher-centred to student-centred teaching (Excerpt 16).

> **Excerpt 16.**
> In the Cypriot community, what is mainly missing is the student-centred teaching methods. Teacher-centred pedagogy does not assist on the same level, due to the lack of interaction and material embracement. Thus, more interaction with the students is needed without diminishing the presence of the figure of the teacher from the course of learning. This can be achieved possibly through providing material beyond that of textbooks (e.g. games, writing or listening), giving more motivation to the students to work effectively on the language they are learning. (Focus group discussion)

They have also commented on the teaching materials, which should include multilingual and multicultural issues (Excerpts 17 and 18).

> **Excerpt 17.**
> Teachers and teaching materials should acquire a crucial role in culture learning. Most of the coursebooks I saw tended to use one specific variety of English. However, they included various locations, and ethnicities of characters. Lastly, there were both familiar and unfamiliar topics, as the books referred to both local and global issues. (Focus group discussion)

> **Excerpt 18.**
> Moreover, as it concerns what culture to teach it would be more affective and productive for the student to learn not only about British culture or the American one, but a bit of every culture that has English as lingua franca, for example Australia. Different cultures and ethics is what manifests one's mind and spirit… (Focus group discussion)

It should be noted that the bi/multicultural background of the students affects their stance and attitudes towards multilingualism in education and in society. Another shared vision is that most of the students are in favour of teaching English as lingua franca.

Finland

The Finnish study comprised a sample of six students (future primary level teachers), chosen from a larger cohort of students taking part in a university course. The sample was chosen to represent a variety in the students' self-identification of their linguistic identity as tripartite (monolingual, bilingual or multilingual), equally distributed between the participants (see Table 5.2).

Although the construction of linguistic identity may seem very static (as shown in Table 5.2), many of the participants refer to their linguistic

Table 5.2 Participants in Finland

	Gender	L1	Linguistic repertoire	DLC
Student teacher 1 (F1)	Female	Swedish	Swedish, English, Finnish, German, Russian, Norwegian (Dari)	Swedish, English, Finnish
Student teacher 2 (F2)	Female	Swedish	Swedish, English, Finnish	Swedish, Finnish, English
Student teacher 3 (F3)	Female	Finnish + Swedish	Swedish, Finnish, English, German, Spanish	Finnish, Swedish (English)
Student teacher 4 (F4)	Female	Swedish + English	Swedish, English, Finnish (Italian)	Swedish, English, Finnish
Student teacher 5 (F5)	Male	Swedish + English + Finnish	Swedish, English, Finnish (German, Russian)	Swedish, Finnish, English
Student teacher 6 (F6)	Female	Swedish + Finnish + English	Swedish, Finnish, English, German (Spanish)	Swedish, Finnish, English

identity as fluid and dynamic (see e.g. Lizardo, 2017). The language repertoire of the Finnish students varied from languages that some participants described as minimal (know some words) to language studies in school over several years. In Table 5.2, the languages in brackets indicate the languages that the participants said they did not know or knew very little of but would like to learn later in life. The DLCs in Table 5.2 represent the researchers' views of the three most expedient languages of the individual participants, based on their accounts of language use. Altogether, the linguistic repertoires of the six Finnish participants display somewhat different languages, but their DLCs are very similar (Figure 5.2).

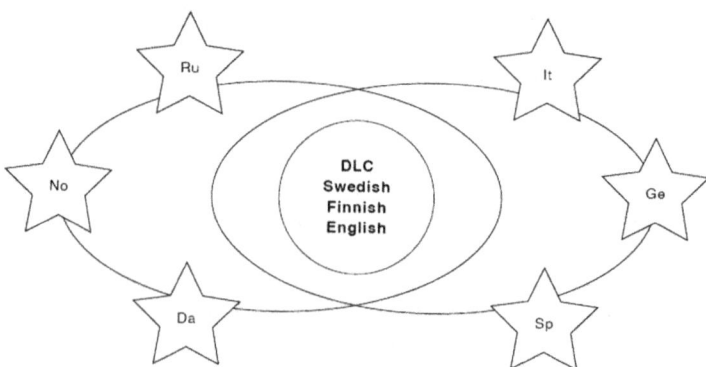

Figure 5.2 DLCs of the participants in Finland (Ru = Russian; No = Norwegian; Da = Dari; Sp = Spanish; Ge = German; It = Italian)

All six participants mentioned the same three languages (Finnish, Swedish and English) as the most prominent languages in relation to their multilingual practices. Although these three languages form a stable DLC constellation, not all participants self-identified with all three languages and the relationship between the languages was noted to be multi-faceted and subject to change.

The other languages included in the participants' linguistic repertoire are traditional languages within the Finnish national language education curriculum (e.g. German, which has lost its ground in language education during recent years, see e.g. Ministry of Education and Culture, 2017, and Russian and Spanish, which are seeing the opposite trend, i.e. growing interest among Finnish pupils). Only one participant (F1) mentioned Norwegian, but knowledge of Swedish implies that one will easily be able to understand most Norwegian, which is probably the reason why neither Norwegian nor Danish was mentioned by the other participants. Italian is not one of the languages traditionally offered by schools in Finland, but F4 considered Italian to be an interesting language and was therefore interested in learning it in the future. The interest in learning Dari is an unexpected language choice in light of all the other European languages represented in the DLC constellation. In this case, personal relations with families speaking Dari motivated the interest in learning the language.

Linguistic self-identification as a mirror of multilingual practices

The six Finnish participants identified themselves as monolingual (F1 and F2), bilingual (F3 and F4) and multilingual (F5 and F6). Participant F1, who identified herself as monolingual, estimated that, daily, she uses mostly Swedish (70%), English (20%) and Finnish (10%). Although Swedish is her most expedient language, she reported reading in all three languages as well as in Norwegian. English is her language of music, and she recognises that Finnish is a viable option to be widely used in society and she sometimes seeks for opportunities to speak more Finnish.

Excerpt 19.
Swedish with family and friends. English with friends from America and other people who do not know Swedish. We celebrated Christmas in English last year since we had a family from Afghanistan visiting us. I study in Swedish, read in English, Finnish and Norwegian if need be. English I use a lot in music. In [city in Finland] I use Swedish if I do not suddenly get inspired to practise my Finnish. And I have attended youth meetings in Finnish to be able to hear and speak Finnish more. (F1)

The other participant who defined herself as monolingual (F2) called herself monolingual at this point of her life since she uses mainly one language in her daily life. She would not like to call herself multilingual as she seldom uses the other languages in her daily life. When younger, she would also have named herself monolingual but in the future she sees herself becoming multilingual. In this case, the monolingual lens of F2 seems to depend on both few multilingual practices and language competence. By contrasting, competence does not seem to be in the foreground in F1's mind when she defines herself as monolingual.

Participants F3 and F4 defined themselves as bilingual even though they also use a third language very frequently. F3 sees Finnish and Swedish as her most expedient languages. Daily, she uses Finnish (60%) more frequently than Swedish (40%), has grown up in a Finnish-speaking family and learnt Swedish via Swedish-medium education. When reasoning about her bilingual identity, she motivated her self-evaluation with high language competence in Finnish and Swedish and frequent bilingual practices (Excerpt 20).

> Excerpt 20.
> In my own studies I speak Swedish. At work I can speak Finnish or/and Swedish depending on what the language of instruction is. In customer service situations, I can serve customers in both domestic languages and be served in both languages. I can participate without problems in both Swedish and Finnish dominated situations and during leisure time I meet both Finnish-speaking and Swedish-speaking friends, acquaintances and family. (F3)

F4 estimates her daily use of Swedish at 90%. None of the other participants estimated such a high percentage of one dominant language. F4 further noted that both English and Finnish are used approximately 5% daily, but Swedish and English are the languages she identifies with. Like F2, she does not include Finnish in her identity and explained this stance by referring to competence ('even though I am not good in Finnish, I do manage'). However, at the time of the study, she perceived herself to be at the edge of developing a multilingual identity.

Interestingly, the two participants who identified as multilingual (F5 and F6) did not deviate in terms of their percentage daily use of Swedish, Finnish and English, unlike the other Finnish participants. They estimated Swedish to be the most dominant language at the time of the study and regarded their multilingualism as a result of multilingual practices in childhood. F5 learnt Finnish by using the language in his hobby and he spent some early years in an English school in Cyprus where English was the main medium of interaction.

> Excerpt 21.
> I feel multilingual since I can choose between using Swedish, Finnish and English when needed and I could manage to use one of those languages as my main medium of communication [...] Before school in English or starting a hobby in Finnish I had answered that I am monolingual. I think that I will have little use of Finnish when I no longer have a hobby in Finnish and live in a city where you manage well in Swedish. For a long time already I have had little use of English and I think that my English will be weaker. That's why I think I will be more monolingual in the future. (F5)

In contrast to participant F5, who expressed a flux in linguistic identification, from monolingual in childhood to present perceptions of being multilingual and from multilingualism to anticipated monolingualism in the future, participant F6 described her linguistic identification as bilingual (Finnish–Swedish) in childhood but at present and in the future as multilingual since she uses English daily and thinks that she is 'doing well' in all three languages.

Stance towards teacher pedagogy as a mirror of self-experienced multilingualism

Self-experienced multilingualism was very prominent when the six Finnish participants engaged in the fourth theme about their experiences of language and culture in the teaching profession. Both F1 and F2 pointed out the importance of their own experience of multilingualism and interculturalism for inclusion of pupils with other languages than the school's language of instruction (Excerpts 22 and 23).

> **Excerpt 22.**
> An engaged and enthusiastic teacher also activates the class. Thorough experience gives confidence in oneself and one's knowledge. Experience diminishes prejudices. More experience will put flesh on the bones when teaching and enrich it. Also the approach to students/pupils from another cultural or linguistic background depends on the experiences of the teacher. (F1)

> **Excerpt 23.**
> The teachers' own experience of language and culture […] is likely to be reflected in the teaching since the more comfortable the teacher is to use languages, the more inclined s/he will be to use those languages that will lead to better teaching. (F2)

In addition, F2 noted that teachers who know several languages may benefit from using all those languages especially if they are able to give instructions in many languages to pupils with special needs. F4 shared a similar attitude towards acting as a language model and stressed the need for cross-linguistic and translanguaging pedagogy (e.g. Cummins, 2019) without confusing the pupils. While a teacher's language competence seems crucial for successful teaching in language-diverse classrooms according to F1, F2 and F4, participant F3 stressed the importance of positive attitudes.

> **Excerpt 24.**
> Teacher's own attitudes will easily show sooner or later. Pupils as young as in primary school are sensitive to noticing what kind of attitudes the teacher possesses. A professional teacher does not have a negative attitude towards another language or another culture. At least, s/he does not show them during teaching. When teachers have a positive and encouraging attitude it will more easily lead to a positive attitude and ways of thinking among the pupils. (F3)

F5 did not explicitly talk about teachers' attitude but raised teachers' unease as an important aspect for using language-aware teaching methods (Excerpt 25).

> **Excerpt 25.**
> In case there are languages that the teacher feels uncomfortable to use, the use may automatically be less visible as the teacher's unease influences how much the language will be used by the teacher. Consequently, the teacher's unease with this language will transfer to the pupils if the teacher does not feel secure enough to give pupils the support they need to learn the language. (F5)

Based upon his own experience of using Finnish predominantly in his hobby F5 believed that his Finnish knowledge will not be a big advantage and visible in his future teaching. On the other hand, he considers that his experiences of another culture in childhood offer him a versatile experience of and a great deal of understanding of different cultures that he thinks he can share with his pupils. In a similar way, F6 shared several pieces of advice on acting multilingually in classroom teaching (Excerpt 26).

> **Excerpt 26.**
> English will be there as a base and as a scaffold in case newly arrived children have difficulties with Swedish. Another thing you can do to include the [new] language in the school is to ask the pupils to count 1–10 in a foreign language instead of rhymes about food or teach rhymes about food in another language. One can also display different posters with different languages in the classroom, and try to find material in different languages [...] All these things assist to act in multiple languages. (F6)

Conclusion

In this comparative qualitative study regarding DLCs, we have studied linguistic repertoires, identities and future trajectories. To illustrate the dynamic and fluid nature of multilingualism within education, we used multilingual university student teachers in Cyprus and Finland as target groups.

Analysis of the data from Cyprus showed that minority language speakers and second-generation immigrants have hybrid language identity, perceptions regarding citizenship, inclusion and belonging. They try to assimilate to the target society, but at the same time they have a strong link with the community of residence, with their L1 country, their heritage or their home language. The participants also have hybrid language practice as they use mixed/multiple languages at home and in society. Furthermore, most of the student teachers support linguistically and culturally responsive teaching (Lucas & Villegas, 2011) and pedagogical translanguaging (Cenoz & Gorter, 2020; Cenoz & Santos, 2020). Being emergent multilinguals themselves, due to their life experience, they promote the idea of diversity in language classrooms and that their learners can become emergent bilinguals or multilinguals, which is in line with previous research by Conteh and Meier (2014).

Among the six Finnish participants, language identification is varied and dynamic in the sense that the participants do not perceive their individual linguistic identification as static but closely associated with age-related life cycles of childhood, school and studies, and the future (see Aronin, 2020). Some of the participants foresee a more monolingual identity later in life, while others assume a growing multilingual identity. In addition, there is a tendency for those participants who have grown up in bilingual Finnish–Swedish homes to readily include Finnish as one of their expedient languages, whereas those with more Swedish-dominant home backgrounds acknowledge the need for use of Finnish but express some doubt about Finnish serving as one of their most expedient languages. Thus, for the simultaneously Finnish–Swedish bilingual participants, it seems that socialisation in Swedish language within Swedish-medium school functions well as a tool to feel secure and comfortable in using Swedish as well as Finnish. English is clearly conceived as the language of (social) media, music, the internet and television, and is presented as a dominant language, albeit not the most expedient language, by all participants. Somewhat surprisingly, there was no consistency between reported daily and frequent use of multilingual practices and self-reported linguistic identification. All six participants reported approximately the same percentage for daily use of Swedish, Finnish and English, but identified themselves differently. In addition, the Finnish participants stress the importance of teachers being comfortable with multiple languages in the classroom and having positive attitudes towards languages (cf. Cenoz & Gorter, 2020). Further, they highlight their own experiences of multiple language use as a fundamental resource for acting appropriately in the classroom.

There are certain similarities and differences regarding the DLC patterns of the student teachers in Cyprus and Finland. It should be noted that English is one of the vehicle languages in both countries, which can be explained by globalisation and the status of English as a worldwide lingua franca. In the case of Finland, other expedient languages are Swedish and Finnish, the two official languages of the country. In Cyprus, core components of the DLCs are Greek (both Cypriot Greek and Standard Modern Greek) and the L1s of minority and immigrant students, in particular Romanian, Bulgarian, Lebanese, Arabic, Russian, Ukrainian, Georgian and Armenian, which reflects the complex and unique situation of bilectalism and multilingualism in Cyprus.

The linguistic repertoires and language identities of the participants are closely related with their language trajectories. In Cyprus, immigrant and minority students have rich linguistic repertoires and DLCs based on their L1 origin and multilingual/bilectal environment. Nevertheless, not all students have hybrid language identity. With regard to foreign languages (e.g. German, French, Spanish), they are few and have only peripheral roles in the DLCs. In Finland, the DLCs are quite stable (Swedish, Finnish and English as the most expedient languages) whereas additional languages are included in linguistic repertoires, consisting of three to five languages. This fact does not preclude some of the students from having a monolingual identity. The students in Finland had a wider range of foreign languages (German, Norwegian, Russian, Spanish, Danish, Dari) than the participants in Cyprus. This difference seems to stem largely from their interest in and possibilities for learning languages at school, alongside personal preferences and social networks.

The results from this study further indicate that the student teachers' DLCs depend on factors such as geographical and social contexts, minority and majority language statuses and their legitimisation, politics, ideology and education, which is in line with previous research conducted by Cenoz and Gorter (2015) and Aronin (2015, 2019, 2020). Via implementing the concept of *longue durée* proposed by Aronin (2020), DLCs seem to be a useful tool for providing insight into diversity, individual dynamic multilingual, multimodal practices of the participants and their life trajectories associated with linguistic, cognitive, physiological and material dimensions. Their personal multilingual experiences, agency and subjective needs and motivations affect their attitudes towards multilingualism and inclusive teaching/learning/assessment (De Angelis, 2011; Haukås, 2016; Heyder & Schadlich, 2014; Jakisch, 2014; Otwinowska, 2014).

A new generation of (language) teachers who daily encounter multiple languages in dynamic ways will have a positive view on multilingualism, will implement multilingual pedagogies and will be able to overcome monolingual ideologies (Alisaari *et al.*, 2019; De Angelis, 2011; Rodríguez-Izquierdo *et al.*, 2020) in teaching and in teacher education programmes (e.g. Alisaari *et al.*, 2019; De Angelis, 2011). Although this experience is no doubt enriching for understanding language diversity, we note that the participants of our study did not explicitly refer to strategies for multilingual pedagogy gained within teacher education (cf. Chapter 4 of this book), nor did they claim to have experienced the role of acting multilingually in professional roles as student teachers.

References

Alisaari, J., Heikkola, L.M., Commins, N. and Acquah, E.O. (2019) Monolingual ideologies confronting multilingual realities. Finnish teachers' beliefs about linguistic diversity. *Teaching and Teacher Education* 80 (1), 48–58.

Aronin, L. (2006) Dominant language constellations: An approach to multilingualism studies. In M. Ó Laoire (ed.) *Multilingualism in Educational Settings* (pp. 140–159). Hohenhehren: Schneider Publications.

Aronin, L. (2015) Current multilingualism and new developments in multilingual research. In P. Safont-Jorda and L. Portoles (eds) *Multilingual Development in the Classroom: Current Findings from Research* (pp. 1–27). Newcastle upon Tyne: Cambridge Scholars Publishing.

Aronin, L. (2016) Multicompetence and dominant language constellation. In V. Cook and Li Wei (eds) *The Cambridge Handbook of Linguistic Multicompetence*. Cambridge: Cambridge University Press.

Aronin, L. (2017) Conceptualizations of multilingualism: An affordances perspective. *Critical Multilingualism Studies* 5 (1), 7–42.

Aronin, L. (2019) What is multilingualism? In D. Singleton and L. Aronin (eds) *Twelve Lectures on Multilingualism* (pp. 3–34). Bristol: Multilingual Matters.

Aronin, L. (2020) Dominant language constellations as an approach for studying multilingual practices. In J. Lo Bianco and L. Aronin (eds) *Dominant Language Constellations: A New Perspective on Multilingualism* (pp. 19–35). Cham: Springer Nature.

Aronin, L. and Jessner, U. (2015) Understanding current multilingualism: What can the butterfly tell us? In C. Kramsch and U. Jessner (eds) *The Multilingual Challenge* (pp. 271–291). Berlin: De Gruyter.

Aronin, L. and Vetter, E. (eds) (2021) *Dominant Language Constellations Approach in Education and Language Acquisition*. Cham: Springer Nature.

Arvaniti, A. (2010) Linguistic practices in Cyprus and the emergence of Cypriot standard Greek. *Mediterranean Language Review* 17, 15–45.

Baker, C. and Prys Jones, S. (1998) *Encyclopaedia of Bilingualism and Bilingual Education*. Clevedon: Multilingual Matters.

Banda, F. (2020) Shifting and multi-layered dominant language constellations in dynamic multilingual contexts: African perspectives. In J. Lo Bianco and L. Aronin (eds) *Dominant Language Constellations: A New Perspective on Multilingualism* (pp. 75–97). Cham: Springer Nature.

Bergroth, M. and Hansell, K. (2020) Language-aware operational culture – Developing in-service training for early childhood education and care. *Apples – Journal of Applied Language Studies* 14 (1), 85–102, https://doi.org/10.17011/apples/urn.202006043978

Björklund, M. (2007) The multilingual competence outlined in the curricular assessment criteria for learners in Swedish-medium schools in Finland. Paper presented at the L3-Conference, Stirling, Scotland, 3–5 September 2007.

Björklund, S., Björklund, M. and Sjöholm, K. (2020) Societal versus individual patterns of DLCs in a Finnish educational context – Present state and challenges for the future. In J. Lo Bianco and L. Aronin (eds) *Dominant Language Constellations: A New Perspective on Multilingualism*. Cham: Springer Nature.

Boland, C. (2020) Hybrid identity and practices to negotiate belonging: Madrid's Muslim youth of migrant origin. *Comparative Migration Studies* 8, 26, https://doi.org/10.1186/s40878-020-00185-2

Braudel, F. (1958) History and the social sciences: The *longue durée*. *Review* 32 (2), 171–203.

Buschfeld, S. (2013) *English in Cyprus or Cyprus English? An Empirical Investigation of Variety Status*. Amsterdam: John Benjamins.

Capra, F. and Luisi, P. (2014) *The Systems View of Life: A Unifying Vision*. Cambridge: Cambridge University Press.

Cenoz, J. and Gorter, D. (2015) Towards a holistic approach in the study of multilingual education. In J. Cenoz and D. Gorter (eds) *Multilingual Education: Between Language Learning and Translanguaging* (pp. 1–15). Cambridge: Cambridge University Press.

Cenoz, J. and Gorter, D. (2020) Teaching English through pedagogical translanguaging. *World Englishes* 39 (2), 300–311.

Cenoz, J. and Santos, A. (2020) Implementing pedagogical translanguaging in trilingual schools. *System* 92, 102273. https://doi.org/10.1016/j.system.2020.102273

Chatzikyriakidis, S. (2012) A dynamic account of clitic positioning in Cypriot Greek. *Lingua* 122 (6), 642–672.

Conteh, J. and Meier, G. (eds) (2014) *The Multilingual Turn in Languages Education: Opportunities and Challenges*. Bristol: Multilingual Matters.

Creese, A. and Blackledge, A. (2010) Translanguaging in the bilingual classroom: A pedagogy for learning and teaching. *The Modern Language Journal* 94 (1), 103–115.

Cummins, J. (2019) The emergence of translanguaging pedagogy: A dialogue between theory and practice. *Journal of Multilingual Education Research* 9 (13), 19–36.

De Angelis, J. (2011) Teachers' beliefs about the role of prior language knowledge in learning and how these influence teaching practices. *International Journal of Multilingualism* 8 (3), 216–234.

Eracleous, N. (2015) Linguistic landscape of Limassol: Russian presence. Unpublished MA thesis, University of Cyprus.

Flick, U. (1998) *An Introduction to Qualitative Research*. London: Sage.

Gorter, D. and Arocena, E. (2020) Teachers' beliefs about multilingualism in a course on translanguaging. *System* 92, 102–272.

Grohmann, K.K., Papadopoulou, E. and Themistocleous, C. (2017) Acquiring clitic placement in bilectal settings: Interactions between social factors. *Frontiers in Communication* 2 (5). https://doi.org/10.3389/fcomm.2017.00005

Hadjioannou, X., Tsiplakou, S. and Kappler, M. (2011) Language policy and language planning. *Current Issues in Language Planning* 12 (4), 503–569.

Hatch, J.A. and Wisniewski, R. (eds) (1995) *Life History and Narrative*. London: Falmer.

Haukås, Å. (2016) Teachers' beliefs about multilingualism and a multilingual pedagogical approach. *International Journal of Multilingualism* 13 (1), 1–18.

Hellgren, J., Silverström, C., Lepola, L., Forsman, L. and Slotte, A. (2019) *Hur hanteras två- och flerspråkigheten i de svenskspråkiga skolorna? Resultat av en utvärdering i åk 1-6 läsåret 2017–2018*. Publikation 8/2019. Helsinki: Finnish Education Evaluation Centre

Heyder, K. and Schadlich, B. (2014) Mehrsprachigkeit und Mehrkulturalität – eine Umfrage unter Fremdsprachenlehrkraften in Niedersachsen. *Zeitschrift für Interkulturellen Fremdsprachenunterricht* 19 (1), 183–201.

Ioannidou, E. (2009) Using the 'improper' language in the classroom: The conflict between language use and legitimate varieties in education. Evidence from a Greek Cypriot classroom. *Language and Education* 23, 263–278.

Ioannidou, E., Karatsareas, P., Lytra, V. and Tsiplakou, S. (2020) Why and how to integrate non-standard linguistic varieties into education. *Languages, Society and Policy*. https://doi.org/10.17863/CAM.54137

Jakisch, J. (2014) Lehrerperspektiven auf Englischunterricht und Mehrsprachigkeit. *Zeitschrift für Interkulturellen Fremdsprachenunterricht* 19 (1), 202–215.

Jessner, U. (2008) A DST model of multilingualism and the role of metalinguistic awareness. *Modern Language Journal* 92, 270–283.

Jessner, U. (2012) Complexity in multilingual systems. In *The Encyclopedia of Applied Linguistics*. Hoboken: Wiley-Blackwell.

Kachru, B. (1985) Standards, codification and sociolinguistic realism: English language in the outer circle. In R. Quirk and H. Widowson (eds) *English in the World: Teaching and Learning the Language and Literatures* (pp. 11–36). Cambridge: Cambridge University Press.

Kannangara, S. (2020) The evolution of personal dominant language constellations based on the amount of usage of the languages. In J. Lo Bianco and L. Aronin (eds) *Dominant Language Constellations: A New Perspective on Multilingualism* (pp. 169–187). Cham: Springer Nature.

Karoulla-Vrikkis, D. (2010) Fifty years of language policy in the Republic of Cyprus. Promotion of Greek, Cypriot or European identity? In C. Perikleous (ed.) *Republic of Cyprus 50 Years: A Painful Path* (pp. 130–157). Athens: Papazisi.

Karpava, S. (2015) *Vulnerable Domains for Cross-linguistic Influence in L2 Acquisition of Greek*. Frankfurt am Main: Peter Lang.

Karpava, S. (2020) Dominant language constellations of Russian speakers in Cyprus. In J. Lo Bianco and L. Aronin (eds) *Dominant Language Constellations: A New Perspective on Multilingualism* (pp. 187–209). Cham: Springer Nature.

Karpava, S. (2022) Multilingual linguistic landscape of Cyprus. *International Journal of Multilingualism*. https://doi.org/10.1080/14790718.2022.2096890

Karpava, S., Ringblom, N. and Zabrodskaja, A. (2018) Language ecology in Cyprus, Sweden and Estonia: Bilingual Russian-speaking families in multicultural settings. *Journal of The European Second Language Association* 2 (1), 107–117.

Karpava, S., Ringblom, N. and Zabrodskaja, A. (2019) Translanguaging in the family context: Evidence from Cyprus, Sweden and Estonia. *Russian Journal of Linguistics* 23 (3), 619–641.

Kirby, A. (2009) *Digimodernism: How New Technologies Dismantle the Postmodern and Reconfigure our Culture*. New York: Continuum.

Lamnek, S. (1989) *Qualitative Sozialforschung, Vol. 2*. Munich: Psychologie Verlags Union.

Larsen-Freeman, D. (2012) Complex, dynamic systems: A new transdisciplinary theme for applied linguistics? *Language Teaching* 45 (2), 202–214.

Larsen-Freeman, D. (2016) Classroom-oriented research from a complex systems perspective. *Studies in Second Language Learning and Teaching* 6 (3), 377–393.

Leppänen, S., Nikula, T. and Kääntä, L. (eds) (2008) *Kolmas Kotimainen – Lähikuvia Englannin Käytöstä Suomessa*. Helsinki: Suomalaisen Kirjallisuuden Seura.

Lizardo, O. (2017) Improving cultural analysis: Considering personal culture in its declarative and nondeclarative modes. *American Sociological Review* 82 (1), 88–115. https://doi.org/10.1177/0003122416675175

Lo Bianco, J. (2020) A meeting of concepts and praxis: Multilingualism, language policy and the dominant language constellation. In J. Lo Bianco and L. Aronin (eds) *Dominant Language Constellations: A New Perspective on Multilingualism* (pp. 35–57). Cham: Springer Nature.

Lo Bianco, J. and Aronin, L. (2020) *Dominant Language Constellations: A New Perspective on Multilingualism*. Cham: Springer Nature.

Lucas, T. and Villegas, A.M. (2011) A framework for preparing linguistically responsive teachers. In T. Lucas (ed.) *Teacher Preparation for Linguistically Diverse Classrooms* (pp. 35–52). New York: Routledge.

May, S. (ed.) (2014) *The Multilingual Turn: Implications for SLA, TESOL, and Bilingual Education*. New York: Routledge.

May, S. (2019) Negotiating the multilingual turn in SLA. *The Modern Language Journal*, 103 (Supplement), 122–129.

Ministry of Education and Culture (2017) *Multilingualism as a Strength. Procedural Recommendations for Developing Finland's National Language Reserve*. Helsinki: Ministry of Education and Culture.

Newton, B. (1972) *Cypriot Greek: Its Phonology and Inflections*. The Hague: Mouton.

Oker-Blom G., Geber, E. and Backman, H. (2001) *Språklig mångfald i skolan. Språkbakgrund och muntlig språkkompetens i de svenska lågstadieskolorna i Finland*. Helsinki: Finnish National Agency for Education.

Otwinowska, A. (2014) Does multilingualism influence plurilingual awareness of Polish teachers of English? *International Journal of Multilingualism* 11 (1), 97–119.

Papapavlou, A. and Satraki, M. (2013) Language of advertising in bidialectal settings: Does the code matter? *Multilingual Academic Journal of Education and Social Sciences* 2 (1), 1–14.

Pappas, P. (2014) Exceptional clitic placement in Cypriot Greek: Results from an MET study. *Journal of Greek Linguistics* 14 (2), 190–211.

Peltoniemi, A., Kvist, M. and Björklund, S. (2020) Om int vi sku prata finska med varandra, så sku vi ju int ha finska här. Språkbadsklasslärarstudenters språkval i studiemiljön. In: S. Haapamäki, L. Forsman and L. Huldén (eds) *Svenskans Beskrivning 37* (pp. 230–241). Turku: Skrifter från Svenska institutionen vid Åbo Akademi.

Revithiadou, A. (2006) Prosodic filters on syntax: An interface account of second position clitics. *Lingua* 116 (2), 79–111.

Rodríguez-Izquierdo, R.M., Gonzàlez Falcón, I. and Goenechea Permisán, C. (2020) Teacher beliefs and approaches to linguistic diversity. Spanish as a second language in the inclusion of immigrant students. *Teaching and Teacher Education* 90, 103035, https://doi.org/10.1016/j.tate.2020.103035

Rowe, C. and Grohmann, K.K. (2013) Discrete bilectalism: Towards co-overt prestige and diglossic shift in Cyprus. *International Journal of the Sociology of Language* 224 119–142.

Rowe, C. and Grohmann, K.K. (2014) Canaries in a coal mine: Native speakerhood and other factors as predictors of moribundity, death, and diglossic shift in Cypriot Greek. *Mediterranean Language Review* 21, 121–142.

Schneider, E. (2003) The dynamics of New Englishes: From identity construction to dialect birth. *Language* 79 (2), 233–281.

Schneider, E. (2007) *Postcolonial English: Varieties Around the World*. Cambridge: Cambridge University Press.

Singleton, D., Fishman, J., Aronin, L. and Ó Laoire, M. (eds) (2013) *Current Multilingualism: A New Linguistic Dispensation*. Berlin: Mouton de Gruyter.

Slavkov, N. (2020) Language background profiling at Canadian elementary schools and dominant language constellations. In J. Lo Bianco and L. Aronin (eds) *Dominant Language Constellations: A New Perspective on Multilingualism* (pp. 117–139). Cham: Springer Nature.

Statistics Finland (2021a) Förhandsuppgifter om befolkningen. Helsinki: Official Statistics of Finland. See http://www.stat.fi/til/vamuu/2021/08/vamuu_2021_08_2021-09-21_tie_001_sv.html

Statistics Finland (2021b) Befolkningsstruktur 2020, Tabellbilaga 2., Befolkningen efter språk 1980–2020. Helsinki: Official Statistics of Finland. See http://www.stat.fi/til/vaerak/2020/vaerak_2020_2021-03-31_tau_002_sv.html

Themistocleous, C. (2019) Conflict and unification in the multilingual landscape of a divided city: The case of Nicosia's border. *Journal of Multilingual and Multicultural Development* 40 (2), 94–114.

Tsiplakou, S., Ioannidou, E. and Hadjioannou, X. (2018) Capitalising on linguistic variation in Greek Cypriot education. *Linguistics and Education* 45, 62–71.

Vertovec, S. (2007) Super-diversity and its implications. *Ethnic and Racial Studies* 30 (6), 1024–1045.

Vertovec, S. (2014) Reading 'super-diversity'. In B. Anderson and M. Keith (eds) *Migration: A COMPAS Anthology*. Oxford: COMPAS.

Young, A.S. (2014) Unpacking teachers' language ideologies: Attitudes, beliefs, and practiced language policies in schools in Alsace, France. *Language Awareness* 23 (1–2), 157–171.

6 Supporting Multilingual Learning in Educational Contexts: Lessons from Poland, Finland and California

Agnieszka Otwinowska, Mari Bergroth and Eve Zyzik

The chapter addresses how multilingual learning can be supported in educational contexts. We argue that all children need support for their languages and opportunities to become familiar with linguistic diversity. We briefly define multilingualism and highlight selected linguistic and cognitive features of multilingual children. Then we zoom in on educational solutions in three very different contexts, two in the EU (Poland and Finland) and one in the USA (California). With the provided contextual background we discuss some of the challenges that learners might experience at school, depending on how support for multilingual learning is implemented in a given context. Finally, we argue that supporting multilingual learning can be enhanced in everyday practices and discuss solutions for supporting multilingual learning from the perspective of teachers and teacher training.

Introduction

Supporting multilingual learning is increasingly important in a variety of educational contexts since it is essential for promoting students' academic achievement and overall wellbeing. For instance, many countries in the EU emphasize the value of national and local languages, as well as the importance of global languages such as English (Breidbach, 2003). This creates the foundations for the teaching of those languages, leading students towards multilingualism (i.e. the opportunity to learn and the ability to use several languages). The language policy of the EU promotes multilingualism as the key to personal success (European Commission, 2019), but implementation of the policy differs across countries. In the USA, language policies at the federal level center on equal access to education for all learners, including those who do not understand English. These policies, under the purview of the Office for Civil Rights, establish the legal obligations of schools with respect to English learners (ELs), but they do not have a specific goal of promoting multilingualism. Nevertheless, some US states (e.g. California, New York and Washington) have adopted initiatives such as the Seal of Biliteracy, which is intended to recognize bilingual students by means of an official designation on their high school diplomas (see Heineke & Davin, 2020).

Despite policies that are intended to promote and incentivize multilingualism, monolingual standards are deeply rooted in many educational contexts. In other words, despite good intentions, many teachers and educators are not prepared to support bilingual and multilingual students. In this chapter we present some of the challenges related to multilingual learning that children might experience at school, depending on how educational policies are implemented. To that end, we focus on educational solutions in three contexts – two in the EU (Poland and Finland) and one in the USA (California). All three regions are of comparable size territorially, but have diverse populations, demographics, language policies and teaching traditions. We will show examples of effective policy implementation and pinpoint some problem areas. We will focus on successful support for multilingual learning that all teachers can employ and present some lessons to be learnt from the three contexts. Before showing how multilingualism is supported in those diverse contexts, let us first clarify the concepts of bilingualism and multilingualism.

Characteristics of Multilingual Learners

Increasing numbers of children are growing up in bilingual or multilingual settings (Armon-Lotem *et al.*, 2015). Simultaneous bilingualism occurs when a child acquires two languages (L1 and L2) simultaneously before the age of three in a home where two languages are used. On the other hand, in sequential bilingualism, a child begins to acquire a new language (L2) in kindergarten or at school after having developed some knowledge of the first language (L1) spoken at home (Zurer Pearson, 2009). Thus, within sequential bilingualism, any foreign language learner can also be considered bilingual if they use their languages regularly (Cook, 2007). Contrary to popular belief, bilingualism does not imply an equal and perfect knowledge of two languages, as proposed by Bloomfield (1933) almost 100 years ago. Being bilingual means that a given person uses two languages on a regular basis, regardless of the level of proficiency in these languages (Grosjean, 1992). Bilingualism is now perceived as a special case of multilingualism, defined as the ability to use several languages by a given person, the mutual interactions of these languages in the user's mind and the entire linguistic and cultural experiences that make up the user's communicative competence (Jessner, 2008). Migrants, members of regional minorities, native speakers of sign languages and spoken languages, as well as people learning foreign languages and using them regularly can all be called multilingual. Those multilinguals whose home language is different from the societal language(s) and the language(s) of schooling are often called heritage speakers, especially in the US context (see also the definition of heritage speakers in Chapter 1 of this book). They acquire the heritage language by exposure to the L1 in their home environment (Benmamoun et al., 2013), generally without the support of formal academic exposure (Zyzik, 2016). In the case of heritage speakers, some misconceptions regarding bilingualism as a hindrance for a child's successful language development and integration within society may lead to abandoning the home language(s) (De Houwer, 2015; Del Valle, 2009).

Childhood bilingualism may, however, show some disadvantages if bilinguals are directly compared to monolinguals in one of their languages (Armon-Lotem et al., 2015; Haman et al., 2017). For example, compared with monolingual children, bilingual children may exhibit a smaller vocabulary range in each of their languages. Bialystok et al. (2010) surveyed a total of 1738 English-speaking children aged 3–10 years in Canada, including monolinguals and children of immigrants who spoke English at school. The results of the study showed that monolingual children knew more English words than their bilingual peers, and that effect was sustained in all age groups. Importantly, however, the groups of children did not differ when only the vocabulary related to the school context was compared. This means that vocabulary knowledge is closely related to the specific language material of different domains (e.g. school, home) and smaller vocabulary size among bilinguals is not due to bilingualism *per se*.

The benefits of bilingualism are linguistic and cognitive. Regarding linguistic benefits, languages in the user's repertoire and affective factors provide powerful resources available to L3 learners who already have bilingual experience. These include knowledge and awareness of another foreign/second language, motivation to learn, a wealth of learning strategies and growing confidence and decreased language anxiety in comparison with less experienced learners (Otwinowska, 2016). Bilinguals and multilinguals may also have enhanced metalinguistic awareness or a better understanding of 'how languages work' (Aronin & Singleton, 2012). Cumulative language knowledge affects noticing the existing similarities and differences across languages (Jarvis & Pavlenko, 2008). All factors combined – that is, language knowledge and proficiency, learning experience and metalinguistic awareness – add to strategic reliance on cross-linguistic similarities in language learning. Thus, we can say that bilingualism and multilingualism facilitate the acquisition of additional languages (for discussion, see Jessner, 2008; Otwinowska, 2016).

The most important cognitive benefit of bilingualism is mental flexibility resulting from the use and interaction in several languages and the need to switch between them. The cognitive benefits of bilingualism were initially observed in children aged 4–6 years. For instance, in experiments involving the need to switch to a different type of task (sorting objects by color or shape), bilingual children did much better than their monolingual peers (Bialystok & Martin, 2004). A similar advantage was observed in older children and adults in many other tasks that required ignoring one rule or an irrelevant stimulus and applying a new rule or paying attention to a new stimulus. For example, bilingual children outperformed monolinguals in recognizing ambivalent figures (Bialystok & Shapero, 2005), sorting cards (Bialystok & Martin, 2004), understanding the interlocutor's perspective and responding to a request in an appropriate way (Fan et al., 2015), and understanding a command when disturbed by some noise (Filippi et al., 2015).

These experimental tasks, despite their differences, have an important common denominator. They require adequate cognitive control (i.e. the involvement of certain control functions of the brain). In order to perform these tasks, one needs to stop one type of exercise and start another (flexibility), adopt the perspective of another person (empathy) or inhibit irrelevant noise and focus on understanding the message (functioning in noise). Bilinguals who regularly use their languages also use these cognitive control mechanisms. In order to use two or more languages, a bilingual person has to decide which one to use and effectively inhibit the unnecessary language (inhibition, flexibility). They must also pick out words and sentences in one language between words and sentences in another language (better understanding in noise). Thus, living in a bilingual/multilingual context and juggling languages supports the mechanisms of cognitive control, which results in easier accomplishment of some tasks that require switching. This is shown in Figure 6.1.

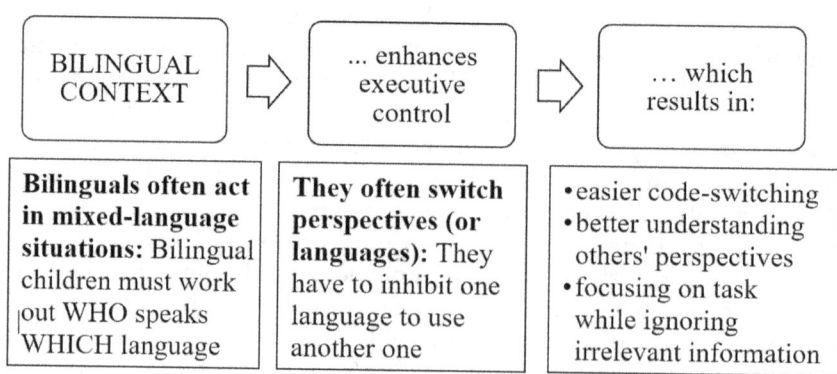

Figure 6.1 The mechanism of developing the cognitive consequences of bilingualism

In the educational realm, it is important to distinguish between subtractive (impoverishing) bilingualism and additive (enriching) bilingualism. Subtractive bilingualism involves acquiring a second language at the expense of not developing or forgetting the first language. Additive (enriching) bilingualism occurs when a child acquires a second language, but also strengthens the first, home language (Li, 2000). It is assumed that additive bilingualism should become the goal of language acquisition and education. If all a child's languages are being developed, they support each other's development and lead to greater academic achievement. According to Cummins' (1979, 2000) interdependence hypothesis, there are areas of shared extra-linguistic knowledge (common underlying proficiency) that develop through the interaction of languages and form the basis for a child's linguistic development. An example of common underlying proficiency is the ability of bilingual preschoolers to narrate in any of their languages. If a child can tell a coherent story in their home language, the child will also be able to narrate coherently in the L2 used at school. Such abilities have been shown for bilinguals with English and Spanish (Zurer Pearson, 2002), Polish and English (Otwinowska *et al.*, 2020), Finnish and Swedish (Kunnari *et al.*, 2016) and many other language pairs, e.g. Russian–German (Gagarina, 2016), Swedish–English (Bohnacker, 2016), English–Hebrew (Iluz-Cohen & Walters, 2012) and Russian–Norwegian (Rodina, 2017). Such coherent storytelling translates into children's later success in writing and reading (Dickinson & McCabe, 2001; Uccelli & Páez, 2007).

In sum, a child's languages will support each other only if both languages are used frequently (Bialystok *et al.*, 2010) and their development is supported in the family and at school so that the child receives enough input in each language (De Houwer, 2015; Zurer Pearson, 2002). Adequate input and interaction in both languages leads to additive bilingualism. In educational contexts, additive bilingual programs such as CLIL (content and language integrated learning), where additional languages are used for content teaching, are popular options in many European countries. In the USA, dual-language immersion programs also pave the way for additive bilingualism. Supporting multilingual learning in both mainstream and bilingual education will be discussed in the next section with relation to the three educational contexts of Poland, Finland and California. First, we present the background of the three educational contexts.

Bilingualism Across the Three Contexts: Who and Where?

Poland

Poland is a large central European country with 38.1 million inhabitants. For centuries, Poland was highly multilingual but became monolingual during and after World War II, which forced large-scale migrations, deportations and territorial changes (Komorowska, 2014). Compared with other European countries, contemporary Poland is very homogeneous in terms of nationality or ethnicity (European Union, 2021). Only around 1% of Poland's population are national minority citizens (Byelorussian, Czech, Lithuanian, German, Armenian, Russian, Slovak and Ukrainian) or ethnic minority citizens (Karaim, Lemko, Romany and Tatar). In north-western Poland there is a small bilingual community that uses the regional Kashubian language. Polish is spoken by the vast majority of the society and is also the predominant language of schooling. For instance, only 1.1% of Polish 15-year-old students speak a different language at home to the language of schooling (Eurydice, 2017). Childhood bilingualism in Poland is still not a common phenomenon, although Polish teachers are now encountering multilingual students much more often than before joining the EU.

There is, however, elective, elite bilingualism, which involves learning languages considered to be prestigious (e.g. English, Spanish and German). In Poland, more than 90% of students learn English from first grade until school graduation (Eurydice, 2017). English is regarded as a highly prestigious language and an investment in a child's future. Elite multilingualism is the result of foreign language teaching and bilingual education (CLIL), which is widely promoted among the middle class in Poland. Bilingual education in prestigious languages is quite elitist and, in many cases, only affordable for wealthy families (Otwinowska, 2013; Otwinowska & Foryś, 2017) who send their children to classes in which they learn with the children of affluent foreign expats living in Poland. Bilingual education in foreign languages can also be free, mostly at secondary level, but many renowned state schools conduct entrance language exams alongside the compulsory content subject exams. Thus, such education is quite selective and is restricted to those children who have already achieved a certain proficiency level and have passed exams (Eurydice, 2017).

A small population of children from national and ethnic minorities (Belarusian, Czech, Lithuanian, German, Armenian, Russian, Slovak and Ukrainian, as well as Lemkos, Karaims and Kashubian) have the right to education in their minority languages, as guaranteed by the Polish constitution (Eurydice, 2017). At parents' request, teaching may be organized in separate groups, classes and schools, or in groups, classes and schools with additional language, history and culture classes. The network of schools teaching in languages of national minorities or offering additional classes in these languages to pupils from national minorities has increased four times since the fall of Communism in 1989 (European Union, 2021). Minority and ethnic languages are mainly taught at the primary level; the number of secondary schools teaching these languages is much smaller. Bilingual children with minority languages are 'absorbed' by Polish-medium schools, using the language of the majority (Komorowska, 2014). To illustrate this, in the school year 2018/2019, before the start of the war in Ukraine, there were 70,700 pupils in 1065 primary schools learning a mother tongue other than Polish, but only 1900 students in 71 post-primary and upper-secondary schools (Central Statistical Office, 2020).

Within the speakers of minority languages, a distinct group are children with Roma as their L1. Roma–Polish children often come to school with poor knowledge of the Polish language and culture. This, unfortunately, often results in a misdiagnosis of their intellectual abilities if they are tested only in Polish. For instance, a shocking report on the cognitive and linguistic development of Roma–Polish children in Poland (Kołaczek & Talewicz-Kwiatkowska, 2011) indicated that more than 50% of those diagnosed with intellectual disability and placed in special education schools were, in fact, within the intellectual norm.

Two separate groups that are not included in the official statistics are the children of immigrants to Poland as well as those born abroad to Polish families and returning to Poland (returnees). Immigrants from Ukraine, Russia, Kazakhstan, Chechnya, Vietnam and China often know Polish only at a basic level, so they cannot cope with Polish lessons without adequate linguistic support. Unfortunately, there are no education programs for pupils with a limited command of Polish. There are also no official rules on how to assess foreign immigrants, so they are often assessed in the same way as Polish-speaking children, despite the fact that they may not understand the instructions (Szybura, 2016). Much depends on school directors and local administrations, who have to deal with the education of foreigners themselves, for example by organizing additional adaptation lessons. Similar problems are experienced by returnees, whose number is difficult to pinpoint, but is estimated to be several thousand students (Grzymała-Moszczyńska *et al.*, 2015). Like immigrants, returnees often cannot cope with lessons conducted in Polish without linguistic support. In addition to language difficulties, there may be cultural differences that affect the returnees' success in schools. For example, Polish–English children are used to being rewarded for their efforts in British schools; they are also used to expressing their own opinions and engaging in debates with the teacher. Since Polish schools have a completely different educational culture, they have problems with both language and behavior, which are inadequate in the Polish school reality (Grzymała-Moszczyńska *et al.*, 2015).

Another group invisible in the system is children of deaf adults (CODA) (or hearing children of deaf parents). In Poland, sign language is not recognized as a minority language, unlike in many European countries, such as Finland. CODA can struggle with the Polish language or they might act as interpreters and guides for their deaf parents, for example in contacts between their school and their parents. While school boards keep records of deaf students, CODA as a group with special linguistic needs are invisible to the Polish education system (CODA Poland, 2021).

To summarize, there are two contexts in Polish schools in which we can find bilingual and multilingual students. The first is the context of formal language learning and teaching (e.g. CLIL), where languages perceived as prestigious (e.g. English, German, French and Italian) are taught. Such education is socially desirable but often only available to children from wealthy families. Bilingual education is also available for some children in minority languages, but this is not common at all stages of education. In the second context, a student's bilingualism develops naturally through contact with a society that speaks a language other than the child's home/minority language. In this case, bilingualism is not the goal but a side effect, and the home language may have a lower prestige relative to the societal/majority language.

Finland

Finland, a north European country approximately the size of Poland, has only 5.5 million inhabitants, which is no exception to other Nordic countries. Finland is a bilingual country with two official national languages – Finnish and Swedish (see Saarinen & Ihalainen, 2018, for more information on Finland's constitutional bilingualism). The Sami, as an indigenous group, and the Roma, as well as 'other' language groups and users of sign languages are also acknowledged in the Constitution of Finland. According to the most recent official statistics (Statistics Finland, 2021), the two national languages are spoken by 92.1% of the population. Foreign languages are spoken by 7.8% of the population, including Russian (1.5%), Estonian (0.9%), Arabic (0.6%), English (0.4%) and Somali (0.4%).

The focus in this chapter is on Swedish, the lesser spoken national language of Finland. The number of registered Swedish speakers is 5.2% (Statistics Finland, 2021) and this number has been steadily declining during the 100 years of Finnish independence. While the status of Swedish as a school language is undoubtedly strong (Oker-Blom, 2021), its linguistic vitality cannot be taken for granted in the same manner as English in the USA or Polish in Poland. Thus, a focus on Swedish-medium education provides an opportunity to address supporting multilingual learning from the viewpoint of the numerical minority.

Finnish-speakers and Swedish-speakers share a similar ethno-cultural background and have equal linguistic rights in society, including in the education realm. Municipalities are obligated to arrange education in parallel school systems for each language group from early childhood education through to higher education (Williams, 2013). At birth, individuals can, by right, be registered as either a Finnish-speaker or a Swedish-speaker. However, the possibility of a person entering several mother tongues in the Population Information System has recently been investigated to provide a fuller picture of a person's language identity and to avoid situations where parents who speak different languages have to choose a language to register for their child (Tammenmaa, 2020). The idea of better acknowledging and identifying all languages as resources and harnessing multilingualism as a potential positive resource for both economic growth as well as individual wellbeing has been promoted in recent reports and recommendations (Pyykkö, 2017).

The provision of Swedish-medium education provides an important mechanism to prevent language shift (Kovero, 2011). Children registered as Swedish speakers enroll in Swedish-medium education by default, but pupils with other linguistic backgrounds can also enroll. Mixed language families (Finnish–Swedish) tend to choose Swedish-medium education (Finnäs, 2012) and more than 40% of pupils in primary school now constitute bilingual children in Swedish-medium schools (Hellgren *et al.*, 2019). The identity of Finnish–Swedish bilinguals is often reserved to those with mixed family backgrounds, making it difficult for others to identify themselves as bilinguals in these languages. In many cases, it might be easier to identify oneself as multilingual rather than bilingual (Smith-Christmas *et al.*, 2019). A survey conducted in 2013 showed that pupils with a monolingual Swedish background varied from 29% to 83% between the Swedish-speaking regions of Finland. The number of pupils with a mixed Swedish–Finnish language background varied from 11% to 62% (Hyvönen & Westerholm, 2016). This means that, in some schools, the number of bilinguals exceeds the number of Swedish monolinguals in clear numbers, making this type of bilingualism a very common phenomenon.

However, Swedish-medium schools also have the obligation of catering to the growing diversity within Finnish society. Immigrants are entitled to choose Swedish as their first integration language, but integration in Finnish is promoted, especially in regions where Finnish has a strong majority position (Creutz & Helander, 2012). Despite this, the number of speakers of foreign languages has steadily increased, even in Swedish-medium education, and is now 3–7% depending on the region (Hyvönen & Westerholm, 2016). The issues with integration language pathways add to the complexity of multilingualism in the Swedish-medium educational path. For example, it can be that guardians/parents had Finnish as their integration language, but their children (second-generation immigrants) are now enrolled in Swedish-medium schools and study in Swedish (Bergroth & Hansell, 2020).

The needs of a multilingual society can be seen in the core curriculum. In Finland, 12 syllabi for different languages are described within the school subject Mother Tongue and Literature (Finnish National Agency for Education, 2016). These languages are Finnish, Swedish, Sami, Roma, sign language, other mother tongue of the pupil, Finnish and Swedish as a second language, Finnish and Swedish for Sami speakers and Finnish and Swedish for sign language users. We can thus conclude that supporting various linguistic groups is very well addressed in Finland on a policy level (Eurydice, 2019). Furthermore, it is obligatory for all pupils to study at least two additional languages. In Swedish-medium schools almost all pupils (99%) study both Finnish and English as advanced syllabi, while only 20% do this (Swedish and English) in Finnish-medium schools. According to recent statistics, within Finnish-medium education, 79% of pupils study only the two obligatory languages; in Swedish-medium education, 65% do not choose to study additional, voluntary languages. Schools can also receive separate funding to provide extra-curricular instruction in the pupil's mother tongue (Finnish National Agency for Education, 2019).

Bilingual education is possible in both educational strands. However, the fear of language shift in the Swedish-speaking population, especially if the target language is Finnish, is frequently brought up in public debates (Bergroth, 2016). In regions with strong societal support for Swedish outside school, bilingual options are generally deemed less problematic and English-medium CLIL education and Finnish-medium language immersion programs are provided. Fear of language shift is not discussed within Finnish-medium education and various languages are offered in bilingual programs (including Spanish, Russian, German, French, Sami), although the most widespread programs are CLIL education in English and early total Swedish language immersion. The programs vary from small scale, with less than 25% in the target language, to large scale, with over 25% in the target language in both educational strands (Bergroth, 2016). Unlike the Polish case presented earlier, almost all children in Finland attend publicly funded schools and bilingual education is provided without any additional cost.

Finally, mediated (online) communication plays an increasingly important role in societal multilingualism. In Finland, home and school have been found to be strong Swedish-medium domains for Swedish-speaking youth and both Swedish and English are used predominantly online; the use of Finnish is almost non-existent online, especially for young people who are not bilinguals (Stenberg-Sirén, 2018).

California

California is the most populous US state, with an estimated population of 39.5 million (US Census, 2020), which is comparable to that of Poland. The population of California represents a wide variety of ethnic, racial, national and linguistic backgrounds. The most recent statistics (for the 2019/2020 school year) indicate a total of 2,555,951 students who speak a language other than English at home – this represents about 41.5% of the state's public-school enrollment. It is important to note that this very large number of bilingual children includes those that are already proficient in English as well as those who are classified as ELs. Any student who speaks a language other than English in the home, as determined by a home language survey, must take a state-mandated test to determine their level of English proficiency in both oral and written language. Based on the results of this initial test, those classified as ELs have to take a summative test each year until they meet the reclassification criteria (for additional information see Hill *et al.*, 2021).

In the 2019/2020 school year, California public schools enrolled 1.148 million ELs, which is 18.63% of the total enrollment. The majority (68.6%) were elementary school students (kindergarten through Grade 6). Although more than 75 languages are spoken in the homes of California students, 93% speak one of the following: Spanish, Vietnamese, Mandarin, Arabic, Cantonese, Filipino, Russian, Korean, Punjabi or Farsi. Within this group, Spanish speakers constitute the largest group (81.44%) of ELs (California Department of Education, 2022). It is important to recognize the heterogeneity of the ELs in terms of family background, the English language abilities of their parents, and socioeconomic status. It is this confluence of factors, in addition to their developing English proficiency, which undoubtedly impacts the academic achievement of these students.

The question of how best to serve the needs of ELs in Californian schools has generated heated debates over the years, culminating with the approval of Proposition 227 in 1998. This statewide ballot initiative was intended to severely restrict the use of bilingual instruction for ELs. In practice, this law did not completely eliminate bilingual education since parents could still request an 'alternative course of study' through a waiver. It did, however, drastically reduce the number of such programs. Carver-Thomas and Darling-Hammond (2017) report that, prior to Proposition 227, about 30% of ELs were in bilingual programs, but a decade later this proportion dropped to 5%. This means that the overwhelming majority of ELs were taught in regular classes with some instructional modifications designed to provide access to the core curriculum and accelerate their English language development. This model is known as English immersion or structured English immersion. The orientation that underlies English immersion is that students who spend more time 'on task' will make faster gains in English than students who spend some portion of instructional time in their home language.

Proposition 227 was overturned in 2016 with the passage of Proposition 58, which repealed the restrictions on bilingual education. Thus, it seems that public opinion on multilingualism shifted from aversion (with the passage of Proposition 227) to support (with the passage of Proposition 58). Simon-Cereijido (2018) argues that the recent passage of Proposition 58 in California represents not only the public's embrace of multilingualism, but also the way in which the proposition was presented to the general public. Specifically, proponents of Proposition 58 emphasized parental choice, meaning that everyone would have the chance (but not an obligation) to raise multilingual children. Furthermore, proponents relied on bilingual research showing the cognitive advantages of bilingualism. In other words, bilingualism was presented as a potential benefit to all children, not just those of ethnic minorities. This is in sharp contrast to the messaging that had been influential in garnering support for Proposition 227. In 1998, the political message focused on the poor educational achievement of immigrant children, especially Latino children. The intended message was that bilingual education was a costly (and detrimental) program for a subset of the California population.

Since the passage of Proposition 58, the creation of new dual-immersion (DI) and bilingual programs in California's public schools no longer faces legal barriers. Thus, schools can now offer various instructional models, including transitional bilingual programs, developmental bilingual programs and DI programs. Some larger school districts offer all these options, in addition to English immersion, allowing parents to rank program preferences. Valentino and Reardon (2015) provide details of these options for Spanish and Chinese in the San Francisco Unified School District. In this context, the transitional bilingual program uses the home language of the student to support access to the core curriculum, but the amount of English increases quickly in the elementary school years. Developmental bilingual programs, in contrast, are intended to develop proficiency in English while maintaining the home language. Accordingly, developmental bilingual programs are longer term, often lasting through to Grade 5. DI programs are unique in that they enroll both native English speakers and ELs in the same classroom. The long-term goal of these programs is to develop bilingualism and biliteracy among both groups. In the DI programs studied by Valentino and Reardon, early elementary classes were more heavily weighted toward the non-English language (e.g. 80–90% of instructional time), with a gradual increase in English as students progressed through the grades.

The demand for DI programs has skyrocketed in California and throughout the USA. Many analysts claim that the popularity of DI programs is being driven by interest from middle-class, English-dominant families who see bilingualism as a type of academic enrichment (Williams, 2017; see also Flores *et al.*, 2021). As the demand for DI education is often greater than the number of seats available, there is concern that ELs may be displaced by native English speakers from more affluent families (Lam & Richards, 2020). Another challenge is staffing these programs, as the shortage of bilingual teachers in California remains particularly acute. According to Carver-Thomas and Darling-Hammond (2017), 14% of 200 California school districts reported a bilingual teacher shortage in 2016 prior to the passage of Proposition 58. Gándara and Mordechay (2017) maintain that the teacher shortage is one of the harmful legacies of Proposition 227, which depleted the number of bilingual teachers by more than two-thirds. The dearth of bilingual teachers in California will inevitably limit the availability of DI programs. Briceño and colleagues argue that recruiting and developing bilingual teachers 'has become a matter of social justice' (Briceño *et al.*, 2018: 213) given the academic promise of DI programs (cf. Collier & Thomas, 2017; Valentino & Reardon, 2015).

What Challenges Can Linguistically Non-Aware Schools Cause for Bilinguals?

In schools where multilingual learning is not actively supported, bilingual children may experience several types of difficulties. First, students with migration experiences may have difficulty learning the content matter in the language of schooling. Second, bilingual children can even experience difficulties in communicating with their peers and school staff. This may result in problems with peer integration, educational difficulties, and socio-affective challenges.

In Poland, the common denominator of these difficulties is problems with the Polish language as a tool for everyday communication, learning and social development (Grzymała-Moszczyńska *et al.*, 2015; Szybura, 2016). Although the official national exams are carried out in the languages of schooling, including the minority languages, the majority of everyday exchanges and learner assessments takes place in Polish. In Finland, the national core curriculum (Finnish National Agency for Education, 2016) explicitly states that assessment needs to account for any shortcomings in pupils' skills in the language of instruction. Similarly, it is stated that the developing language skills in the instructional language for pupils with an immigrant background or other foreign language speakers are accounted for. This is to be done, for example, by using versatile and flexible assessment methods that are suited to the pupil's situation. This means that the responsibility for supporting multilingual learning is placed on the pedagogical staff at the schools. In California, ELs run the risk of becoming long-term ELs, a label that designates students who have not been reclassified out of EL status after six years in a US school. Thus, by the time they reach Grade 6 or secondary school, they are struggling academically even though they can function socially in English and have strong oral skills. Moreover, these students often feel stigmatized in their status as ELs and, as noted by Olsen (2010), may have developed habits of non-engagement and low personal expectations. Many researchers contend that the proficiency tests used with ELs are problematic in that they include academic content, thus constituting a barrier for children who are struggling with academic reading and/or writing tasks (cf. Clark-Gareca *et al.*, 2020).

It is worth noting that lack of support for multilingual learning may result in problems both within mainstream education as well as within any type of bilingual education. Children may experience a proficiency gap, understood here as 'the difference between the level and type of L2 proficiency the students have and the target or "threshold level" they require in order to be able to engage effectively with the curriculum they are required to study' (Johnson & Swain, 1994: 211). As demonstrated by Otwinowska and Foryś (2017), these difficulties are influenced not only by linguistic factors (weaker knowledge of the language of instruction, experiencing a proficiency gap), but also by affective factors (stress caused by high competition and pressure, aversion to difficult tasks in a foreign language) and cognitive factors (disturbed attention and information processing caused by stress). These factors may form a cause-and-effect sequence, leading some children to experiencing learned intellectual helplessness (see Figure 6.2). The concept of intellectual helplessness (Sędek & McIntosh, 1998) refers to cognitive, motivational and emotional disorders caused by situations in which a student cannot influence the course of events because his/her learning attempts do not bring the expected results. In the case of a bilingual or multilingual child, the mechanism works as follows. The child needs to cope with linguistically difficult material in the language of instruction and experiences a lack of progress despite intense intellectual effort. These experiences may lead to cognitive exhaustion, manifested by worse performance on complex tasks ('blank mind') and loss of creativity and internal motivation. These are exactly opposite results to those assumed by bilingual education and CLIL (Dalton-Puffer, 2011).

In order to find out what is difficult for children at a bilingual school and what can cause intellectual helplessness in CLIL lessons, Otwinowska and Foryś (2017) examined 10-year-olds and 11-year-olds learning science and mathematics in English at a prestigious school in Poland. One of the tools used by the researchers was a set of sentence frames that the children could complete with information about their feelings concerning lessons conducted in the L2, English. In Excerpts 1 and 2, we present two fragments of the 140 answers obtained, where children comment on the

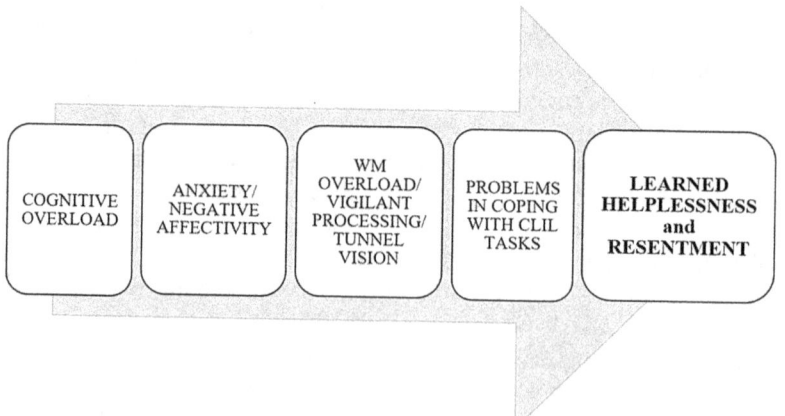

Figure 6.2 Mechanism leading to intellectual helplessness in the case of a child who has problems with the language of instruction (after Otwinowska & Foryś, 2017: 463)

CLIL tasks that were difficult for them both linguistically and intellectually (as cited in Otwinowska & Foryś, 2017: 468).

> Excerpt 1.
> [difficult in CLIL Science] everything with a few exceptions; [easy in CLIL Maths] few things, I prefer to learn in Polish; [on CLIL Maths I liked] nearly nothing; [it wasn't nice/interesting/cool because] I don't like them, [difficult because] I don't know English well, I didn't understand 90%; [What would you like to add?] I hate English! I want to have such lessons once a year! (Pupil 4a8, compiled from two questionnaires)

> Excerpt 2.
> [difficult in CLIL Science] to remember some things and to stay focused, to understand some notions; [I'd like to] speak more Polish and to slow down with the pace of the topics; [difficult in CLIL Maths] that we always rush with the next topic [What would you like to add?] I don't like English, so such lessons are BORING for me! (Pupil 4b15, compiled from two questionnaires)

Clearly, due to a proficiency gap and lack of adequate instructional support to scaffold learning, these children showed symptoms of stress and reluctance to perform difficult tasks in a foreign language. Extrapolating from the examples above, we can imagine what children with migration experiences might feel if they do not know the language of instruction and do not get support for their multilingual learning. If, in addition, they do not receive emotional support from teachers and peers, their school experiences can lead to cognitive impairment.

This leads to the following questions:

- Why do some bilingual children find it difficult to learn in the school language if not adequately supported?
- Why do returnees, even when they speak the heritage language relatively well, have problems with using this language in school contexts?

Cummins (1979, 2000) notes that there is a difference between the use of language in casual conversation and the use of language for academic learning purposes. Specifically, we use basic interpersonal communication skills (BICS) in everyday conversations that are strongly context-dependent and that use gestures and body language. In contrast, in school lessons, we use language for learning purposes (i.e. cognitive academic language proficiency, CALP). CALP has more difficult vocabulary (specific to the discipline) and more complex syntax than everyday language (e.g. passive voice, conditionals). Furthermore, it is often about abstract concepts and is not contextualized. Since Cummins' influential proposal more than 40 years ago, the BICS/CALP distinction has been much debated (see Cummins, 2021 for an extensive discussion). It has been criticized on the grounds that BICS/CALP might oversimplify conversational interactions and the notion of academic language (e.g. Bailey, 2007), or that the general construct of academic language and different proficiency types should be rejected (e.g. García & Solorza, 2021). Still, researchers have worked to identify the specific language skills that are encompassed by academic language (cf. Schleppegrell, 2004; Snow & Uccelli, 2009). Recently, Barr *et al.* (2019) presented the construct of core academic language skills (CALS) and the development of an assessment (in English) for Grades 4–8 that measures the various domains of this construct. Included in CALS are skills such as 'unpacking dense information' (2019: 987), which involves understanding morphologically complex words (e.g. relating 'invasion' to 'invade'), and 'connecting ideas logically' (2019: 987), which refers to how ideas are related to one another and the language that signals these connections (e.g. consequently, as a result).

Awareness of the linguistic dimensions of academic language is needed by all teachers in order to adequately support multilingual learning. As CALP/CALS is not necessarily acquired 'along the way', it needs to gain explicit focus in instruction (Cammarata & Haley, 2017; Morton, 2017). This topic needs to be addressed in the initial training of teachers as well, because it is precisely the use of CALP/CALS that causes the greatest difficulties for students. The development of CALP/CALS, or language for academic purposes, should be ensured by all teachers (Otwinowska & Foryś, 2017). A major obstacle in both mainstream and bilingual education is the lack of attention devoted to CALP/CALS, throwing children (and teachers) in at the deep end and assuming they will 'manage somehow'. Unfortunately, this is not always the case and lack of linguistic support in the education system may cause frustration in children and even symptoms of intellectual helplessness.

Supporting Multilingualism in Schools

What should a teacher be aware of when supporting multilingual learning? A well-established model by Lucas and Villegas (2013) includes two distinct parts – teacher orientations and pedagogical knowledge and skills. The former emphasizes that the teacher is oriented towards values and beliefs of seeing multilingualism as a resource. Furthermore, multilingualism is not seen as affecting individual learners and their learning processes only, but rather as a wider phenomenon connected to social cohesion. Supporting multilingualism means giving all students opportunities to learn and participate in society, with teachers inclined to advocate for L2 learner needs.

Lucas and Villegas (2013) point out that, without these orientations, teachers will not be able to utilize the pedagogical knowledge and skills needed for supporting multilingualism. The essential starting point for all teachers is therefore to challenge beliefs and attitudes, especially regarding the deficit view of multilingualism (cf. Armon-Lotem *et al.*, 2015; De Houwer, 2015; Jessner, 2008). When teachers are oriented towards multilingualism, they understand the importance of the linguistic and academic backgrounds of their students and how to support their learning. This includes both noticing the language skills required for completing learning tasks and supporting learning by applying key language learning principles (Otwinowska, 2017). The orientation also challenges teachers to notice which specific parts of instruction are challenging so that they can provide sufficient scaffolding techniques to support learning.

Similarly, Meier's (2018) approach to multilingual socialization is a critique of monolingual norms in education. Her framework, which combines views from multilingual education, sociolinguistics and language socialization, consists of practical suggestions that can be reflected upon in a variety of sociopolitical and linguistic contexts. For example, Meier (2018) discusses affective factors such as encouraging positive self-evaluation and normalizing multilingualism. Likewise, this framework advocates developing student awareness of linguistic differences and similarities, as well as explicitly talking about multilingual learning goals. In short, the aim of this approach is not only supporting school language learning for all, but also supporting multilingualism more broadly.

Although linguistic diversity is increasing and has gained more attention in society, the provision of solutions for multilingual classrooms is still fragmented in initial teacher education (European Commission, 2017; Vetter, 2012). It is a common misconception that supporting multilingualism in a classroom requires the teacher to know all the languages present in the classroom (see Chapter 4 of this book). It is also a common fear that allowing other languages in the classroom opens possibilities of bullying if the teacher does not understand all the languages that are used. These kinds of fears might be related to uncertainty in classroom management, which highlights the need to discuss multilingual classroom practices. If a teacher feels uncertain about multilingual practices, a good starting point may be to map the languages present in the classroom, but also to bring in foreign languages that the teacher is familiar with. It might feel easier for the teacher to bring in languages they know themselves, thus showing all students that multilingualism is accepted and valued in the classroom (Bergroth & Hansell, 2020). This means that a teacher working in linguistically diverse classrooms does not have to start from the big issues, such as speaking multiple languages fluently. Even including some multilingual aspects in instruction may have a positive effect on the classroom atmosphere and make room for educational innovations (Bergroth & Hansell, 2020).

Finally, we include some previously unpublished voices from student teachers, in-service teachers and teacher educators in the Swedish-medium context in Finland reflecting on supporting multilingual learning within the European project Listiac (Linguistically Sensitive Teaching in All Classrooms) (see Bergroth *et al.*, 2022). In Excerpts 3 and 4, teacher educators are reflecting upon the importance of building good relationships, in this case with parents or other guardians.

> Excerpt 3.
> I am afraid to make a mistake, [...] because I don't know that culture, because of my lack of knowledge. [...] (Teacher educator 1)
>
> Excerpt 4.
> That relationship, if you manage to create it, there will be an understanding that you cannot know everything. [...] [We] cannot handle all cultures knowledge-wise but [we have] to build on the idea about 'the will to create a relationship'. (Teacher educator 2)

The teacher educators share their fear of accidentally causing cultural clashes, because they may lack the knowledge base for different cultures present in their classrooms. They conclude that it would not be realistic for teachers to know everything about different cultures from the start. However, they underline the will to build relationships, meaning that the teacher must be open to discussing and negotiating expectations about languages and multilingualism with parents/guardians (Bergroth & Palviainen, 2016).

In other reflections, student teachers discussed the importance of being responsive to a pupil's own wishes on how to approach linguistic and cultural diversity in classrooms.

> Excerpt 5.
> [...] I have also thought a lot about that it can be uncomfortable for some if you bring up the fact that 'you have a different home language' too often. (Student teacher 1)
>
> Excerpt 6.
> Yes, because not everyone likes that attention, if you're somehow made into an example, representing that entire culture somehow. (Student teacher 2)

These examples show that it is important for teachers to be empathetic and understanding of the needs of the pupils in the classroom, so that well-intentioned messages of acknowledging linguistic diversity do not result in accidental othering (emphasizing differences) (cf. Dervin, 2016). For these reasons, it may be good to normalize the approach to multilingualism: the responsibility of catering to linguistic diversity is not to be placed on the shoulders of individual pupils but becomes the responsibility of the school. This also means that it is not obligatory to have multiple languages in classrooms to use a multilingual approach to teaching.

The benefits of supporting multilingual learning become apparent in Excerpts 7 and 8, in which an experienced primary school teacher and a teacher educator reflect on pre-service teacher education and the role of multilingual language awareness as a way to support learning for all students. The teacher is concerned that monolingual teachers may lack a certain sensitivity to the multilingual repertoires of their students and thus lack an understanding of some concepts.

> Excerpt 7.
> I had some American students [...], they have come and done their teacher practicum here. [M]ost exchange students are very monolingual. They cannot draw parallels in that way and benefit from another language, so to speak. I think they are very weak at reinforcing any language these exchange students, because they are not used to multilingualism in that way. (In-service teacher/teacher educator)

This reflects Meier's (2018) call for multilingual socialization and Otwinowska's (2017) plea for training teachers in the use of several languages to help them get a better grasp of cross-linguistic issues. The teacher quoted above concludes that the foundation for this type of understanding should be established in pre-service teacher education. The teacher sees it as a solution for better language learning, which can enhance the learning of content-specific concepts across the curriculum. The teacher says:

> Excerpt 8.
> A lot of effort has to be put into teacher education. [...] I see some parallels, I think of mathematics which has also decreased very much, it is also about a certain language awareness in mathematics as well. A little parallel there in that way, to become more aware of the concepts, the use of them and get them reinforced a little more than just showing that 'this is a square', and that's it. 'Why is it square, quadra, quatro, what is it, so it's four, Audi Quattro, it's a four-wheel-driven car' and like keep going all the time to get those connections. And that is very much lacking today. (In-service teacher/teacher educator)

This type of awareness helps teachers to draw parallels between languages and different kinds of associations. Learning to group words that go together and making connections between languages and associating concepts with different languages will generally help students build vocabulary. This is also a part of normalizing multilingualism in classroom practices, which supports multilingual learning (Little & Kirwan, 2019). This way of working is useful to all pupils and thus does not take time away from content teaching. For some teachers this type of approach may come naturally, but others can acquire the skills in connection to some key concepts of the lessons. If the teacher does not know where to start, language teachers can be consulted. Subject teachers and language teachers working together in professional teams or even opting for co-teaching (Mård-Miettinen *et al.*, 2018) can be highly efficient in noticing and highlighting opportunities to support multilingual learning. However, support from language teachers should not be understood as the language teacher stepping in to teach the language or subject-specific vocabulary while the subject teacher proceeds to teach the content. Co-teaching and partnerships in teaching should naturally be equally rewarding for both teachers.

Conclusion

In this chapter we have examined multilingual learning from various angles. As a point of departure, we argued that both monolingual and multilingual children need support in the development of their languages and opportunities to become familiar with linguistic diversity for their growth to balanced citizens in modern societies. Although the need for support and opportunities to become familiar with linguistic diversity may sound somewhat self-evident, we also argued that there is still a long way to go in supporting multilingual learning in everyday practices in educational contexts across the globe so that all learners obtain both acceptance and support from their families, peers and teachers.

In the theoretical framework for the chapter, we showed how childhood bilingualism can bring educational benefits, but we also discussed what can happen when multilingual learning is not adequately supported. We made an effort to show that benefits and risks may occur in both mainstream and bilingual education alike and thus highlighted the constant need for educators to be aware of the linguistic dimension in all types of educational contexts. By focusing on three vastly different sociolinguistic contexts, Poland and Finland in the EU and California in the USA, we were able to address a variety of topics closely connected with the need to support multilingual learning. We also relied on voices from teacher education and pupils in CLIL education. In this final section we draw upon these insights and formulate lessons worth considering when considering different aspects of supporting multilingual learning in education as a broad concept.

First, education systems cannot be treated in isolation from their surroundings; policymakers and educators need some awareness of historical developments and current political trends. All the contexts discussed in this chapter show how an understanding of background issues is necessary to situate educational practices. In Poland, it was WWII and communism. In Finland, it was constitutional bilingualism. In California, legal propositions have had a radical impact on educational provisions.

Second, across the systems, policymakers and educators need to be aware that educational culture is differently conceptualized, which may lead to serious misunderstandings, especially in the case of migrants and returnees. Bilingual children may behave differently than expected, but they cannot be looked at as 'having problems'.

Bilingual and multilingual students, especially those with migration and re-emigration experiences, must not be made invisible in the education system. A lack of support for multilingual learning may result in many challenges for families, the students themselves and their teachers. It is schools that are obliged to support multilingual learning, as shown by the Finnish examples. Building on relationships within classes and schools, despite the fear of cultural clashes, and valuing multilingual repertoires and all languages brought in by students is the starting point. Cherishing multilingualism means acknowledging students' languages, drawing some parallels between languages and normalizing multilingual language use in classrooms. It is also crucial to problematize the dichotomy between languages of high and low prestige.

All of this cannot be achieved without acknowledging the essential role of teacher education. In all three contexts examined, we have foregrounded the crucial role of linguistically aware and responsive teachers as the ones who can either cause or alleviate problems. Although a child may have mastered the everyday language of schooling well, teachers must understand that, to succeed in reading and writing tasks (especially in the higher grades), they must provide support with respect to the academic aspects of language. In light of this, we highlighted some issues with the assessment of bilinguals and the affective states that some CLIL tasks may evoke. Without linguistically aware teachers it is hard to support multilingual learning and student wellbeing. Educating teachers and teacher educators to understand and support multilingualism is thus a crucial goal to achieve across continents.

References

Armon-Lotem, S., de Jong, J. and Meir, N. (eds) (2015) *Assessing Multilingual Children: Disentangling Bilingualism from Language Impairment.* Bristol: Multilingual Matters.

Aronin, L. and Singleton, D. (2012) *Multilingualism.* Amsterdam: John Benjamins.

Bailey, A. (2007) Introduction: Teaching and assessing students learning English in school. In A. Bailey (ed.) *The Language Demands of School: Putting Academic English to the Test* (pp. 1–26). New Haven: Yale University Press.

Barr, C.D., Uccelli, P. and Phillips Galloway, E. (2019) Specifying the academic language skills that support text understanding in the middle grades: The design and validation of the core academic language skills construct and instrument. *Language Learning* 69 (4), 978–1021.

Benmamoun, E., Montrul, S. and Polinsky, M. (2013) Heritage languages and their speakers: Opportunities and challenges for linguistics. *Theoretical Linguistics* 39 (3–4), 129–181.

Bergroth, M. (2016) Reforming the national core curriculum for bilingual education in Finland. *Journal of Immersion and Content-Based Language Education* 4 (1), 86–107.

Bergroth, M. and Hansell, K. (2020) Language-aware operational culture: Developing in-service training for early childhood education and care. *Apples – Journal of Applied Language Studies* 14 (1), 85–102.

Bergroth, M. and Palviainen, Å. (2016) The early childhood education and care partnership for bilingualism in minority language schooling: Collaboration between bilingual families and pedagogical practitioners. *International Journal of Bilingual Education and Bilingualism* 19 (6), 649–667.

Bergroth, M., Dražnik, T., Llompart Esbert, J., Pepiot, N., van der Worp, K. and Sierens, S. (2022) Linguistically sensitive teacher education: Toolkit for reflection tasks and action research. See https://urn.fi/URN:NBN:fi-fe2022021018583

Bialystok, E. and Martin, M.M. (2004) Attention and inhibition in bilingual children: Evidence from the dimensional change card sort task. *Developmental Science* 7 (3), 325–339.

Bialystok, E. and Shapero, D. (2005) Ambiguous benefits: The effect of bilingualism on reversing ambiguous figures. *Developmental Science* 8 (6), 595–604.

Bialystok, E., Barac, R., Blaye, A. and Poulin-Dubois, D. (2010) Word mapping and executive functioning in young monolingual and bilingual children. *Journal of Cognition and Development* 11 (4), 485–508.

Bloomfield, L. (1933) *Language*. New York: Holt.

Bohnacker, U. (2016) Tell me a story in English or Swedish: Narrative production and comprehension in bilingual preschoolers and first graders. *Applied Psycholinguistics* 37 (Special Issue 01), 19–48.

Breidbach, S. (2003) *Plurilingualism, Democratic Citizenship in Europe and the Role of English*. University of Bremen Language Policy Division. Council of Europe: Strasbourg.

Briceño, A., Rodriguez-Mojica, C. and Muñoz-Muñoz, E. (2018) From English learner to Spanish learner: Raciolinguistic beliefs that influence heritage Spanish speaking teacher candidates. *Language and Education* 32 (3), 212–226.

California Department of Education (2022) English learners. See https://www.cde.ca.gov/sp/el/

Cammarata, L. and Haley, C. (2017) Integrated content, language, and literacy instruction in a Canadian French immersion context: A professional development journey. *International Journal of Bilingual Education and Bilingualism* 21 (3), 332–348.

Carver-Thomas, D. and Darling-Hammond, L. (2017) *Bilingual Teacher Shortages in California: A Problem Likely to Grow*. Palo Alto: Learning Policy Institute.

Central Statistical Office (2020) Education in the 2018/2019 school year. See https://stat.gov.pl/en/topics/education/education/education-in-the-20182019-school-year,1,15.html

Clark-Gareca, B., Short, D., Lukes, M. and Sharp-Ross, M. (2020) Long-term English learners: Current research, policy, and practice. *TESOL Journal* 11 (1), 1–15.

CODA Poland (2021) See http://www.codapolska.org (accessed May 2021).

Collier, V.P. and Thomas, W.P. (2017) Validating the power of bilingual schooling: Thirty-two years of large-scale, longitudinal research. *Annual Review of Applied Linguistics* 37, 203–217.

Cook, V. (2007) The goals of ELT: Reproducing native-speakers or promoting multicompetence among second language users? In J. Cummins and Ch. Davison (eds) *International Handbook of English Language Teaching* (pp. 237–248). New York: Springer.

Creutz, K. and Helander, M. (2012) *Via svenska: Den svenskspråkiga integrationsvägen (Through Swedish: The Swedish Integration Path)*. Helsinki: Think Tank Magma.

Cummins, J. (1979) Cognitive/academic language proficiency, linguistic interdependence, the optimum age question and some other matters. *Working Papers on Bilingualism* 19, 121–129.

Cummins, J. (2000) Putting language proficiency in its place. In J. Cenoz and U. Jessner (eds) *English in Europe: The Acquisition of a Third Language* (pp. 54–83). Clevedon: Multilingual Matters.

Cummins, J. (2021) *Rethinking the Education of Multilingual Learners: A Critical Analysis of Theoretical Concepts*. Bristol: Multilingual Matters.

Dalton-Puffer, C. (2011) Content-and-language integrated learning: From practice to principles? *Annual Review of Applied Linguistics* 31, 182–204.

De Houwer, A. (2015) Harmonious bilingual development: Young families' well-being in language contact situations. *International Journal of Bilingualism* 19 (2), 169–184.

Del Valle, S. (2009) The bilingual's hoarse voice: Losing rights in two languages. In M.R. Salaberry (ed.) *Language Allegiances and Bilingualism in the US* (pp. 80–109). Bristol: Multilingual Matters.

Dervin, F. (2016) *Interculturality in Education: A Theoretical and Methodological Toolbox*. London: Palgrave Macmillan.

Dickinson, D.K. and McCabe, A. (2001) Bringing it all together: The multiple origins, skills, and environmental supports of early literacy. *Learning Disabilities Research and Practice* 16 (4), 186–202.

European Commission (2017) *Preparing Teachers for Diversity: The Role of Initial Teacher Education*. Luxembourg: Publications Office of the European Union.
European Commission (2019) Council Recommendation of 22 May 2019 on a Comprehensive Approach to the Teaching and Learning of Languages (2019/C 189/03). *Official Journal of the European Union* C189/15. See https://eur-lex.europa.eu/legal-content/EN/TXT/?uri=CELEX:32019H0605(02)
European Union (2021) See https://eacea.ec.europa.eu. (accessed May 2021).
Eurydice (2017) *Key Data on Teaching Languages at School in Europe*. Luxembourg: EU.
Eurydice (2019) *Integrating Students from Migrant Backgrounds into Schools in Europe: National Policies and Measures*. Luxembourg: EU.
Fan, S., Liberman, Z., Keysar, B. and Kinzler, K. (2015) The exposure advantage: Early exposure to a multilingual environment promotes effective communication. *Psychological Science* 26 (7), 1090–1097.
Filippi, R., Morris, J., Richardson, F.M., Bright, P., Thomas, M.S., Karmiloff-Smith, A. and Marian, V. (2015) Bilingual children show an advantage in controlling verbal interference during spoken language comprehension. *Bilingualism: Language and Cognition* 18 (3), 490–501.
Finnish National Agency for Education (2016) *National Core Curriculum for Basic Education* 2014. Finnish National Board of Education Publications, 5. Helsinki: Finnish National Agency for Education.
Finnish National Agency for Education (2019) Facts express 1C /2019. What languages do pupils study in basic education? See https://www.oph.fi/en/statistics-and-publications/publications/facts-express-1c2019-what-languages-do-pupils-study-basic
Finnäs, F. (2012) *Finlandssvenskarna 2012. En statistisk rapport (Finnish-Swedes 2012. Statistics Report)*. Helsinki: Folktinget.
Flores, N., Tseng, A. and Subtirelu, N. (eds) (2021) *Bilingualism for All? Raciolinguistic Perspectives on Dual Language Education in the United States*. Bristol: Multilingual Matters.
Gagarina, N. (2016) Narratives of Russian–German preschool and primary school bilinguals: Rasskaz and Erzaehlung. *Applied Psycholinguistics* 37 (1), 91–122.
García, O. and Solorza, C.R. (2021) Academic language and the minoritization of US bilingual Latinx students. *Language and Education* 35 (6), 505–521.
Gándara, P. and Mordechay, K. (2017) Demographic change and the new (and not so new) challenges for Latino education. *The Educational Forum* 81 (2), 148–159.
Grosjean, F. (1992) Another view of bilingualism. *Advances in Psychology* 83, 51–62.
Grzymała-Moszczyńska, H., Grzymała-Moszczyńska, J., Durlik-Marcinowska, J. and Szydłowska, P. (2015) *(Nie)łatwe powroty do domu? Funkcjonowanie dzieci i młodzieży powracających z emigracji ((Un)easy Comebacks Home? The Functioning of Children and Adolescents Returning from Migration)*. Warsaw: Fundacja Centrum im. prof. Bronisława Geremka.
Haman, E., Wodniecka, Z., Marecka, M., Szewczyk, J., Białecka-Pikul, M., Otwinowska, A., Mieszkowska, K., Łuniewska, M., Kołak, J., Miękisz, A., Kacprzak, A., Banasik, N. and Foryś-Nogala, M. (2017) How does L1 and L2 exposure impact L1 performance in bilingual children? Evidence from Polish–English migrants to the United Kingdom. *Frontiers in Psychology* 8, 1444.
Heineke, A.J. and Davin, K.J. (eds) (2020) *The Seal of Biliteracy: Case Studies and Considerations for Policy Implementation*. Charlotte, NC: Information Age Publishing.
Hellgren, J., Silverström, C., Lepola, L., Forsman, F. and Slotte, A. (2019) *Hur hanteras två- och flerspråkigheten i de svenskspråkiga skolorna? Resultat av en utvärdering i åk 1–6 läsåret 2017-2018 (How is Bi- and Multilingualism Handled in the Swedish-medium Schools? Results from a Survey at Grades 1–6 School Year 2017–2018)*. Helsinki: The National Center for Educational Evaluation.

Hill, L., Lee, A. and Hayes, J. (2021) *Surveying the Landscape of California's English Learner Reclassification Policy*. San Francisco: Public Policy Institute of California.

Hyvönen, S. and Westerholm A. (2016) Elevernas språkbakgrund i årskurs 1–6 i de svenskspråkiga skolorna (Language background of pupils in grades 1–6 in the Swedish-medium schools). In A. Westerholm and G. Oker-Blom (eds) *Språk i rörelse: skolspråk, flerspråkighet och lärande (Language in Motion: Language of Schooling, Multilingualism and Learning)* (pp. 12–35). Helsinki: Finnish National Agency for Education.

Iluz-Cohen, P. and Walters, J. (2012) Telling stories in two languages: Narratives of bilingual preschool children with typical and impaired language. *Bilingualism: Language and Cognition* 15, 58–74.

Jarvis, S. and Pavlenko, A. (2008) *Crosslinguistic Influence in Language and Cognition*. London: Routledge.

Jessner, U. (2008) Teaching third languages: Findings, trends and challenges. *Language Teaching* 41 (1), 15–56.

Johnson, R.K. and Swain, M. (1994) From core to content: Bridging the L2 proficiency gap in late immersion. *Language and Education* 8 (4), 211–229.

Kołaczek, M. and Talewicz-Kwiatkowska, J. (eds) (2011) *Raport końcowy z projektu badawczego. Funkcjonowanie poznawcze i językowe dzieci romskich uczęszczających do szkół podstawowych specjalnych i masowych – konteksty społeczne (Final Report on the Research Project. Cognitive and Linguistic Functioning of Roma Children Attending Special and Mass Primary Schools – Social Contexts]*. Oświęcim: Stowarzyszenie Romów w Polsce.

Komorowska, H. (2014) Analyzing linguistic landscapes. A diachronic study of multilingualism in Poland. In A. Otwinowska and G. De Angelis (eds) *Teaching and Learning in Multilingual Contexts: Sociolinguistic and Educational Perspectives* (pp. 19–31). Bristol: Multilingual Matters.

Kovero, C. (2011) *Språk, identitet och skola II (Language, Identity and School II)*. Rapporter och utredningar 6. Helsinki: Finnish National Board of Education.

Kunnari, S., Välimaa, T. and Laukkanen-Nevala, P. (2016) Macrostructure in the narratives of monolingual Finnish and bilingual Finnish–Swedish children. *Applied Psycholinguistics* 37 (Special Issue 01), 123–144.

Lam, K. and Richards, K. (2020) More US schools teach in English and Spanish, but not enough to help Latino kids. *USA Today*, 2 January 2020.

Li, W. (2000) Dimensions of bilingualism. In W. Li (ed.) *The Bilingualism Reader* (pp. 3–25). London: Routledge.

Little, D. and Kirwan, D. (2019) *Engaging with Linguistic Diversity: A Study of Educational Inclusion in an Irish Primary School*. London: Bloomsbury.

Lucas, T. and Villegas, M. (2013) Preparing linguistically responsive teachers: Laying the foundation in preserve teacher education. *Theory Into Practice* 52 (2), 98–109.

Meier, G. (2018) Multilingual socialisation in education: Introducing the M-SOC approach. *Language Education and Multilingualism: The Landscape Journal* 1, 103–125.

Morton, T. (2017) Reconceptualizing and describing teachers' knowledge of language for content and language integrated learning (CLIL). *International Journal of Bilingual Education and Bilingualism* 21 (3), 275–286.

Mård-Miettinen, K., Palviainen, Å. and Palojärvi, A. (2018) Dynamics in interaction in bilingual team teaching: Examples from a Finnish preschool classroom. In M. Schwartz (ed.) *Preschool Bilingual Education*. Multilingual Education, vol. 25. Cham: Springer.

Oker-Blom, G. (2021) *Swedish-Language Education in Finland: Special Features, Challenges, Development Needs and Proposed Measures*. Helsinki: Finnish Ministry of Education.

Olsen, L. (2010) *Reparable Harm Fulfilling the Unkept Promise of Educational Opportunity for California's Long Term English Learners.* Long Beach, CA: Californians Together.

Otwinowska, A. (2013) CLIL lessons in the upper-primary: The interplay of affective factors and CALP. In D. Gabryś-Barker and J. Bielska (eds) *The Affective Dimension in Second Language Acquisition* (pp. 211–225). Bristol: Multilingual Matters.

Otwinowska, A. (2016) *Cognate Vocabulary in Language Acquisition and Use: Attitudes, Awareness, Activation.* Bristol: Multilingual Matters.

Otwinowska, A. (2017) English teachers' language awareness: Away with the monolingual bias? *Language Awareness* 26 (4), 304–324.

Otwinowska, A. and Foryś, M. (2017) They learn the CLIL way, but do they like it? Affectivity and cognition in upper-primary CLIL classes. *International Journal of Bilingual Education and Bilingualism* 20 (5), 457–480.

Otwinowska, A., Mieszkowska, K., Białecka-Pikul, M., Opacki, M. and Haman, E. (2020) Retelling a model story improves the narratives of Polish–English bilingual children. *International Journal of Bilingual Education and Bilingualism* 23 (9), 1083–1107.

Pyykkö, R. (2017) *Monikielisyys vahvuudeksi. Selvitys Suomen kielivarannon tilasta ja tasosta* (Multilingualism into a strength. A report of the status and levels of language competences in Finland). Helsinki: Finnish Ministry of Education and Culture.

Rodina, Y. (2017) Narrative abilities of preschool bilingual Norwegian–Russian children. *International Journal of Bilingualism* 21 (5), 617–635.

Saarinen, T. and Ihalainen, P. (2018) Multi-sited and historically layered language policy construction: Parliamentary debate on the Finnish constitutional bilingualism in 1919. *Language Policy* 17 (4), 545–565.

Schleppegrell, M.J. (2004) *The Language of Schooling: A Functional Linguistics Perspective.* Mahwah, NJ: Lawrence Erlbaum Associates.

Sędek, G. and McIntosh, D.N. (1998) Intellectual helplessness. Domain specificity, teaching styles, and school achievement. In M. Kofta, G. Weary and G. Sędek (eds) *Personal Control in Action. Cognitive and Motivational Mechanisms* (pp. 419–443). New York: Plenum Press.

Simon-Cereijido, G. (2018) Bilingualism, a human right in times of anxiety: Lessons from California. *International Journal of Speech-Language Pathology* 20 (1), 157–160.

Smith-Christmas, C., Bergroth, M. and Bezcioğlu-Göktolga, I. (2019) A kind of success story: Family language policy in three different sociopolitical contexts. *International Multilingual Research Journal* 13 (2), 88–101.

Snow, C.E. and Uccelli, P. (2009) The challenge of academic language. In D.R. Olson and N. Torrance (eds) *The Cambridge Handbook of Literacy* (pp. 112–133). Cambridge: Cambridge University Press.

Statistics Finland (2021) Population structure. Helsinki: Statistics Finland. See http://www.stat.fi/til/vaerak/index_en.html

Stenberg-Sirén, J. (2018) *Den svenskspråkiga ungdomsbarometern 2018. Språk och internet* (The Swedish-Speaking Youth Survey 2018. Language and the Internet). Helsinki: Think Tank Magma. See http://magma.fi/wp-content/uploads/2019/06/111.pdf

Szybura, A. (2016) Nauczanie języka polskiego dzieci imigrantów, migrantów i reemigrantów (Teaching Polish to children of immigrants, migrants and returnees). *Języki Obce w Szkole* 1/2016, 112–117.

Tammenmaa, C. (2020) *Report on Entering Several Languages in the Population Information System.* Helsinki: Ministry of Justice.

Uccelli, P. and Páez, M.M. (2007) Narrative and vocabulary development of bilingual children from kindergarten to first grade: Developmental changes and associations among English and Spanish skills. *Learning, Speech, and Hearing Services in Schools* 38, 225–236.

US Census (2020) See www.census.gov (accessed March 2020).
Valentino, R.A. and Reardon, S.F. (2015) Effectiveness of four instructional programs designed to serve English learners: Variation by ethnicity and initial English proficiency. *Educational Evaluation and Policy Analysis* 37 (4), 612–637.
Vetter, E. (2012) Multilingualism pedagogy: Building bridges between languages. In J. Hüttner, B. Mehlmauer-Larcher, S. Reichl and B. Schiftner (eds) *Theory and Practice in EFL Teacher Education: Bridging the Gap* (pp. 228–246). Bristol: Multilingual Matters.
Williams, C. (2013) *Minority Language Promotion, Protection and Regulation. The Mask of Piety*. New York: Palgrave Macmillan.
Williams, C. (2017) The middle-class takeover of bilingual schools. *The Atlantic*, 28 December 2017.
Zurer Pearson, B. (2002) Narrative competence among monolingual and bilingual school children in Miami. In D.K. Oller and R. Eilers (eds) *Language and Literacy in Bilingual Children* (pp. 135–174). Clevedon: Multilingual Matters.
Zurer Pearson, B. (2009) Children with two languages. In E.L. Bavin (ed.) *The Cambridge Handbook of Child Language* (pp. 379–398). Cambridge: Cambridge University Press.
Zyzik, E. (2016) Toward a prototype model of the heritage language learner. In S. Beaudrie and M. Fairclough (eds) *Innovative Strategies for Heritage Language Teaching: A Practical Guide for the Classroom* (pp. 19–38). Washington, DC: Georgetown University Press.

7 Researching Adolescents' Linguistic Repertoires in Multilingual Areas: Case Studies from South Tyrol and Finland

Lorenzo Zanasi, Karita Mård-Miettinen and Verena Platzgummer

In this chapter we present and compare two research experiences in the domain of linguistic repertoires (LRs) applied to the field of education. Our aim is to elucidate how we used different combinations of methods for data generation in the trilingual (German, Italian and Ladin) Italian province of South Tyrol and the bilingual (Finnish and Swedish) coastal regions of Finland in order to map the LRs of young multilingual participants aged 10 to 19. We investigated different aspects of their LRs (representations, use and trajectories) with multiple methods, ranging from more traditional sociolinguistic surveys such as questionnaires and interviews to multimodal and task-based methods such as language portraits, photographs and simulated contexts for multilingual interaction. We describe these methods and share some of the insights they enabled us to gain into the LRs of adolescents in two multilingual contexts in Europe.

Introduction

This contribution is related to sociolinguistic studies on linguistic repertoires (LRs) as flexible and dynamic resources that are not bound to specific languages (Blommaert & Backus, 2013). As Blommaert and Backus (2013) point out, individuals may develop their LR through formal learning in educational contexts but also through more informal encounters with languages when meeting people live or online, when travelling, via media and so on. This is true in particular for bi- or trilingual areas where young people experience language diversity and contact not only at school but also in everyday life. Blommaert and Backus (2013) further argue that the learning that takes place through short-term informal encounters is seldom perceived as language learning even though its outcomes form part of a person's LR. Alongside the adoption of a historical-biographical and developmental perspective on the LR, researchers such as Busch have sought to further expand the notion in order to foreground a subject perspective that 'encompasses the body dimension of perceiving, experiencing, feeling, and desiring' (Busch, 2012: 510).

In this chapter we aim to display different methodological ways to map different aspects of the LR, including participants' representations and use of their repertoires as well as a biographical perspective on their repertoires as trajectories. In doing so, we also aim to take emotional and bodily dimensions as well as the fluid nature of LRs into account. We approach the methodologies through two projects that researched adolescents learning multiple languages in Italian, German and Ladin schools in South Tyrol and in Swedish immersion schools in Finland. By adolescents we mean persons aged between 10 and 19 years (World Health Organization, 2022). The point of departure for both projects is the fact that, in both contexts, children study multiple languages in school from an early age. Additionally, the participating young students also have a unique possibility of learning and using many languages even outside of school since they live in multilingual environments consisting of two or three official languages (German, Italian and Ladin in South Tyrol and Finnish and Swedish in the southern and western coastal regions of Finland) as well as a large number of other languages spoken by inhabitants with an immigrant background. Hence, both projects focused especially on the use of LRs both in and outside school. Furthermore, since the schools are situated in multilingual areas, some of the students have a bi- or multilingual rather than a monolingual background when entering the school. Of course, the degree of multilingualism varies depending on whether pupils are placed in specific language immersion pathways (as in the Finnish project) or in a non-specific, mainstream education system in which second- or third-language learning is normally encouraged (as in the South Tyrol project).

The geographic areas addressed in this chapter, the Italian province of South Tyrol and the bilingual regions of Finland, represent an ideal research context as these territories are characterised by a very diverse linguistic landscape and they share a long history of approaches to multilingualism and multiple language learning. Due to their geographical locations and historical development, both South Tyrol and the southern and western coast of Finland have always been multilingual areas. This is evident today not only because of the deep-rooted presence of the official languages (Italian, German and Ladin in South Tyrol and Finnish and Swedish in Finland) but also because of the appearance of numerous languages of the new minorities. Moreover, both areas are influenced by neighbouring countries: the bilingual coastal regions of Finland are influenced by Sweden and South Tyrol is influenced by Austria and Germany. For instance, many young adults in Finland complete their university studies in Sweden and many in South Tyrol go on to study in Austria or Germany.

A special methodological challenge in the two projects was formed by the ages of the participants (10–19 years). Conducting research with adolescents has been found to be challenging when it comes to motivating participants to provide information, capturing their lives and overcoming the power imbalance between young participants and adult researchers (e.g. Waugh *et al.*, 2014). By drawing on the experience of two projects carried out in different times and contexts, in this chapter we seek to illustrate a path to describing LRs that goes beyond enumerating linguistic resources.

The chapter begins with a discussion of the concept of the LR, after which we introduce the two projects and their contexts. In the following three sections, we present the methodological approaches for data generation used in the projects and the results gained with them in relation to the different dimensions of LRs they were addressing, before drawing more general conclusions.

The Linguistic Repertoire

The notion of the LR dates to Gumperz's work from 1964, who defined the verbal repertoire as 'the totality of linguistic forms regularly employed in the course of socially meaningful interaction' (Gumperz, 1964: 137), taking as the starting point for his analyses the speech community. Linguistic forms are thereby not investigated for their own sake, but as social action and with the aim of observing their social meanings for the groups of people who employ them.

Since Gumperz, the focus on the notion of LR has gradually shifted from the speech community to individual speakers, supported in recent years by theoretical elaborations by Blommaert and Backus (2013) and Busch (2012, 2015). These researchers agree on the need to question two central concepts – that of speech communities and that of delimited and separable languages. In the context of globalisation and new communication technologies, speech communities can no longer be considered homogeneous, and real-life language practices are fluid and do not correspond to the socially constructed boundaries between languages. This idea also underlies approaches such as translanguaging (e.g. Canagarajah, 2011; Otheguy *et al.*, 2015) or polylanguaging (Jørgensen *et al.*, 2011), and has also been more widely discussed in sociolinguistics in general (Heller, 2007; Makoni & Pennycook, 2007).

Busch's notion of the LR represents a 'move away from the idea that the repertoire is a set of competences, a kind of toolbox, from which we select the "right" language, the "right" code for each context or situation' (Busch, 2015: 17), and in this, her notion differs from other reconceptualisations such as that of Blommaert and Backus (2013). Busch's concept of the LR in particular can be mobilised as a theoretical notion to address how people experience, and potentially also subvert, categorisations along axes such as legitimacy, authenticity, inclusion or exclusion in connection with linguistic variation (Busch, 2015, 2020).

For Busch, the point of departure of the LR is the speaking subject that moves through different social spaces and assumes different positions within these spaces. She understands the LR 'not as something the individual possesses but as formed and deployed in intersubjective processes located on the border between self and the other' (Busch, 2015: 7). Accordingly, the LR is constituted in interaction just like the subject itself. Busch additionally merged these insights with a phenomenological perspective on the subject by introducing the concept of the lived experience of language. This notion brings to the fore the bodily and emotional dimension of experiencing language in intersubjective interaction, aspects that remained under-researched (see e.g. Kramsch, 2009).

In this context, Busch (2012, 2015) underlines that a LR is not only determined by the linguistic resources we use, but also by the ones we do not use. These may be resources that we do not yet use, and are relevant as objects of desire, or they may be experienced in bodily-emotional terms as threats in encounters with high stakes (e.g. asylum procedures). They may also be resources we no longer use but are inextricably linked to past experiences. Consequently, the LR does not only point backwards along a biographical trajectory, but also forwards to possible futures that speakers are imagining.

This complexity of the notion of LR has obvious repercussions in empirical research. In other words, if we aim to investigate adolescents' LRs, it is appropriate to investigate their different dimensions. We will thus discuss methods by which we investigated how students represent their own LRs, how they use them in interaction in typical adolescent domains (family, school, free time) both online and offline, and how their repertoires developed along their biographical trajectories. Before we do so, however, we present the two projects and contexts providing the basis for this chapter.

Two Projects, Two Contexts

This section begins with an introduction to the two sociolinguistic contexts and the two projects or case studies addressed in this chapter and ends with a discussion of the main common and distinctive features between them in connection with the research reported on in this chapter.

Case study 1: RepertoirePluS in South Tyrol

South Tyrol is an autonomous province in northern Italy. It is an officially trilingual territory with Italian, German and Ladin as official languages. According to data from the last census in 2011, about 69% of the population declares itself to be a member of the German language group, 27% of the Italian language group and 4.5% of the Ladin language group (Astat, 2012) – which, of course, does not necessarily provide any insight into the population's LRs. As far as geographical distribution is concerned, declared members of the German language group are in the majority throughout most of the province, apart from the capital of the province, Bolzano, where the Italian language group prevails (74%). The latter is also well represented in the second and third largest cities Merano (49%) and Bressanone (26%). Ladin-speaking communities are historically located in the valleys of Val Gardena and Val Badia. In the province, German has been put on equal footing with Italian and bilingualism is therefore present in public administration, in toponymy and in dealings with judicial offices. It should be noted that the German-speaking population widely uses local dialects belonging to the Southern Bavarian group in both public and private contexts.

The South Tyrolean education system exhibits a tripartite structure with three school boards (Italian, German and Ladin), which guarantees the right to education in the 'mother tongue' for Italian and German (see Platzgummer, 2021, for a critical discussion), as well as the right and obligation to learn the respective second language of the territory (German for Italian schools, Italian for German schools). Education in the Ladin valleys, on the other hand, includes all three languages, with German and Italian serving as languages of instruction to the same degree. In South Tyrol, this system has resulted, on the one hand, in the possibility for each language group to have its own school and, on the other, in the separation of the school population, starting from kindergarten. In order to overcome this distance, since the 1980s and 1990s (Gelmi & Saxalber, 1992), German and Italian schools have promoted mutual encounters. In addition, they enhanced the offer of L2 lessons with the use of content and language integrated teaching (CLIL) for German, Italian and English.

As far as new minorities are concerned, the three systems of schooling in South Tyrol have been affected by the wave of migration that began in Italy in the 1990s and has been progressively increasing ever since. Tools such as the multilingual curriculum implemented at some schools (Schwienbacher *et al.*, 2016) and the creation of a competence area called Intercultural and Citizenship Education are currently used in the schools' curricular planning and in the design of teacher training. The most significant result of the synergy between the three school systems is the establishment of so-called Language Centres in 2007, aimed at all schools in the province at all levels, with the function of promoting the integration of pupils with a migrant background.

In this context, within the Institute of Applied Linguistics of Eurac Research, the project RepertoirePluS matured. The aim of the project was to study the LRs of a group of students aged 12–16 years, enrolled in lower and upper secondary schools in South Tyrol. The project, which included schools with Italian or German as the language of instruction as well as schools in the Ladin valleys, focused on the operationalisation and evaluation of individual LRs and observed their use during multilingual interaction. RepertoirePluS was structured around three research questions aimed at investigating qualitative and quantitative aspects of local students' LRs.

(1) How diverse are the LRs of students in South Tyrol?
(2) What kind of multilingual skills do the students have?
(3) How do the students use their multilingualism in interactive learning scenarios and how do they perceive this experience?

The first question was answered by means of a questionnaire, while the other two questions were addressed with a 'language village' – a specifically adapted research method – and with focus groups. The research was an opportunity to test, empirically, the appropriateness of methodological tools for collecting and analysing self-declarations, representations and feelings associated with multilingualism and examples of multilingual communication.

In connection with RepertoirePluS, Platzgummer (2021) also conducted a PhD project aiming to investigate adolescents' self-positionings in relation to their LRs. For this purpose, she carried out language-biographical interviews with 24 participants, taking the RepertoirePluS questionnaire as a point of departure.

Case study 2: Multi-IM in Finland

The other context in this chapter, Finland, is a bilingual country by constitution with Finnish and Swedish as official languages (Ministry of Justice, 1999). At the end of 2020, 86.9% of the population was registered as Finnish speakers, 5.2% as Swedish speakers and 7.8% as speakers of other languages (Statistics Finland, 2021). The latter percentage has steadily grown in Finland during the 2000s, from 1.9% in 2000 to 7.8% in 2020, and includes the immigrant population as well as speakers of the three indigenous Sami languages spoken in Finland and speakers of Roma and sign language, which are also mentioned in the language legislation in Finland. In the regions where this research was conducted, this average is similar to or higher than the national average (Statistics Finland, 2021). Geographically, the two national languages are not evenly distributed in Finland. There are bilingual Swedish–Finnish municipalities in the southern and western coastal regions of Finland whereas other regions in mainland Finland are monolingual Finnish-speaking and the municipalities on the Åland Islands are monolingual Swedish-speaking.

In the bilingual municipalities, signs, important documents and public services need to be in both languages. Moreover, the Language Act

(423/2003) guarantees speakers of Finnish and Swedish the right to use their language in public services, even in the monolingual municipalities. However, the realisation of linguistic rights is continuously debated in Finland (see e.g. Prime Minister's Office, 2018). Furthermore, Finland has separate national and local newspapers in the two national languages and the Finnish Broadcasting Company (YLE) is required to provide media services in both languages. Both national and local theatres and other cultural institutions and societies as well as sport clubs are run either monolingually in one of the two languages or bilingually. Both Finnish and Swedish are also used in many workplaces in the bilingual regions, even though companies within the private sector do not have any language-related obligations in Finland (Malkamäki & Herberts, 2014).

With regard to education, Finland has a system of parallel monolingual education, meaning that schools and early childhood education institutions are administratively either Finnish-medium or Swedish-medium but follow the same national curriculum guidelines. The 'other' national language (i.e. Swedish in Finnish-medium schools and Finnish in Swedish-medium schools) is an obligatory school subject in all schools in Finland and has to be studied at the latest from the age of 12 onwards. There is, however, ongoing debate in Finland on the obligatory status of Swedish as a subject in Finnish-medium schools due to low learning motivation and low learning results (e.g. Hult & Pietikäinen, 2014). For newcomers to Finland, the tendency is to enrol them in Finnish-medium schools even in the bilingual municipalities. Multilingual students are supported in various ways in Finnish schools; for example, they are offered preparatory education and teaching of their mother tongue. Furthermore, the newest national curriculum guidelines oblige schools to support the multilingual and multicultural development of all students (Finnish National Agency for Education, 2016).

In order to provide students with better learning results in Swedish in the bilingual coastal regions, Finnish-medium schools started to provide early total Swedish immersion education in 1987 (e.g. Bergroth, 2015; Björklund & Mård-Miettinen, 2011a). Swedish immersion addresses mainly majority language (Finnish) children who do not have Swedish as their home language. Despite the growing number of immigrant-background students in Finland, the Swedish immersion population is still Finnish-dominated due to the enrolment criteria used (Mård-Miettinen et al., 2020). Swedish immersion is an optional programme that starts in early childhood education (ages 3–5 years) and continues throughout preschool and basic education (Grades 1–9, ages 6–16 years). In early childhood education, teaching is 100% in Swedish, gradually diminishing to 50% by Grades 5–6 (Bergroth, 2015; Björklund & Mård-Miettinen, 2011a). The main goal of Swedish immersion is to provide students with functional language proficiency and literacy in the immersion language (Swedish) and L1 level proficiency and literacy in Finnish as well as age-level proficiency and literacy in one to three foreign languages that are introduced in different grades of basic education.

Internationally, one of the core features of immersion is language separation by teacher (one teacher–one language) and subject (one subject–one language each school year) (e.g. Johnson & Swain, 1997). Hence, some researchers (e.g. Heller, 1999) label immersion as an educational programme that fosters individual multilingualism through parallel monolingualism. Students in immersion are, however, allowed to use all their languages for communication and learning, but they are often explicitly asked to only use the immersion language during certain lessons to support its development to a strong language for content learning as it is a minority language and a new language to the students (e.g. Ballinger *et al.*, 2017).

The project Multilingualism in Swedish immersion (or Multi-IM) was set up at the University of Vaasa by Professor Siv Björklund and PhD Karita Mård-Miettinen in 2011 with the aim of studying the use of multiple languages among 10–16-year-olds attending primary and secondary school Swedish immersion education in the bilingual regions of Finland. Prior to this, immersion research in Finland had mainly focused separately on the development and use of the immersion language (Swedish) and Finnish (as first language) as well as on learning results in foreign languages in order to investigate whether immersion education fulfils its objectives. Research on immersion students' whole LRs was expected to give an interesting point of departure to the study of the use of multiple languages, as immersion students belong to the language majority but live in bilingual municipalities with an increasing number of multilingual speakers. For a majority speaker, the use of multilingual repertoires is not in the same way obvious and a prerequisite as it is for students who belong to a linguistic minority. Immersion students' LRs were approached from different angles and hence the Multi-IM project consists of several data sets and different cohorts of Swedish immersion students living in different parts of the bilingual coastal parts of Finland. The initial quantitatively oriented mapping of Swedish immersion students' LRs was carried out with a written questionnaire followed by individual and focus group interviews. This was followed by case studies where data were generated with two types of visual methods and self-recordings to examine the students' use of LRs outside the school context. The latest data generation was completed within the scope of a larger research project financed by the Society of Swedish Literature in Finland that aimed to investigate the relation between language practices, linguistic identity and language ideology within the context of Swedish immersion (Björklund *et al.*, 2022).

Common Features in the Two Contexts

The two research projects on LRs addressed in this chapter were set up in contexts with a number of shared features regarding multilingualism on societal and individual levels (cf. Herberts & Laurén, 1998). Both research contexts are historically bi- or trilingual border areas and issues around bi- or trilingualism are legally regulated in both areas: in Finland both on a national and local level and in South Tyrol on a provincial level within the framework of the Italian Constitution. Language policies in both areas are built on ideas of language separation, which results in rather complex provisions regulating language on a societal level. For instance, there are separate newspapers and theatres, and public documents are translated between the languages. Regarding education, the two or three language groups mainly have separate schools up to university level and it is compulsory for all to study the respective second language of the region/country in both contexts.

Another common feature is that both contexts have recently seen an increase in their resident immigrant populations and, consequently, in the immigrant student population. This has also resulted in changes in the multilingual situation in education, as students' LRs became more diverse. Hence, more recently established policies were added to the long-term policies and established practices with bi- and multilingualism in educational contexts in these regions in order to adjust to the changing situation.

Moreover, both national contexts are not uniform as far as their sociolinguistic situation is concerned and neither are the smaller regions we are interested in. Italy is officially monolingual, with provisions for linguistic minorities, and Finland is officially bilingual, with provisions for other linguistic minorities. Along the coastal regions of Finland, there are monolingual Finnish-speaking and Finnish–Swedish bilingual regions. These regions, in turn, are also not uniform. The southern and southwestern coastal regions are Finnish-dominated whereas (particularly) the north-western coastal region is Swedish-dominated. Furthermore, Finland has an autonomous Swedish-speaking region, the Åland Islands, with its own language legislation as well as a region called the Sami Homeland in the northernmost Finland, which is autonomous on issues relating to Sami language and culture. In South Tyrol, too, the sociolinguistic profile changes in connection with locality, with a large portion of the countryside being German-dominant (apart from an Italian–German bilingual South and the Ladin valleys), the capital city being Italian-dominant and other larger cities being Italian–German bilingual to differing degrees.

Due to the long history of societal and individual bi- and multilingualism in the two contexts, there is also a considerable tradition of research studies, especially of bi- and multilingual practices in education and administration. The multilingualism experienced on a daily basis and the coexistence of very different communities in delimited territories have prompted all those in society who deal with languages and education (schoolteachers, administrators, researchers, policymakers) to develop a sensitivity towards tools, methodologies and theoretical approaches that are grounded in the lives of speakers. For this reason, both South Tyrolean and Finnish research experiences converge towards multimodal and versatile methods for research in the field of applied linguistics. As to the two projects focused on in this chapter, there is a common interest in researching children's and adolescents' LRs, particularly to identify combinations of methods that are adequate for use in a complex multilingual context and with the challenging age group of young multilinguals.

Researching Representations of Linguistic Repertoires

In the two projects, several methods were used to generate and analyse verbal or visual representations of LRs, i.e., the participants were asked to describe and portray their repertoires.

Exploring repertoires with questionnaires

The questionnaire is a classic tool for sociolinguistic research and continues to be a formidable means of data collection, including for the investigation of individual LRs. Using a questionnaire to explore the representations that participants have of multilingualism means being able to relate their daily world to the diversity of languages and thus direct their attention to a reality in which multilingualism is often hidden, taken for granted or undervalued. To bring out the personal linguistic experience, as suggested by the research approach of the LR (Busch, 2015), presupposes that the items on the questionnaire cover different periods of the informants' lives, various contexts of use, an attention to the emotions linked to languages and that they offer the respondents considerable degrees of freedom to develop their representations. Analysis of the questionnaires makes it possible to interpret the data on two levels. The first is that of the entire student sample considered as a homogeneous group in order to get an overview of the LRs at group level. The second focuses on the representations of the multilingualism of each individual and constitutes an important resource in the triangulation with other sources of data.

RepertoirePluS (South Tyrol)

Based on these assumptions, in the course of the RepertoirePluS project, researchers at Eurac Research developed a questionnaire that was completed by 240 secondary school students. It consisted of 47 items, including creative elements (e.g. a language portrait), closed, semi-open and open questions, and was divided into five sections. The first two sections covered aspects of the participants' language biography (past, present and future) and self-assessments of language skills, accompanied by information about frequency of use, favourite or non-preferred languages and varieties, and language learning experiences. The third section focused on language use in everyday life and specifically on representations of receptive and productive language use at home, at school, in their personal surroundings and in the digital world. The fourth section asked students to reflect on the meaning and benefits of being multilingual and then to imagine how they would react in plausible multilingual situations. The questionnaire ended with a section about the students' metadata.

Analysis of the sociolinguistic questionnaires revealed that the group of participating students was multilingual in its entirety (all 240 participants), all together mentioning knowledge of 29 different languages. Taking only named standard languages into account, the most frequent combination was Italian, German and English (30%), followed by combinations of these three languages with Ladin (16%), Latin (14%) and Spanish (8%). Participants also mentioned a total of 32 non-standard language varieties in the questionnaires. Most of these were related to the German standard languages (e.g. Bavarian, Swiss German, Viennese, one of the South Tyrolean dialects) or to the Italian standard language (e.g. regional varieties such as Calabrese, Roman, Trentino, Sicilian). When asked about language use at school, however, pupils tended to mention only the languages taught in their respective schools, with the exception of local varieties of German and Italian. Language use at home, in turn, was described as multilingual by the majority of students (81%), with 49% using two languages (often a combination of Italian and German standard language and/or varieties) and the remaining 32% using three or more languages. Regarding their free time, an even higher percentage of students (94%) stated that they use more than one language.

In conclusion, the questionnaire analysis showed that the observed sample used multilingualism proactively and confidently. Students associated positive experiences with learning and using languages and were convinced that their multilingual skills would continue to be important and useful in the future and in many personal, social and professional situations (for further details on the findings see Engel *et al.*, 2020).

Multi-IM (Finland)

A questionnaire was also developed in the Multi-IM project in order to map multilingual patterns among Swedish immersion students in three municipalities along bilingual coastal Finland. The questionnaire consisted of 26 closed and open-ended questions addressing the participants' language learning history and experiences, past and present language use in different contexts and their conceptions of language learning. They were also asked to self-assess their language skills and to indicate if they considered themselves multilingual. The questionnaire was completed by 182 Grade 4–6 students (ages 10–13) in 2011 and by 203 Grade 7–9 students (ages 13–16) in 2014. In each municipality, this was accompanied by structured interviews with volunteering students to gain more insight into the themes brought up in the questionnaire, resulting in a total of 11 interviews with Grade 5 students (ages 11–12) and 22 interviews with Grade 8 students (ages 14–15).

In the Multi-IM project, the sociolinguistic questionnaire data showed the knowledge of 12 different languages by the participating immersion students as a group. Furthermore, all the students felt they knew the two languages used for content teaching in the immersion programme (Finnish and Swedish), as well as English, which is a compulsory foreign language for them. Most of those students who studied other foreign languages in school (German, French, Italian, Spanish or Russian) reported that they knew those languages. This goes against the national trend that not even several years of language studies in school (up to six years) gives Finns the confidence to say they know these languages (except English) or that they are multilingual (e.g. European Commission, 2012).

Secondly, the questionnaire and interview data allowed the project researchers to study in more detail to what extent immersion students head towards multilingualism by studying elective languages offered within the programme. The results showed that 55% of the responding students studied at least one elective language besides the three compulsory languages. This indicates that students in the immersion programme are, nationally, an important group of multilingually oriented individuals compared with students in mainstream education, with national statistics showing that the study of elective languages has dramatically declined in schools in Finland since its peak in the 1990s (Ministry of Education and Culture, 2017).

As to reported use of the LR, even in the youngest cohort (Grades 4–6 students, $n = 97$), more than half (57%) reported using at least two languages in their repertoire for activities such as reading books, watching TV or using the internet; many (43%) also indicated they dreamt in several languages. Furthermore, in the oldest cohort (Grades 7–9 students, $n = 114$) with the longest experience of language learning, 75% of the students felt that they were multilingual, meaning that participation in immersion education had made them multilingual language users. Cross-linguistic influence was also brought up by 93% of the immersion students, who found that the knowledge of the immersion language (Swedish) helped them learn subsequent languages (for further details on the results see Björklund & Mård-Miettinen, 2011a, 2011b; and Björklund et al., 2015).

Representing repertoires through visual methods

Another way of eliciting data on multilingual repertoires is visual methods. These are typically based on photographs, commercials or videos and films that are either produced by the researcher or the subject of the study or are naturally occurring visual products (Heath et al., 2009). Visual methods have been employed in the field of language research for only a relatively short time, but they have a long tradition in social sciences in researching social worlds of everyday life (Pitkänen-Huhta & Pietikäinen, 2017; Rose, 2016). In recent years, visual methods have also been used more frequently in ethnographic research concerning language learning and language use (for some examples see Kalaja & Pitkänen-Huhta, 2018). Pitkänen-Huhta and Pietikäinen (2017) emphasise that visual data can make language experiences and practices visible without the need to use restricting classifications of languages or language skills.

RepertoirePluS: Language portraits

One method of eliciting visual data is a language portrait. This was originally conceived as a didactic method aimed at language awareness but has been adapted and widely used as a research method over the last decade. While the uses differ in modes of elicitation and methods of analysis, they share a common interest in investigating speakers' perspectives on their LRs and lived experience of language (see e.g. Kusters & De Meulder, 2019; Prasad, 2014).

The language portrait method consists of participants colouring a body silhouette to represent their linguistic resources and language practices and the meanings they attach to them. Kusters and De Meulder (2019: 2) highlight the participant-centred nature of the method and state that it 'allows and aids researchers to see languages as embodied, experienced and historically lived'. More so than other interviewing methods, the language portrait gives participants time for reflection as they create a visualisation of their LRs. The visual representation and its concurrent or subsequent verbal explanations exist in tandem and the research interest does not lie in the portrait itself, but rather in the interaction during which it serves as a prompt and point of reference. In fact, Busch (2018: 7) conceives the language portrait 'as a situational and context-bound production that is created in interaction between the participants, framed by the specifications [...] and the setting'.

In the RepertoirePluS project, language portraits were used as an icebreaker activity at the beginning of the questionnaire described previously in order to prepare the ground for participants to reflect on their repertoires. They were then reintroduced to the students in focus group interviews during the second phase of data generation as well as in the 24 individual language, biographical interviews conducted by Platzgummer (2021). As the focus of the latter interviews was a perspective on LRs as trajectories, we will present the results of this investigation only before the conclusions.

Multi-IM: Language trees

Another possible method for eliciting visual data on LRs is the language tree, developed by Østern (2004). The method is inspired by family trees and was originally used by Østern as coursework on a university

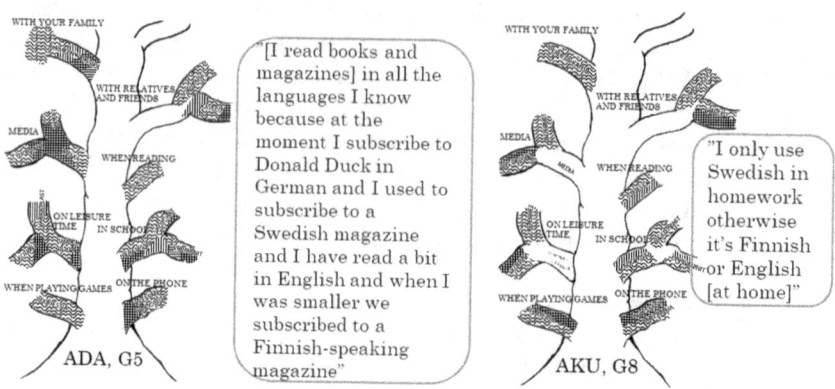

Figure 7.1 Language trees of Ada (Grade 5) and Aku (Grade 8). Waves stand for Finnish, vertical stripes for Swedish, checkered for English and horizontal stripes for German.

course on child language and bilingualism in order to develop student teachers' awareness of language and culture to prepare them to better understand their future pupils. In the original language tree method, the participants were asked to think about their language background, language competence and current LRs, represent their reflections in a language tree and comment on their drawing in writing.

In the Multi-IM project, the language tree method was used with certain modifications to generate more detailed data on the use of LRs among immersion students and to allow for method triangulation. In 2015, a group of ten primary and secondary school immersion students were given a drawing of a tree silhouette and asked to complete it to make their own language tree. The tree silhouette was accompanied with a short, written instruction that encouraged the students to think about the languages they use in certain places, with certain people and in certain activities in order to inspire them to think more broadly on the issue. Some examples of places, people and activities mentioned in the European language portfolio in Finland (Finnish National Board of Education, 2014) were written on the branches in the tree silhouette and the students were encouraged to draw more branches and to add more situations of language use (see next section). Furthermore, the students were given coloured pencils and asked to use different colours for different languages in their language tree. They were also asked to write a short explanation about their language tree. Prior to drawing the language tree, they also answered three questions on their LR. To gain deeper knowledge about the language trees, the students were engaged in a 15-minute structured individual elicitation interview one week after drawing the language tree.

The results generated through the visual language tree method were in accordance with the quantitative findings in the questionnaires: most of the participating students reported using three languages in their repertoire (Finnish, Swedish and English), both in school and in their leisure time. The data also revealed that, for some, the immersion language (Swedish) was mainly a language used in school and the only other language widely used outside the school besides their first language (Finnish) was English (see Figure 7.1). No languages other than those studied at school appeared in the drawings or in the elicitation interviews.

Discussing repertoires through focus group interviews

In addition to individual interviews, focus group interviews were also conducted to investigate the participants' reflections on issues related to use of their LRs.

RepertoirePluS

In the RepertoirePluS project, focus groups were designed to serve a dual purpose. First, participants were asked to reflect on their LRs generally and also on their use of their LRs in the language village activity (described later in this chapter). Second, the focus groups served as a method of triangulation. For this reason, the focus group interviews were conducted after the conclusion of the mentioned activity. Students were invited to discuss a set of questions in small groups with the assistance of an interviewer taking the role of moderator. Participants were free to use any language or dialect from their repertoire and it was specified that they could also alternate between and mix languages. The focus groups were designed to last for up to 45 minutes and were audio and video recorded.

Multi-IM

In the Multi-IM project, focus groups were used for method triangulation to enable the ten primary and secondary school immersion students who had drawn a language tree and had been individually interviewed about it in Autumn 2015 to collaboratively reflect on the use of their LRs as well as to demonstrate the use of their repertoires in Spring 2016. Focus groups of five primary and five secondary school students were set up and they were given a set of five topics that they discussed independently. The discussions were audio recorded and they lasted for approximately 15 minutes. The topics concerned languages they felt they would need in the future, imagined language use in a number of given situations in and outside school, reflections on who can be considered a multilingual person and actual language use when figuring out the language and content of a Dutch text. The topics were written down on separate sheets and a moderator gave the groups one sheet at a time but did not interfere with the discussion. For this reason, each student was instructed to act as chairperson for one topic.

The students' reflections on their individual multilingualism in the focus group discussions yielded similar results to the questionnaire and interview data and the language tree data: the participating Grade 9 students considered themselves to be multilingual as they knew Finnish, Swedish and English well; the Grade 5 students had some doubts about their own multilingualism as they felt they only knew two languages well (Finnish and Swedish) and, according to them, a multilingual person would need to know at least three languages well and have some basic knowledge of a fourth language. It seemed important for both groups that a multilingual person knows their languages well and can use them with other speakers of these languages. These relatively high standards may be linked to the fact that the participating students attend multilingual schooling and live in a multilingual area where several languages are used in their environment.

Researching Linguistic Repertoires in Use

Employing methods designed to observe the use of LRs aims to fill the gap between what young people say about their languages (the ones they claim to speak and know) and the real, everyday use they make of them.

Documenting LRs through photographs

In the Multi-IM project, another way of using visual methods for researching LRs was the use of photographs taken by the participants. This method was implemented in an attempt to model the students' use of their multilingual repertoires. Data generation focused on informal school spaces (breaks) and out-of-school spaces (e.g. home, hobbies, with friends etc.) – in other words, contexts that are challenging to map with other forms of data generation (questionnaires, interviews, drawings). According to Heath *et al.* (2009), using visual data produced by participants makes the participants active agents, opens access to more private spaces than other methods and also gives access to information that is hard to illustrate with words.

In 2016, ten Grade 5 (11–12 years) and ten Grade 8 (14–15 years) students were first asked to fill in a short questionnaire to indicate which languages they used at school and in their spare time. They were then engaged in data production with the instruction to use their mobile phones to take photographs of typical situations when they used their different languages over the course of a week. They were asked to send two or three photographs each day to the researchers by email or WhatsApp, with a short comment to describe each photograph. This medium of data generation was selected as, in 2015, over 90% of Finnish school children were reported to have a mobile phone and to use WhatsApp daily (DNA, 2015). The total number of photographs sent by each student varied between two and 11, and the research data comprised a total of 71 photographs. To gain a deeper understanding of the photographs and to support the analysis, the students were engaged in individual 15-minute structured photo elicitation interviews two weeks after taking the photographs.

When documenting the use of their LRs in their leisure time with photographs and through photo elicitation interviews, the students reported diverse contexts for language use that were also connected to languages other than those studied at school (Mård-Miettinen & Björklund, 2019). Finnish, Swedish and English were a part of many of the immersion students' everyday lives, even outside school. The other foreign languages studied at school (German and Spanish) also appeared regularly in the immersion students' lives, but mainly in connection with doing homework or holidays. Interestingly, Swedish had also brought another Nordic language (Norwegian) into the everyday lives of many students as they reported reading in Norwegian and communicating with Norwegians using Swedish in these situations and, when necessary, using English as support. Additionally, some students reported using French, Estonian or Chinese, which they did not study at school. Some students also described situations where they had noticed the presence of certain languages in their environment that they did not know themselves (e.g. Japanese).

As to the consequences of immersion being a programme that fosters individual multilingualism through parallel monolingualism, the students' descriptions in the elicitation interviews included discourses of both language separation and dynamic language use. Concerning language separation, the students talked about using one language at a time, so that a specific language was used with a specific person or in a specific situation or activity. The same activity was often reported to be done (separately) in several languages. The students also gave examples of parallel use of two languages, so that they simultaneously spoke in one language and wrote in another language. Dynamic use of different languages was mainly reported when talking with their friends. In these situations, English and/or Swedish words appeared in their Finnish speech. The students also reported using Finnish as support when doing their homework in Swedish.

Observing repertoires in interaction

In order to observe how LRs are used in interaction, communicative tasks can serve to simulate multilingual social interactions close to real-life situations. The 'language village' is a task-based method originally developed in the Netherlands as a method for foreign language learning and assessment at school (Adrighem et al., 2006). It was adapted in the course of the RepertoirePluS project in order to investigate participants' use of their LRs and their multilingual competences. A language village generally consists of small groups of participants entering a physical environment (a classroom or a lecture hall) in which they are set communicative tasks at different stations. The time spent at each of these stations is predetermined; when it expires, the groups change stations. While the tasks are set by researchers, the participants are left free to express themselves according to their linguistic abilities and resources in order to meet the task demands.

In a revised format of the language village, carried out with 131 participants in 32 groups in the spring of 2018, each station was centred around a precise communicative task designed in accordance with the principles of multilingual assessment discussed by Lenz and Berthele (2010). Three of the four 'areas' identified as crucial for the assessment of multilingual competences were taken into account for the language village:

(1) mediation, which involves mediating between people and/or texts in different languages;
(2) polyglot dialogue, which concerns interactions with the simultaneous use of several languages;
(3) intercomprehension, which involves drawing on one's linguistic resources in one language to understand a related other language.

We now describe one of the five stations (called Lost and Found) used within the RepertoirePluS project in order to illustrate how we investigated strategies for using the entire LR in complex communicative situations (for further information on the language village, see Engel *et al.*, 2021). The setting for the Lost and Found station is the lost and found office of Disneyland Paris. The participants' task is to explain to the French-speaking clerk that they have lost a member of their group, who in turn is looking for his/her lost wallet. When this interaction nears completion, a very agitated lady who speaks only Albanian enters the office asking for help in finding her lost daughter in the park. The group has to fill in two forms for the two missing persons, and the clerk asks the group for help in recording a message to be transmitted through loudspeakers in the park. The task therefore requires activation of the areas of mediation (between the participants), polyglot dialogue and intercomprehension when filling out the form. The fact that both the clerk and the supposed worried mother played their roles in a realistic manner allowed some participants to also identify with the situation on an emotional level.

Regarding the students' use of their LRs during the language village task and their narration of their interactive performance during the focus group (for more details see Lopopolo & Zanasi, 2019; Lopopolo *et al.*, forthcoming), the analysis showed the following:

(1) A strong recourse of students to transversal plurilingual skills (i.e. the ability to combine their own languages and varieties), both in production and reception, in order to cope with an unexpected situation.
(2) The emergence of mediation strategies determined by participants' roles within the group.
(3) The use of non-verbal semiotic strategies (gestural language, physical proximity or distance, eye contact).

Looking more specifically at the Lost and Found station, Engel *et al.* (2020) noted that, among themselves, the lower secondary school students communicated mainly in Italian, German dialect or German. In their interaction with the clerk, they frequently used English, quite often French and, in two groups, Albanian. The upper secondary school students mainly used English and Italian to communicate with the clerk and, to a lesser extent, French and German. Italian often served as a bridge language to French, and many students tried to include French terms and phrases in conversation. Communication was balanced between oral and written modes, and the station received generally positive feedback.

During the focus group, students were able to recall specific moments of the language village activity, to reflect on their communicative strategies and on the outcome of certain situations. This allowed the identification of different factors that affect the activation of the students' LRs. In addition to the languages and varieties present in the various stations, other factors that guided the speakers' choices were the context of each station, the students' perceptions of each task and of those who animated the stations and, of course, the type of behaviour of each student (extroverted or introverted, involved or detached) within the group dynamics.

The focus groups also allowed the students to clarify information previously stated in the language portraits and thus to update and recalibrate the data collected through qualitative commentary by the students themselves. Finally, the discussion that arose in the focus groups revealed additional details about what students think about language. First-person accounts of life experiences brought out opinions on language policy as perceived by students in their social relationships and on the future of languages. The focus groups were therefore very useful for collating different elements and reflections on the students' own LRs in order to draw up individual profiles of the relationships, attitudes and uses of languages.

Researching Linguistic Repertoires as Trajectories

As underlined earlier in this chapter, LRs develop as subjects move through different social spaces along their biographical trajectory. Consequently, language biographical interviews are a means of capturing this aspect of LRs along life trajectories (Busch, 2017). Language biographies have been referred to as 'life histories that focus on the languages of the speaker and discuss how and why these languages were acquired, used, or abandoned' (Pavlenko, 2007: 165) and language-biographical interviews have been a popular research method since the 1990s (Franceschini, 2004). A key principle in this context is that this kind of research is not primarily interested in the singularity of biographical experience, but in what individuals' language biographies 'reveal about specific dimensions of language practices and ideologies that are neglected when taking an assumed "average" speaker as representative of a certain group' (Busch, 2017: 55).

Language biographical interviews were conducted in the course of Platzgummer's (2021) PhD project. The aim thereby was to investigate the LRs of adolescents in South Tyrol, as well as how these adolescents position themselves with respect to their linguistic resources. For this purpose, 24 adolescents were interviewed, using the creation of a new language portrait as well as the language portraits previously created for the RepertoirePluS questionnaire by the respective adolescents as interview prompts (see Figure 7.2). The latter introduced a quasi-longitudinal element to the study, as contemplation of the earlier portraits offered an entry to reflections on changes and continuities in the participants' LRs.

An interactional analysis of these language biographical interviews provided additional insights into the participating adolescents' LRs, shedding light on the ways in which they perceived their language practices to have changed or remained the same over time. For instance, they mostly described their language practices at school in static terms (i.e. invariable over time), even though potentially multilingual. The few instances in which participants did describe school language practices as changing revolved around transitional moments of moving from one school to the other, which has already been demonstrated as a common pattern in language biographical research (Busch, 2015). Family language practices, on the other hand, were more likely to be constructed as changing over time. For instance, one participant recounted how her mother seemingly decided at some point that her father should stop speaking Italian in the family in order to prepare her for going to an elementary school of the

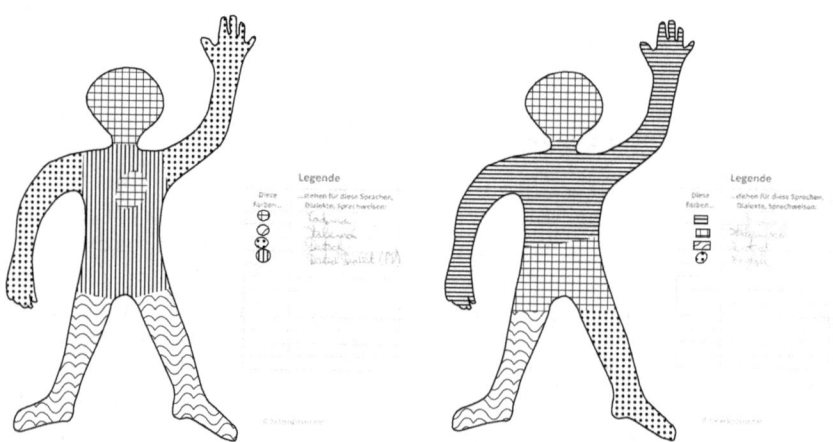

Figure 7.2 The 2017 questionnaire language portrait (left) and 2018 interview portrait (right) created by Lukas. Both portraits include Ladin, Italian and German, whereas a local German variety is only included on the left and English only on the right.

German track. Another participant narrated how she only ever wanted to speak Italian when she was little, even when her mother and grandmother spoke German to her, while now she not only spoke German in the family but was also attached to the language in emotional terms.

The narration of such changes in language practices finally points to key moments along a biographical trajectory during which a subject's LR is – often rapidly – reconstituted. Analysis of such narrations allows the identification of salient factors that bring about such reconstitutions, such as transitioning from one school to another, parents' choices with respect to family language policy, or migration and displacement. Other ways in which the LR becomes reconstituted were narrated as more gradual in the interviews, with an example being narrations of language learning processes.

Conclusion

In this chapter we have given examples of methods for data generation that were used to capture the LRs of young multilinguals attending multilingual schooling in two different geographical contexts with a long history as multilingual societies. The contexts are the trilingual (German, Italian, Ladin) Italian province of South Tyrol and the bilingual (Finnish, Swedish) coastal regions of Finland. The two cases discussed in the chapter especially focused on language learning and the use of LRs in school and outside school when living in a multilingual environment. The aim of both projects was to capture the multidimensional nature of LRs in terms of extension, quality and use in space and time (i.e. to describe LRs in a way that goes beyond enumerating linguistic resources).

Regarding the RepertoirePluS project in South Tyrol, the combination of looking at LRs in representations (sociolinguistic questionnaires and focus group interviews) and in use (the language village task) yielded a number of interesting results for the participating multilingual adolescents. Their LRs included, at the very least, the three languages provided for in all South Tyrolean school curricula (i.e. Italian, German and English) and, in many cases, additional languages and local or non-local varieties. Moreover, a complex picture emerged when considering which functions these languages and varieties served for the individual participants, ranging from everyday communication to education to language use in the digital world. In relation to the language village, it is interesting to underline the students' reactivity towards unexpected situations: new languages and new words or phrases were added to the repertoire when the opportunity or the need for them arose in this specific context (e.g. students with no previous skills in French picked up French terms and used them). By comparing the students' answers in the questionnaires with their behaviour in the language village, we also found that the ways in which they stated that they would solve a hypothetical problem in the questionnaire often did not coincide with the strategies they applied in the language village scenarios. Additionally, the language biographical interviews conducted by Platzgummer (2021) opened a third perspective on LRs as trajectories, showing how the participants' LRs had already been reconstituted at different moments in their biographical trajectories.

In the Multi-IM project, Swedish immersion students in Finland reported a total of 12 languages as languages they know in the sociolinguistic questionnaire. Most of them also reported to use at least Swedish and English (and many of them also other languages) outside of school, alongside Finnish. This indicates that participation in immersion education provided them with a broad LR to use in their multilingual environment. Nevertheless, mainly the languages studied at school were mentioned when reporting on language use in school and in leisure time in both the questionnaires and the connected interviews. The same result was also gained when generating data using language trees and focus group discussions as well as in the questionnaire part of the photo elicitation study. However, the use of photographs accompanied with an elicitation interview when collecting data led to a better balance between the participants and the researcher (cf. Waugh *et al*., 2014) and this turned out to be a successful way of engaging students to give more versatile information on their LRs. The adolescent students were highly motivated to take photographs and to describe their language use even outside the situations in the photos. The results from the photographic data showed that many students in fact regularly used languages other than those they studied in various contexts outside school.

In the two projects, multiple methods for data generation were used and triangulated. The methods ranged from more traditional sociolinguistic surveys such as questionnaires and interviews to the application of multimodal and task-based approaches such as photographs and recreated multilingual interaction environments. This allowed for an investigation of the different aspects of LRs among the participants and thus the acquisition of more reliable and valid insights. In addition to showing the value of method triangulation, the results of these projects highlight the importance of using methods that make participants active agents in order to allow for more participant-centred perspectives. Such methodological approaches can motivate teenage participants to elaborate more deeply on their LRs and thus help gain a situated understanding of their individual multilingualism.

The research experiences described in this chapter show that, while the two European research contexts are geographically distant and different in many respects, they share a history of societal bi- and trilingualism that impacts on individuals' LRs. In both contexts, there are education policies that strive to foster the learning and use of multiple languages, with a focus on the official languages of the respective context as well as other prestigious languages, in particular English. However, our research has also shown that students' LRs go beyond these languages. This points to a need for education policies that adopt a more inclusive approach to multilingualism and respect and promote the resources in everyone's LR, which is of central importance for individual wellbeing and social equity.

References

Adrighem, I., Härtig, J., Chlosta, C. and Iordanidou, C. (2006) Taaldorp – Von der Idee zu den ersten Versuchen. See https://www.daf-netzwerk.org/download.php?id=675 (accessed May 2021).

Astat (2012) *Volkszählung/Censimento della popolazione 2011: Berechnung des Bestandes der drei Sprachgruppen in der Autonomen Provinz Bozen-Südtirol/ Determinazione della consistenza dei tre gruppi linguistici della Provincia Autonoma di Bolzano-Alto Adige*. Bolzano: Astat.

Ballinger, S., Lyster, R., Sterzuk, A. and Genesee, F. (2017) Context-appropriate crosslinguistic pedagogy. Considering the role of language status in immersion education. *Journal of Immersion and Content-Based Language Education* 5 (1), 30–57.

Bergroth, M. (2015) *Kotimaisten kielten kielikylpy. Vaasan yliopiston julkaisuja. Selvityksiä ja raportteja 202*. Vaasa: University of Vaasa.

Björklund, S. and Mård-Miettinen, K. (2011a) Integrating multiple languages in immersion: Swedish immersion in Finland. In D.J. Tedick, D. Christian and T. Williams Fortune (eds) *Immersion Education: Practices, Policies, Possibilities* (pp. 13–35). Bristol: Multilingual Matters.

Björklund, S. and Mård-Miettinen, K. (2011b) Kielikylpylasten ja -nuorten monikielinen toimijuus. In N. Mäntylä (ed.) *Lapset ja nuoret yhteiskunnan toimijoina* (pp. 154–169). Vaasan yliopiston julkaisuja. Tutkimuksia 297. Vaasa: University of Vaasa.

Björklund, S., Pakarinen, S. and Mård-Miettinen, K. (2015) Är jag flerspråkig? Språkbadselevers uppfattningar om sin flerspråkighet. In J. Kalliokoski, K. Mård-Miettinen and T. Nikula (eds) *Kieli koulutuksen resurssina: vieraalla ja toisella kielellä oppimisen ja opetuksen näkökulmia* (pp. 153–167). AFinLA-e: soveltavan kielitieteen tutkimuksia. University of Jyväskylä.

Björklund, S., Pakarinen, S. and Mård-Miettinen, K. (2022) A language socialisation perspective on Swedish immersion in Finland: Students, teachers, and parents as key actors. *Journal of Immersion and Content-Based Language Teaching* 10 (2), 323–342. https://doi.org/10.1075/jicb.21019.bjo

Blommaert, J. and Backus, A. (2013) Superdiverse repertoires and the individual. In I. de Saint-Georges and J.-J. Weber (eds) *Multilingualism and Multimodality: Current Challenges for Educational Studies* (pp. 11–32). Rotterdam: Sense Publishers.

Busch, B. (2012) The linguistic repertoire revisited. *Applied Linguistics* 33 (5), 503–523.

Busch, B. (2015) Expanding the notion of the linguistic repertoire: On the concept of Spracherleben – The lived experience of language. *Applied Linguistics* 38, 340–358.

Busch, B. (2017) Biographical approaches to research in multilingual settings: Exploring linguistic repertoires. In M. Martin-Jones and D. Martin (eds) *Researching Multilingualism: Critical and Ethnographic Approaches* (pp. 46–59). Abingdon: Routledge.

Busch, B. (2018) The language portrait in multilingualism research: Theoretical and methodological considerations. *Working Papers in Urban Language and Literacies*, WP236, 1–13.

Busch, B. (2020) Discourse, emotions and embodiment. In A. De Fina and A. Georgakopoulou (eds) *The Cambridge Handbook of Discourse Studies* (pp. 327–349). Cambridge: Cambridge University Press.

Canagarajah, S. (2011) Translanguaging in the classroom: Emerging issues for research and pedagogy. *Applied Linguistics Review* 2, 1–28.

DNA (2015) DNA:n kysely esikoulu- ja ala-asteikäisten matkapuhelinten käytöstä. See https://docplayer.fi/15965364-Dna-n-kysely-esikoulu-ja-ala-asteikaisten-matkapuhelinten-kaytosta.html

Engel, D., Platzgummer, V. and Zanasi, L. (2020) *RepertoirePluS – Plurilingual Repertoires of South Tyrolean Students: Survey, Description and Usage in Multilingual Learning Scenarios. Final project report.* Bolzano/Bozen: Eurac Research.

Engel, D., Platzgummer, V., Zanasi, L. and Barrett, J. (2021) Activating linguistic repertoires in the language village. *LEND* 3, 151–166.

European Commission (2012) Europeans and their languages. Special Eurobarometer 386. See https://op.europa.eu/en/publication-detail/-/publication/f551bd64-8615-4781-9be1-c592217dad83

Finnish National Agency for Education (2016) *The Finnish National Core Curriculum for Basic Education.* Helsinki: Finnish National Agency for Education.

Finnish National Board of Education (2014) The European language portfolio. See http://kielisalkku.edu.fi/fi/ (accessed April 2021).

Franceschini, R. (2004) Sprachbiographien: das Basel-Prag-Projekt (BPP) und einige mögliche Generalisierungen. In R. Franceschini and J. Miecznikowski (eds) *Leben mit mehreren Sprachen – Vivre avec plusieurs langues: Sprachbiographien – Biographies langagières* (pp. 121–146). Bern: Peter Lang.

Gelmi, R. and Saxalber, A. (1992) *Integrierte Sprachdidaktik – Didattica Linguistica Integrata.* Bozen: Pädagogisches Institut.

Gumperz, J.J. (1964) Linguistic and social interaction in two communities. *American Anthropologist* 66 (6), 137–153.

Heath, S., Brooks, R., Cleaver, E. and Ireland, E. (2009) *Researching Young People's Lives.* London: Sage.

Heller, M. (1999) *Linguistic Minorities and Modernity: A Sociolinguistic Ethnography.* London: Longman.

Heller, M. (ed.) (2007) *Bilingualism: A Social Approach.* New York: Palgrave Macmillan.

Herberts, K. and Laurén, Ch. (1998) *Urbes linguas suas habent: Bolzano/Bozen, Fribourg/Freiburg, Vaasa/Vasa.* Skrifter utgivna av Svensk-Österbottniska samfundet nr 59. Vaasa: Österbottniska samfundet.

Hult, F. and Pietikäinen, S. (2014) Shaping discourses of multilingualism through a language ideological debate: The case of Swedish in Finland. *Journal of Language and Politics* 13 (1), 1–20.

Johnson, R.K. and Swain, M. (1997) Immersion education: A category within bilingual education. In R.K. Johnson and M. Swain (eds) *Immersion Education: International Perspectives* (pp. 1–16). Cambridge: Cambridge University Press.

Jørgensen, J.N., Karrebæk, M., Madsen, L.M. and Møller, J.S. (2011) Polylanguaging in superdiversity. *Diversities* 13 (2), 23–37.

Kalaja, P. and Pitkänen-Huhta, A. (2018) Visual methods in applied language studies. *Applied Linguistics Review* 9 (2–3), 157–176.

Kramsch, C. (2009) *The Multilingual Subject.* Oxford: Oxford University Press.

Kusters, A. and De Meulder, M. (2019) Language portraits: Investigating embodied multilingual and multimodal repertoires. *Forum Qualitative Sozialforschung/Forum: Qualitative Social Research* 20 (3). https://doi.org/10.17169/fqs-20.3.3239

Lenz, P. and Berthele, R. (2010) *Assessment in Plurilingual and Intercultural Education. Satellite Study No. 2. Guide for the Development and Implementation of Curricula for Plurilingual and Intercultural Education.* Strasbourg: Council of Europe.

Lopopolo, O. and Zanasi, L. (2019) Mediazione e repertori plurilingui nel villaggio delle lingue: nuovi strumenti per la didattica e la valutazione. *Babylonia* 3, 58–63.

Lopopolo, O., Platzgummer V. and Zanasi L. (forthcoming) Trasformare la classe in un Villaggio delle lingue: un metodo per la didattica del plurilinguismo. *Proceedings of the*

International Conference 'Insegnare (e imparare) l'italiano in contesti germanofoni: ricerca scientifica ed esperienze didattiche a confronto'. Bochum: Frank & Timme.
Makoni, S. and Pennycook, A. (2007) Disinventing and reconstituting languages. In S. Makoni and A. Pennycook (eds) *Disinventing and Reconstituting Languages* (pp. 1–41). Clevedon: Multilingual Matters.
Malkamäki, A. and Herberts, K. (2014) *Case Wärtsilä – Multilingualism in Work Situations*. Proceedings of the University of Vaasa. Report 194. Vaasa: University of Vaasa.
Ministry of Education and Culture (2017) Multilingualism as strength. Procedural recommendations for developing Finland's national language reserve. See https://minedu.fi/documents/1410845/4150027/Multilingualism+as+a+strength.pdf/766f921a-1456-4146-89ed-899452cb5af8/Multilingualism+as+a+strength.pdf (accessed May 2021).
Ministry of Justice (1999) Constitution of Finland 731/1999. See https://www.finlex.fi/fi/laki/kaannokset/1999/en19990731_20111112.pdf (accessed April 2021).
Mård-Miettinen, K. and Björklund, S. (2019) 'In one sentence there can easily be three languages'. A glimpse into the use of languages among immersion students. In A. Huhta, G. Erickson and N. Figueras (eds) *Developments in Language Education: A Memorial Volume in Honour of Sauli Takala* (pp. 239–249). EALTA & University of Jyväskylä.
Mård-Miettinen, K., Arnott, S. and Vignola, M.J. (2020) Early immersion in minority language context: Canada and Finland. In M. Schwartz (ed.) *Handbook of Early Language Education* (pp. 1–26). Cham: Springer.
Østern, A.-L. (2004) 'My language tree': Young Finland-Swedish adults tell us about their linguistic and cultural identities. *Journal of Curriculum Studies* 6 (6), 657–672.
Otheguy, R., García, O. and Reid, W. (2015) Clarifying translanguaging and deconstructing named languages: A perspective from linguistics. *Applied Linguistics Review* 6 (3), 281–307.
Pavlenko, A. (2007) Autobiographic narratives as data in applied linguistics. *Applied Linguistics* 28 (2), 163–188.
Pitkänen-Huhta, A. and Pietikäinen, S. (2017) Visual methods in researching language practices and language learning: Looking at, seeing, and designing Language. In K. King, Y.-J. Lai and S. May (eds) *Research Methods in Language and Education: Encyclopedia of Language and Education* (pp. 393–405). Basel: Springer.
Platzgummer, V. (2021) Positioning the self: A subject-centred perspective on adolescents' linguistic repertoires and language ideologies in South Tyrol. Thesis, University of Vienna.
Prasad, G. (2014) Portraits of plurilingualism in a French international school in Toronto: Exploring the role of visual methods to access students' representations of their linguistically diverse identities. *Canadian Journal of Applied Linguistics* 17 (1), 51–77.
Prime Minister's Office (2018) *Report of the Government on the Application of Language Legislation 2017*. Government publication 10/2017. See http://urn.fi/URN:ISBN:978-952-287-476-4 (accessed May 2021).
Rose, G. (2016) *Visual Methodologies. An Introduction to Researching with Visual Data* (4th edn). London: Sage.
Schwienbacher, E., Quartapelle, F. and Patscheider, F. (eds) (2016) *Auf dem Weg zur sprachsensiblen Schule: Das Mehrsprachencurriculum Südtirol*. Köln: Carl Link.
Statistics Finland (2021) Population structure 2020. Appendix table 2. Population according to language 1980–2020. Helsinki: Statistics Finland. See http://www.stat.fi/til/vaerak/2020/vaerak_2020_2021-03-31_tau_002_en.html (accessed April 2021).
Waugh, A., Ahn, J., Magee, R.M., Bowler, L., Agosto, D.E. and Subramaniam, M. (2014) Youth beyond borders: Methodological challenges in youth information interaction. *Proceedings of ASIST Annual Meeting* 51 (1), 1–5.
World Health Organization (2022) Adolescent health. See https://www.who.int/health-topics/adolescent-health#tab=tab_1 (accessed June 2022).

Creating Synergies in Comparative Multilingualism: An Epilogue

Colin H. Williams

Introduction

Multilingualism has become a keyword in social discourse. It is often used as one of the central elements to describe rapidly changing societies, at least within those advanced liberal democracies which for so long espoused a form of nationalistic monolingualism as the state sanctioned a single and indivisible language as the sole carrier of official and authoritative statements.

In the past two generations, five features have served to further challenge the monolingual hegemony of selected states. The first is the gradual and often grudging recognition of indigenous language minorities and their rights to be respected and incorporated within the state apparatus, particularly within education, local government and the media. Thus, Welsh speakers, Basque, Catalans and Frisians have seen their languages recognised and incorporated at both state and international levels with the passage of domestic legislation and the signing of instruments such as the Council of Europe's Charter for Regional or Minority Languages. The second is the increased mobility of capital and people, especially within the EU with its prized adherence to the free movement of people so as to make market capitalism a functioning reality. This has resulted in major metropolitan cores such as Frankfurt, Paris, London and Rome becoming far more attractive for investment, for mobile (often highly skilled) labour and for major infrastructural developments that often serve a global clientele as well as the state's population. The third is the increased presence of residents whose ancestral home typically would be one of the former European colonies, such as British people of West Indian, African or Asian stock or French citizens of Algerian origin, who in time situate their languages, cultures, faiths and foodways within an increasingly multicultural local context. They may also, in turn, develop access to designated classes designed to reproduce the dominant language of their forebears' country of origin, as happens in the teaching of Urdu in Manchester Islamic Grammar School for Girls, UK. The fourth is the increased presence of dislocated people, whether as migrants, refugees or asylum seekers, fleeing war-torn locales or searching for a more secure and better quality of life. The fifth is the phenomenon of guest workers and their descendants, best represented by the arrival of Turkish guest workers in Germany some 60 years ago, two thirds of whom are not yet German citizens (Anon, 2021).

Cumulatively, these factors induce major changes to the ethnolinguistic and racial makeup of many states. This can be illustrated in the 2021 announcement that a third of pupils in the UK come from an ethnic minority background (33.9% of primary school pupils and 32.1% of secondary school pupils). While 80.3% of pupils were recorded as having a first language known or believed to be English, some 1.6 million (19.2%) were recorded as having a first language other than English (UK Government, 2021). Accordingly, the social character of many states is increasingly multilingual and multicultural as is discussed in Williams (2021a), (2021b), (2022a), (2023).

This volume was derived from the activities of the Workshop on Multilingualism (WoM) network, which had four main aims:

(1) to establish an international network of scholars and practitioners;
(2) to construct a series of comparative case studies to draw out similarities and differences in the application of aspects of multilingualism;
(3) to generate new knowledge;
(4) to establish a task force that would bring the results of the network's research to the attention to selected policy decision makers.

In analysing the contours of multilingualism through a comparative lens, one may discern a number of implicit issues that the network identified, such as:

(1) the impact of language hierarchies, especially in the realm of education;
(2) the role of English within commerce, the media and intercultural affairs;
(3) the differing varying influence generated by whether a language is being used for professional or social reasons within a multilingual context;
(4) and perhaps, most significantly, how the discourse surrounding multilingualism impacts on the public's perception and reaction to a dynamic world order.

Of the many issues discussed within the WoM network, three will feature in this chapter. The first is the conscious adoption of a comparative perspective whereby a sharp focus on the contours of multilingualism can be maintained. The second is the role that policy documents, curriculum design, reform and implementation can have in either promoting or indeed damaging the prospects of a target language within the education system. The third is the increased salience of (metropolitan) multilingualism both for language transmission and for increased interaction within designated spaces, both open and closed.

The first feature of this volume's collection is the comparative perspective involving paired elements of case studies. The WoM participants were consciously paired with others from a markedly different sociolinguistic context so as to foreground the comparative element of their analysis, as in the case of a Swedish–Canadian (Chapter 1) or a Finnish–Cypriot focus (Chapter 5). These comparisons are in the main revealing, but can at times be stretched – both conceptually and empirically – and need to be seen essentially as heuristic devices as we together seek to understand more about the contours of multilingualism. Nevertheless, they do add new material and perspectives, since other analysts often tend to concentrate on their own or cognate societies that are rooted within one of a European, North American or Asian preoccupation, which then tends to be seen as a universal rather than a particular narrative illustration of a phenomenon. Clearly this has not prevented scholars from making generalisations from a limited basis of knowledge, especially when it relates to theory construction in language and education studies.

The second feature, the consequences for bi- and multilingualism of policy document, curriculum design, reform and implementation, is scrutinised in particular in the first three chapters of this volume, while the subsequent four chapters mainly deal with different perspectives on increased salience of multilingualism in education.

Consequences for Bi- and Multilingualism of Policy Documents, Curriculum Design, Reform and Implementation

Diachronic perspectives from Canada and Sweden

An analysis of the Canadian and Swedish experience of language learning identifies the early pioneering initiatives in the field of bilingualism and multilingualism during the 1960s and 1970s as starting points for current educational policies (Cummins & Lainio, Chapter 1). Given its commitment to an official languages regime within a multicultural framework, the Canadian experience has generated a great deal of information, research data and policy formulations.

These not only feed back into Canada's own structural reforms, but also provide proven examples of how initiatives in fields as diverse as language immersion education, employee language awareness training and the regulation of established official language rights may be evaluated and transferred to different levels in the political and administrative hierarchy.

In many ways, both the Canadian and Swedish developments have also offered best practice examples of language learning, which have been transposed to other contexts. However, this set of practices is tempered by a tension surrounding the ideological underpinnings of educational and language reform, especially with regard to the marginalisation of heritage and indigenous languages within the system – a common enough feature in most liberal democratic states at the time of early reforms. In Sweden, Sami and Tornedalen children were the target of assimilation policies, being removed from their families and placed in 'working lodges' for their socialisation into young adults. In Canada, residential schools for indigenous peoples served the same purpose over a longer period and, despite condemnation by earlier generations, it is only recently that the full extent of the harsh and discriminatory, even abusive, nature of some of these institutions has been recognised; so much so that one could describe some of the residential school children as victims of a racist and antipathetic system.

In the decade following the end of World War II, Cummins and Lainio (Chapter 1) argue that significant changes in Swedish labour force demands as a result of industrialisation and modernisation attracted migrants from Finland and southern Europe. This first wave of migration opened up the possibility of additional languages being recognised and taught within the educational system, largely as a consequence of the Social Democrats' belief in the power of the welfare state to produce a redistributive effect based on universalism and a form of social cohesion where basic needs and a relatively equal standard of living should be guaranteed. However, equality of access to services and opportunities did not translate into an equitable approach within language policy. Indeed, and quite ironically, a form of inequality was institutionalised within the educational and language realm as double semilingualism predominated, despite the criticism that the separation of languages had received from scholars. Further evidence of structural inequality was the continued marginalisation of the Sami, which rendered the system an unsympathetic overseer of their affairs.

Under the impress of pending EU membership in 1995, Sweden took the opportunity to revise its approach to both its indigenous language speakers and resident immigrant population. Accordingly, key legislation regarding the role of Swedish as an official language was formulated as the Swedish Language Act in 2009. Together with a steady influx of EU migrants, Sweden also has sought to address the needs of the increasing number of non-EU migrants and asylum seekers, which peaked at 163,000 in 2016, who were attracted in part by relatively generous asylum laws. Thereafter, stricter legislative reforms witnessed a significant decline in numbers, to about 82,500 by 2020. Consequently, approximately one in five of today's 10 million population has Swedish as a second language.

By contrast, the Canadian experience reveals a much longer period of managing multilingualism within an official language duality. The dominant concern of many studies has been to concentrate on the Québec versus

English Canada dualism and authors have adopted terms such as a multinational federation, an unequal partnership and a historical relationship in need of reconciliation to describe this impasse (Gibbins & Laforest, 1998).

A secondary, but increasingly significant, body of research and policy interpretation has focused on the multilingual and multicultural inheritance of the Canadian polity, with early works focusing on ethnic differentiation, immigrant language communities and how the politics of difference influences the quest for a cohesive sense of identity throughout the state (Elliott, 1979; Mackey, 2002). Early critiques of the 'cult of multiculturalism' asked hard-hitting questions about the new orthodoxy and concluded that ethnic communities had little to gain from the multicultural framework because they were more likely to be manipulated by this 'government sanctioned mentality', which was selling an illusion (Bissoondath, 1994). More recent interpretations have been more benign, largely as a result of a great deal of government investment in programmes and initiatives designed to recognise the permanent contribution of residents who do not have either English or French as their home language.

However, the old schisms persist and of great note is that Cummins and Lainio (Chapter 1) draw attention to the east–west split in the handling of multilingualism and multiculturalism, with the four western provinces engaging in several bilingual educational programmes, initially comprising a variety of European languages (e.g. German, Ukrainian, Italian, Polish and Spanish) and, more recently, Mandarin and Arabic. Several other possibilities exist for heritage language instruction outside the formal provincial system, offered by the communities themselves, particularly within metropolitan cores throughout Canada. Evaluations of both types of programmes offer positive encouragement, which is not the case for evaluations of indigenous language programmes that show a more mixed set of attainments and results.

Impacts of national curriculum reforms on the Sami and the Welsh languages

A comparative perspective on the manner in which national curriculum reforms have impacted on both the Sami and the Welsh languages reveals some fundamental similarities regarding the role of parental pressure, national ideology, political empowerment, infrastructure development and legislation, as explained by Özerk and Williams in Chapter 2. Notwithstanding the significant differences in scale, context, demography and institutionalisation, both case studies point to the centrality of formal education and curriculum reform in stimulating language revitalisation efforts. However, questions are raised as to the implication such reforms have on the preponderance of L2 students within the systems and on the degree to which minority languages are used within various socioeconomic domains (Johnson & Swain, 1994). Özerk and Williams pick out two themes that are common in many minority language contexts. The first is the relative lack of throughput of minority language pupils from kindergarten to junior and then secondary school stages, where a significant drop in the number of pupils studying mainly through the target language of Sami or Welsh reduces the potency of the respective languages and – one would assume – the competence of the pupils to maintain their skill sets as they get older. The second theme is a concern over the long-term use of the target language outside the school setting in important socioeconomic domains, including commerce, sport and leisure. This raises questions as to the adequacy of formal schooling in stimulating a close relationship between language competence and multifunctional communication, even when such opportunities are readily available for the widespread use of the minority language. One of the chief challenges faced by language policy formulators in such contexts is to embed the default expectation of using both languages as a matter of choice in many circumstances rather than accepting that the hegemonic language is the only or predominant language available. Language promoters point to the possibilities offered by AI, IT and other media opportunities to enable the target language to be present and grow as technology develops. All the same, this requires constant investment to make the choices realisable and this in turn is dependent largely on the political deployment of public resources.

Curriculum reform in Norway had a direct impact on the number of Sami children who received Sami teaching as either L1, L2 or Sami Language and Culture classes. Curriculum documents NC-87 and NC-97-S induced a growth in the number of participants receiving Sami instruction between 1990 and 2006. The introduction of a new curriculum document in 2006/2007, which did not include Sami Language and Culture as a designated school subject, witnessed the beginning of a trend. This saw a decline in the numbers receiving Sami instruction: during the NC-06 and NC-06-S-period, far fewer children received Sami L1 or L2 teaching compared with the NC-97-S period. In 2016, this decline was partly offset by the significant improvement in distance education, which had a positive impact on the number of children who received Sami teaching as L1 or L2. Given these variations, the overall trend was a 98% increase in the number of Sami children who had access to any kind of Sami language teaching between 1990 and 2020. Curriculum reform has thus ensured the offering of the Sami language as a separate school subject with its own subject curriculum and a specified number of teaching hours per week as part of Sami students' comprehensive/compulsory/basic education. While not being entirely satisfactory, current debates surrounding the reform of the national curriculum among Sami territories are relatively settled, unlike the more urgent debate in Wales where the Welsh Government has committed itself to a wholesale reform of the curriculum within statutory education.

Driven by two considerations, the reform of the national curriculum in Wales was designed to introduce new subjects and to simultaneously achieve the strategic goal of furthering the development of a bilingual society. The latter aim was underpinned by a government commitment to produce a million Welsh speakers by 2050, largely by widening the opportunities to be taught Welsh within a range of school experiences.

In order to free up space within the national curriculum, on 14 October 2021 it was announced that the General Certificate of Secondary Education (GCSE) in English Language and the GCSE in English Literature would be combined into one qualification. Similarly, physics, chemistry and biology will no longer be offered as individual subjects from 2025; they will be replaced by one integrated science award, which combines the three subjects and will be worth two GCSEs. The reformed curriculum will also see the introduction of new GCSEs in Engineering and Manufacturing and Film and Digital Media.

The impact of curriculum reform on the Welsh language is less clear cut as, such was the uncertainty surrounding the Welsh language qualification, a final decision was postponed. One of the controversial issues was the proposal to abolish the distinction between Welsh L1 and L2 levels and to create a single standard of attainment, producing a continuum reflecting varying skills. Critics have argued that this would weaken the salience of Welsh as a mother tongue qualification and lead to a dumbing down of the language standards – an accusation also levelled at the science subject reform. It should also be noted that, in order to achieve these reforms to boost the teaching of Welsh in all schools, a further 500 subject specialist teachers would be required.

In consequence, the reforms of the national curriculum, together with other policy initiatives, may indeed realise the target of achieving a million Welsh speakers by 2050, but at what cost to the quality, idiomatic richness and grammatical accuracy of the language when a significant portion will have been L2 learners, largely within designated English-medium schools? It does not necessarily follow that those who have acquired the skills of communicating in Welsh will automatically embrace it as their *lingua propria*.

Implications for classroom practice and ideology in Finland and Denmark

In Chapter 3, Slotte, Møller and From compare pupils' languaging and negotiation of language policies in the context of institutional education in Finland and Denmark. This offers a welcome opportunity for eliciting the voice and opinions of pupils and for weaving their contribution into a multi-level framework informed by Spolsky's (2004) notion of language policies comprising the interrelated dimensions of macro-level language management, language ideologies and micro-level language practices. The comparative study uses interviews with pupils in a Finnish-medium school and a Swedish-medium school, video recordings from bilingual workshops in Finland and group conversations with pupils with diverse linguistic backgrounds in Denmark. The results demonstrate how language management policies and monolingual normativity ascribe language-based identities to the pupils, shape their ideas of appropriate language practices and determine the value of bilingualism in both contexts.

The comparison highlights the ideological and political influence of national culture on conceptions of bilingualism. Despite an increased awareness of living within an increasingly multilingual world, Slotte *et al.* state that 'it is probably fair to describe most of the Swedish- and the Finnish-medium schools as dominated by a strong monolingual language practice'. Pupils are sensitive to dynamic tensions between normative language policies and the actual practice of their teachers to tend to keep to one language while teaching (Sędek & McIntosh, 1998). In contrast, the Danish evidence is contextualised by the fact that people who have migrated are increasingly viewed as a cultural and economic problem for the welfare state (Padovan-Özdemir & Moldenhawer, 2016). The emphasis on switching between formal Danish and slang in informal, more private communication among pupils ties in with Spolsky's (2004) insights on how pupils attune themselves to teachers' language ideologies. However, Slotte *et al.* claim that in so doing the participants not only risk being ascribed identities as unruly pupils but also as the 'non-Danish other' when using slang. Such stigmatism reveals important social mores and informs the construction of identity. This is more acute in dealing with the relative significance of being described as 'bilingual' or *tosproget*, which – despite sincere attempts in the past generation to conceive of minority language bilingualism as a positive rather than a negative effect – still carries the connotation for many of being disadvantaged within the monolingual and monocultural school system. Such a stigma is not reflected in the Finnish data even if bilingualism is not always necessarily prized. The message from this comparison is that pupil identity constructions, whether regarding 'Finns', 'Swedes' or 'bilinguals' in Denmark are 'outcomes of the monolingual ideologies of the institutions. When monolingual regimes are enforced in educational systems, they do not only result in language policies and practices, but also in categorisations and senses of belonging' (Slotte *et al.*, Chapter 3).

Increased Salience of Multilingualism in Education

Tensions in discourses on plurilingualism among student teachers in Catalonia, Slovenia and Finland

Chapter 4, by Llompart, Dražnik and Bergroth, draws on evidence from Catalonia, Slovenia and Finland. As a part of the European project

Listiac (Linguistically Sensitive Teaching in All Classrooms), data from 173 student teachers enrolled in initial teacher education (ITE) at four universities located in Barcelona, Ljubljana, Vaasa and Jyväskylä were interpreted using reflection instruments based on a qualitative SWOT analysis. This comparative investigation identified a disjuncture between two countervailing tendencies. The first was a positive construction of student teachers accommodating as plurilingual speakers and being committed to a career as a teacher within a pluralistic context. This was the theoretical desiderata to which they aspired. However, this was juxtaposed with a negative construction of their imagined future as teachers whose identity was bound up teaching in a plurilingual context. It was a largely negative perception because they believed that they had not received enough practical training or adequate experience and relational competence with diverse people to enable them to carry out their functions in an effective manner. The authors acknowledge that others have investigated this discrepancy between ambition and perceived reality among teachers and student teachers regarding plurilingualism (Birello *et al.*, 2021; Bredthauer & Engfer, 2016; Haukås, 2016). What is novel in the current context is the finding that such discrepancies may be found within several ITE institutions in Europe, prompting the authors to recommend a rethink on ITE practice so as to make the plurilingual element more manageable and attractive to trainee teachers. This concern echoes the evidence supplied by the Cyprus–Finland comparison as discussed next.

Openings for multilingualism and linguistic identity as mirrors of language aware teaching among future educators in Cyprus and Finland

Chapter 5, by Karpava, Björklund and Björklund, is concerned with identifying dominant language constellations (DLC) in Cyprus and Finland and determining to what extent the participants' multilingual contexts are mirrored in future trajectories for language awareness/multiple language use as educators. This is important because the participants' own experience of multilingualism and interculturalism enables them to be more aware of the need for inclusion of pupils with languages other than the school's designated language of instruction. In the Cyprus and Finland data, such an awareness was reported in general terms rather than as a direct reflection of the participants' acceptance of strategies for multilingual pedagogy or to any experience they may have had of such practices during their period as student teachers. This suggests that, in both contexts, additional attention to the linguistic repertoire of pupils within the teacher training programme would bode well for developing skills to manage linguistically and culturally diverse classroom situations.

Beyond the need for increased sensitivity and awareness, what other similarities could be discerned by such comparative analyses? It is evident that the presence of English influences the language continuum in both cases, even if for markedly different reasons. In Cyprus, in addition to the prevalence of Greek (Cypriot Greek and Standard Modern Greek), there is a far wider range of L1s of minority and immigrant students, in particular Romanian, Bulgarian, Lebanese, Arabic, Russian, Ukrainian, Georgian and Armenian, which Karpava *et al.* aver reflects a complex and unique situation of bilectalism and multilingualism. This does not necessarily confer a hybrid identity. Within Finland, the DLCs and linguistic repertoires are also complex, ranging from three to five languages, including many other largely European languages such as German, Norwegian, Russian, Spanish, Danish, together with Dari, the Afghan dialect of Persian. Understandably, the degree to which individuals acquire additional language fluency depends on their interest in learning a language, personal preferences and social networks.

The student teachers in both Finland and Cyprus affirmed the need to be at ease in using and modelling multilingual language use in a classroom situation, confirming the increasing normalcy of multilingualism as a societal norm. What the case studies in this volume demonstrate is the acute need to equip teachers – in their formative years of training – with the skills, competence and raised awareness to manage increasingly diverse classroom settings. However, several case studies also emphasise the significance of national and local contexts in practising or implementing these skills. It does not necessarily follow those improvements in ITE training and processes will automatically render teachers more effective practitioners in diverse multilingual and multifaith settings, until such time as the ideology and general popular concerns validate multilingualism as a permanent, not an epiphenomenal, element of contemporary society.

Openings for multilingualism in schools in Poland, Finland and California

An investigation into the methods used to support multilingual learning in Poland, Finland and California demonstrates a variety of initiatives and approaches, driven as much by political as by educational factors. In Chapter 6, Otwinowska, Bergroth and Zyzik illustrate the mechanism of developing the cognitive consequences of bilingualism and argue that children's language knowledge is developed by both frequent use and by external institutional and familial support – nothing surprising in that. What is significant is the juridical context that produces the conditions of possibility for supporting bilingual or multilingual learning. Thus, Poland's limited exposure to contemporary multilingual education can be explained in large part by geopolitical events. In 1945 a turbulent, wartorn restructuring of Polish state boundaries saw the Oder–Neisse Line function as its western border and the Curzon Line as its eastern limit. Population exchanges of Polish and German residents witnessed the transfer of millions of people to populate their respective new spaces. For Poland, this resulted in a previously multilingual society becoming a largely homogenous one with only 1% of the population now classed as national minority citizens. While most of the modern language teaching concerns English and German, very few opportunities exist for the formal teaching of minority language instruction, except within the community and at home as a consequence of familial transfer of selected languages.

A more structured approach to the teaching of Swedish in Finland reflects the historical geopolitical salience of Sweden in the broader region, the high status of Swedish as one of the national languages and the arrangements made to support the Swedish-speaking population. Accordingly, the registered Swedish-speaking segment of the population (5.2%) is well protected in law and the resultant educational and local authority infrastructure mitigates somewhat against systematic, historical language shift. Nevertheless, concerns about the vitality of the Swedish-speaking segment are still prevalent and are a constant source of political and social agitation. Within the Finnish education sectors, linguistic diversity has grown apace and the subject Mother Tongue and Literature now includes 12 syllabi for different languages. These are Finnish, Swedish, Sami, Roma, sign language, other mother tongue of the pupil, Finnish and Swedish as a second language, Finnish and Swedish for Sami speakers and Finnish and Swedish for sign language users.

Quite different perspectives and challenges are adduced from the California context, which illustrates a far more diverse and episodic trajectory regarding the promotion of multilingualism. The current position, it would appear, is far more promising than at earlier junctures, with the mission statement of the California Department of Education (CDE) being

> ... to equip students with world language skills to better appreciate and more fully engage with the diverse mixture of cultures, heritages, and languages found in California and the world, while also preparing them to succeed in the global economy. The CDE has set specific goals in the Global California 2030 Initiative. By 2030, half of all kindergarten through grade twelve students will participate in programs leading to proficiency in two or more languages, either through a class, a program, or an experience. By 2040, three out of four students will be proficient in one or more languages, earning them a State Seal of Biliteracy. (California Department of Education, 2021)

The authors' concern with matching contextual background to the organisation of multilingual learning is a ready reminder that what happens outside the formal classroom is a key determinant of the likely success or otherwise of designated programmes depending on how they are implemented and received. One could not argue with their conclusion that supporting multilingual learning can be enhanced in everyday practices and much more attention needs to be given to the solutions for supporting multilingual learning as derived from the perspective of teachers and teacher training. Naturally enough, Otwinowska *et al.* are keen to demonstrate that supporting various linguistic groups is consequently very well addressed in Finland at a policy level (Eurydice, 2019), but one could be forgiven for reminding the reader that, in comparison with the USA, Finnish society appears to be far more stable and regulated and less subject to political challenge as regards the primacy of educational consistency.

Self-Reported Use of Multiple Languages for Increased Awareness of Multilingualism among Adolescents in Italy and Finland

In an intriguing chapter on researching adolescent linguistic repertoires, Zanasi, Mård-Miettinen and Platzgummer pair Finland with South Tyrol (Chapter 7). Using distinct methods of research (the RepertoirePluS project in South Tyrol and the Multi-IM project for Swedish immersion students in Finland), it was observed that both samples were confident in using at least three languages, namely German, Italian and English in South Tyrol and Swedish, Finnish and English in Finland. In addition, a much wider range of linguistic resources were present in both cases.

In order to delve deeper into the linguistic repertoire construct, visual methods of representation and the elicitation of information were employed to good effect. The RepertoirePluS project used language portraits for both the questionnaire and interview stages. By contrast, the Multi-IM project used the language tree method to generate additional data about the participants. In both cases, competence in two or more languages was prized and important clues as to when and where certain languages within their repertoire were obtained. One may question to what extent this sort of visual and perceptive methodology yields sufficient fine-grained data for pedagogical and planning purposes, but when it is utilised as one of a package of investigative tools it can reveal significant insights shared by the pupils, but not necessarily fully appreciated by the teaching staff employed within such programmes.

Language biographies also yield important information about life trajectories and language choices and, although the authors do not use the term *muda*, what they are describing is akin to the findings of Pujolar and Puigdevall (2015) in terms of significant stages in the journey to becoming a new speaker of a particular language.

Conclusion

There are many strengths in this collective endeavour, not least of which is the interdisciplinary skill set of the participants in the WoM, particularly their own linguistic range and knowledge of the case studies under review. A second virtue is the adoption of a comparative approach to multilingualism, consciously pairing specialists from different jurisdictions and thereby compelling them to address issues of commonality and divergence in their thematic explorations. We learn that there are indeed several generic traits that can be identified from such an exercise. These, in turn, can inform the transfer of good practice from one situation to another, thereby assisting in the diffusion of pragmatic solutions to the various challenges that teaching and living in a multilingual environment can produce.

We also acknowledge that ideological and political interventions and processes can severely influence the contours of multilingualism, thereby highlighting the significance of context-dependent trajectories in the life cycle of pedagogical approaches or sociolinguistic programmes of action. Obviously, the political influence and culture of the hegemonic state is most acute in the management of majority–minority relationships within bilingual and multilingual situations (Strani, 2020; Williams, 2013). As demonstrated by the diachronic aspect in Chapter 1, a common feature of many evaluations is to focus on outputs rather than outcomes and so it is pertinent to ask whether or not these reforms have had a beneficial impact. In Sweden, the few available evaluations of Sami, national minority languages and migrant languages cited by Cummins and Lainio in Chapter 1 demonstrate several weaknesses related to the operation of a multilingual curriculum, namely a tendency to collapse all non-native born pupils into a single operational category of immigrant despite their fundamental differences, all of which reduce the purchase of the pupil's mother tongue as a significant component in their linguistic trajectory. It is a moot point whether or not the mother tongue fares as well in educational circles that emphasise the two official languages together with English as the necessary requirements for earning a living and engaging with the wider world. Thus, even such apparently clearly marked identities of majority and minority are subject to qualification and do not always reflect the constituent make up of society, for they may be symbolically important but not sociologically accurate as descriptors of group membership and identity formation. A further caveat is the need to assert that multilingualism is a distinct phenomenon from multiculturalism, even though they are often used in tandem. Multilingual policies do not necessarily accord with or consciously promote cultural pluralism.

We recognise that the key concepts of multilingualism and multiculturalism are subject to quite different interpretations both between and within specific jurisdictions. However, in those societies, such as Canada, that have adopted multiculturalism as a 'national' policy, interpreters such as Gilles Paquet have cautioned against seeing such policies as an unalloyed success. While a multicultural perspective may raise the status of a state's ethnic heritage and conduce to cultural pluralism, it can also be seen both as a containment policy and as a means of reducing communal inequalities as a symbolic policy (Paquet, 2008: 59). The general public, it is claimed, is increasingly cynical about the claims of a multicultural policy and may even grow resentful if the policy does not in fact deliver its putative promises of securing heritage language survival, group solidarity, increased representation within the cultural mosaic and overall recognition of migrants of non-British and non-French stock to the commonwealth and wellbeing of Canada. Multiculturalism has been perceived as a negation of the founding two nations principle of statehood. A second form of opposition emanates from those who wish to support Canadian national unity and see the emphasis on ethnic origins as a distraction perpetuating a historical and politically charged source of division. Yet a third critique sees multiculturalism, the granting of group rights such as linguistic transmission and education within the provincial education system, as damaging to the liberal political tradition and the differentiated discriminatory treatment of individuals. A fourth interpretation sees multiculturalism as a divergence that allows the hegemonic English Canadian polity to progress largely unhindered, relegating ethnic marginals to the side-lines but dressing up their condition as an essential multicultural contribution to the enrichment of society, but one which can be safely marginalised from the real business of running a country (Peleg, 2007: 119–120).

Such considerations, for Canada as elsewhere, are significant as they provide the presumptive political and administrative culture within which multilingual innovations and programmes are introduced, calibrated and judged as to their relevance and efficacy.

This volume's interrogation of multilingualism offers a wide ranging, detailed and thoughtful set of interpretations. Replete with powerful insights that may not have been produced had it not been for the judicious pairing of case studies, this volume is a pioneering attempt to counter the pressing insistence of advocates of monolingual nationalism that a state functions best when it yields to the power of a hegemonic language in its internal affairs. It may not always succeed in convincing many that bilingualism and multilingualism represent a steady state or that plural identities conceived in and through language can coexist in permanent mutual harmony. Such is the nature of historical inequalities and contemporary injustices that tension will always abound unless the separate voices are managed within a flexible and accommodating structure. Here we have examples of how such accommodation has been forged in several distinct societies, which together offer a richness of experience and representation. It is quite a different matter to anticipate to what extent several of the key messages and good practice exemplars will be heeded, even within their own societies as progressive reform measures, let alone transferred to other jurisdictions.

References

Anon. (2021) Sixty years of Turkish 'guest workers' in Germany. *The Economist*, 6 November.
Birello, M., Llompart, J. and Moore, E. (2021) Being plurilingual versus becoming a linguistically sensitive teacher: Tensions in the discourse of initial teacher education students. *International Journal of Multilingualism* 18 (4), 601–618.

Bissoondath, N. (1994) *Selling Illusions: The Cult of Multiculturalism in Canada.* Toronto: Penguin.

Bredthauer, S. and Engfer, H. (2016) Multilingualism is great – but is it really my business? Teachers' approaches to multilingual didactics in Austria and Germany. *Sustainable Multilingualism* 9, 104–121.

California Department of Education (2021) *Multilingual education.* See https://www.cde.ca.gov/sp/el/er/multilingualedu.asp (accessed October 2022).

Elliott, J.L. (ed.) (1979) *Two Nations, Many Cultures: Ethnic Groups in Canada.* Scarborough: Prentice Hall Canada.

Eurydice (2019) *Integrating Students from Migrant Backgrounds into Schools in Europe: National Policies and Measures.* Eurydice report. Luxembourg: EU.

Gibbins, R. and Laforest, G. (eds) (1998) *Beyond Impasse: Toward Reconciliation.* Ottawa: Institute for Research on Public Policy.

Haukås, Å. (2016) Teachers' beliefs about multilingualism and a multilingual pedagogical approach. *International Journal of Multilingualism* 13 (1), 1–18.

Johnson, R.K. and Swain, M. (1994) From core to content: Bridging the L2 proficiency gap in late immersion. *Language and Education* 8 (4), 211–229.

Mackey, E. (2002) *The House of Difference: Cultural Politics and National Identity in Canada.* Toronto: University of Toronto Press.

Padovan-Özdemir, M. and Moldenhawer, B. (2016) Making precarious migrant families and weaving the welfare nation-state fabric 1970–2010. *Race, Ethnicity and Education* 20 (6), 723–736, https://doi.org/10.1080/13613324.2016.1195358

Paquet, G. (2008) *Deep Cultural Diversity: A Governance Challenge.* Ottawa: University of Ottawa Press.

Peleg, I. (2007) *Democratizing the Hegemonic State.* Cambridge: Cambridge University Press.

Pujolar, J. and Puigdevall, M. (2015) Linguistic *mudes*: How to become a new speaker in Catalonia. *International Journal of the Sociology of Language* 231, 167–187.

Sędek, G. and McIntosh, D.N. (1998) Intellectual helplessness. Domain specificity, teaching styles, and school achievement. In M. Kofta, G. Weary and G. Sędek (eds) *Personal Control in Action. Cognitive and Motivational Mechanisms* (pp. 419–443). New York: Plenum Press.

Spolsky, B. (2004) *Language Policy.* Cambridge: Cambridge University Press.

Strani, K. (ed.) (2020) *Multilingualism and Politics.* London: Palgrave Macmillan.

UK Government (2021) *Schools, Pupils and Their Characteristics. Academic Year 2020/21.* London: Department of Education.

Williams, C.H. (2013) *Minority Language, Promotion, Protection and Regulation: The Mask of Piety.* London: Palgrave Macmillan.

Williams, C.H. (2021a) On the side of angels: Dignity and virtue in minority–majority relations. In M. Bufon, T. Malloy and C.H. Williams (eds) *Societies and Cultures in Contact: Between Convergence and Divergence* (pp. 35–64). Bern: Peter Lang.

Williams, C.H. (2021b) Forging hope in the company of cynics. In H. Lewis and W. McLeod (eds) *Language Revitalisation and Social Transformation* (pp. 363–380). London: Palgrave Macmillan.

Williams, C.H. (2022a) Minority language revitalization: European conundrums. In D. Boucher (ed.) *Language, Culture and Colonialism.* Cape Town: HRS Press.

Williams, C.H. (2023) *Language Policy and the New Speaker Challenge.* Cambridge: Cambridge University Press.

Index

Amazigh, 97, 113
Arabic, 15, 21, 23, 27–29, 70, 91, 97, 101, 130–131, 141, 154, 157, 202, 207
assimilation, 13, 17, 32–33, 41–44, 201

bilectal(ism), 124, 126, 129, 141, 207
bilingual, 5–7, 23, 26, 48–49, 51, 62, 68–69, 71–76, 87, 92, 100, 121, 125–127, 129, 133, 141, 148–152, 154–161, 166–167, 173–175, 178–181, 183, 193, 204–205, 207, 210
   education (programme), 6–7, 11–12, 14–17, 19–21, 23–24, 27–29, 33, 40, 49–51, 56–57, 99, 106, 151–152, 154, 156–160, 162, 166, 202
   identity, 128, 130, 135, 137–139
   practice, 76–82, 90, 92, 138
   school, 19, 20, 51, 55–56, 60, 62, 69, 75, 77, 90, 160
bilingualism, 6–7, 9, 31, 41–42, 44–46, 55, 68, 86–88, 90–92, 125, 129, 134, 148–152, 154–155, 158, 166, 177, 186, 200, 205, 207, 211
biliteracy, *see also* literacy, 17, 23, 32, 158

Catalan, 97–98
Chinese (Cantonese), 27–29, 97, 157–158, 189, 202
code-switch(ing), 5, 125, 131, 150
content and language integrated learning (CLIL), 15, 17, 151–152, 154, 156, 160–161, 166–167, 177
culture, 5, 12, 17–18, 24, 27–28, 32, 40, 44–47, 58, 63, 85, 96, 101, 106, 108–109, 113, 125, 129, 133–135, 139–140, 153, 164, 181, 186, 198, 203, 208

curriculum, 7, 30, 32, 41–50, 53–54, 57–60, 62–64, 69–70, 77, 97–99, 101, 103, 105, 108, 110, 126–127, 137, 155, 157–160, 165, 177, 179, 193, 199–200, 203–204, 210
   or curricular reform, 6, 39–67, 202–204
Cypriot Greek, 124–125, 130, 141, 207

Danish, 8, 68–70, 72, 82–92, 137, 142, 205, 207
Dari, 136–137, 142, 207
diversity (cultural, cultural pluralism), *see also* language/linguistic diversity, 96, 98, 101, 108, 110–111, 113–114, 122, 135, 140, 142, 155, 164, 210
dominant language, 12, 29, 33, 42, 69, 130, 138, 141, 198
dominant language constellation (DLC), 8–9, 121–138, 140–142
dual(-language) immersion in the USA, 151, 158–159

education, 19, 56
   basic, 45, 48, 70, 101, 127, 179–180, 203
   comprehensive, 48, 68, 126, 203
   compulsory, 41–42, 45, 48, 203
   further, 50, 53, 62
   higher, 18, 50, 62, 105, 125, 154
   primary, 56, 98
   secondary, 56, 98, 124
   statutory, 41, 50, 53–54, 58, 60, 203
education(al) policy, 5–6, 9, 11–12, 32–33, 54, 96, 99, 101, 126, 200
English, 5–6, 9, 12, 15, 17, 20–21, 24–32, 49, 50–51, 53, 55, 57–60, 71, 84, 91, 97, 98, 101, 105–106, 112, 115, 124–142, 147–149, 151–154, 156–162, 177, 183–184, 186–189, 191–194, 199, 202, 204, 207–210

English *(Continued)*
  medium education/instruction, 50–51, 62, 115, 204
  learner (EL), 148, 156–159

Finnish, 7, 68–71, 73, 75, 77–82, 100–101, 125–127, 136–142, 151, 154–156, 173–174, 178, 181, 184, 186–189, 193–194, 208
  in Sweden, 12, 15–16, 18–20, 23, 33
Finnish-medium school/education, 7, 68–70, 71, 72, 74, 75, 76, 79, 80, 82, 91, 92, 125–126, 156, 179, 205
first language (L1), *see also* mother tongue, home language, 7, 11–12, 20, 24, 30, 31, 33, 39–40, 42, 44–48, 51, 53–54, 57–60, 63, 68–69, 72, 82, 100, 125, 127, 129–130, 132–134, 136, 140–141, 148–149, 151, 153, 179–180, 187, 199, 203–204, 207
French, 6, 12, 25–30, 97–98, 101, 130–131, 142, 154, 156, 184, 189–191, 193, 202, 211
French immersion in Canada, 6, 11–12, 25, 28, 200
foreign language, 16, 96, 100–101, 115, 125–126, 132, 134, 140–142, 148–149, 152, 154–155, 159–161, 163, 180, 184, 189

Georgian, 130, 132–133, 141, 207
German, 27, 97, 130–131, 136–137, 142, 151–152, 154, 156, 173–178, 181, 183–184, 186, 189, 191–193, 202, 207–209
globalisation, 107, 122, 125, 141, 175
Greek, *see also* Standard Modern Greek, Cypriot Greek, 125, 128–132

heritage language, 6, 11–12, 26–30, 33, 127, 130, 133, 140, 149, 161, 201–202, 211
high school, *see also* secondary school, 27, 49, 55, 95, 97–98, 101, 148
home language, 6, 24, 26, 29–31, 100, 109, 126, 140, 149, 151, 154, 156–158, 164, 202
  instruction, 12, 14

identity *see also* language/linguistic identity, 5–6, 8, 21, 24, 28, 32, 55, 70, 72, 92, 96, 101, 106–107, 112, 123, 125, 140, 207, 210–211
  cultural, 33, 109, 127–128, 133
ideology, 7, 39, 41–43, 68–71, 78, 84–86, 92, 97, 102–103, 105–106, 109–110, 115, 122, 127, 142, 202, 204, 207
immigrant, 9, 12, 23–25, 69, 96, 100–101, 124–126, 128–129, 133, 140–141, 149, 153, 155, 158–159, 174, 178–179, 181, 202, 207, 210
indigenous language, 6–7, 12–13, 17, 24–30, 28–32, 39–41, 63–64, 178, 198, 201–202
  community/group/people, 24–25, 28, 42, 44–45, 63, 101, 154, 201
initial teacher education (ITE), *see also* teacher training/education, 6, 8–9, 95–99, 101–102, 104–106, 110–111, 113–115, 163, 206
intercultural(ism), 100, 105, 107, 139, 199, 206
Italian, 27, 97, 99, 136–137, 154, 173–174, 176–178, 181, 183–184, 191–193, 202, 209

Ladin, 173–174, 176–177, 183, 192–193
language/linguistic
  acquisition, 40, 49, 56, 59, 151
  awareness, 96, 105–107, 113, 115, 123, 126, 164, 185, 200, 205
  diversity, 4–6, 8, 12, 69, 72, 95–98, 100–104, 107, 111–114, 122, 142, 147, 163–164, 166, 173, 208
  identity, 8, 33, 121–122, 124, 126–129, 129–133, 135, 140–141, 154, 180, 205–206
  ideology, 7–8, 72–73, 75, 77, 86–90, 92, 103, 115, 180, 191, 205
  management, 4–5, 7, 68–70, 72–73, 75, 85, 90–91, 204–205,
  policy, 7, 98, 100, 103, 105, 123, 127, 181, 191, 193, 201, 203–205
    in Sweden, 13–24
    in Canada, 24–33
    in Norway, 39–49, 62–64
    in Wales, 39–41, 49–64
    in Finland, 68–69, 73–82, 89–92, 100–102, 125–126, 154–156, 173–174, 178–180

in Denmark, 68–69, 82–92
in Catalonia, 97–99
in Slovenia, 99–100
in Cyprus, 124–125
in Poland, 151–154
in California, 148, 156–159
in South Tyrol, 173–174, 176–178
repertoire (LR), 9, 90, 124, 129–132, 136–137, 140–142, 149, 173–178, 180–195, 206–207, 209
revitalisation, 7, 18–19, 28, 39–41, 44, 62, 63
rights, 11, 22, 41, 61, 68, 101, 125, 154, 179, 200
separation, 9, 70, 72, 75, 90, 104, 180–181, 189
shift, 18–20, 122, 155–156, 208
transmission, 41, 61, 133, 200, 211
languaging, 7, 68, 70, 74, 204
lingua franca, 18, 101, 124, 132, 134–135, 141
linguistically sensitive teaching (LST), 8, 96, 97, 100, 102
literacy, 23–24, 28–31, 33, 58, 179–180

mainstream education/school/classroom, 15, 30, 33, 105, 124, 151, 159, 162, 166, 174, 184
majority language, 2, 12–14, 16, 28, 100, 115, 131-133, 142, 154, 179, 210
Mandarin, 27–29, 157
Meänkieli (language), 12, 15–16, 18–19, 23
migrant, 13, 15, 96–99, 111, 149, 166, 177, 199, 201, 211
language, 6, 12–13, 15–17, 19–23, 210
migration, 12–13, 40, 69, 84, 88, 91–92, 95, 122–123, 151, 159, 161, 166, 177, 193, 201
minority (national/recognised/regional/linguistic), 11, 13, 15, 17–18, 21, 99, 149, 152, 174, 177, 181, 208
minority language, 2, 6–7, 10–13, 15, 19, 28, 39–40, 63–64, 92, 96, 99, 128–129, 131, 133, 140–142, 152–154, 159, 180, 202–203, 205, 207
national minority languages in Sweden (NML), 11, 15–17, 19–23, 210
monocultural, 41–42, 70, 88, 92, 205
monolingual(ism), 1, 28–30, 32, 41–42, 49, 63, 68–71, 74, 78, 80, 85, 87–88, 90, 92, 96, 100, 102–103, 109, 115, 126, 129, 138–139, 148–151, 155, 164–166, 174, 178–181, 189, 198, 205, 211
norm, 7, 75–76, 78–79, 81–82, 84, 89–91, 163
identity, 7, 128, 130, 135, 137–139, 141–142
ideology 89–92, 110, 142
mother tongue, 11, 14, 19–21, 23, 45, 59–60, 63, 99, 109, 111, 131, 153–156, 177, 179, 204, 208, 210
instruction (MTI), 6, 14–24, 42
multicultural(ism)/pluricultural, 12–13, 25–26, 30, 41, 45, 57, 63, 96–98, 100, 102, 106, 110, 122–123, 135, 179, 198–200, 202, 210–211
multilingual/polylingual, *see also* plurilingual, 3, 7–9, 25, 27, 30, 41, 45, 68–69, 71, 89, 91, 96–98, 100, 102, 104, 114, 121–129, 131–135, 140–142, 147–150, 152, 154, 160, 164–167, 173–182, 184, 187, 189–190, 192–194, 199, 202, 205–211
classroom, 23, 25, 106, 110, 112–113, 163
education, 7, 10, 11, 71, 103, 163, 207
identity, 5, 9, 128, 131, 135, 137–139, 141, 155, 183, 188
language learner (MLL), 6, 11–12, 16, 17, 32, 33
learning, 9, 12, 147–148, 151, 159, 161–162, 164–167, 207–209
pedagogy, 6, 9, 31, 96, 142, 206
practice, 5, 75, 77–78, 137–138, 141, 163, 181
reality, 6, 25–26, 33, 123
repertoire, 9, 12, 27, 31, 33, 165–166, 180, 184, 188
school(ing), 6, 15, 188, 193
society, 3, 24, 155, 193, 208
multilingualism/polylingualism, *see also* plurilingualism, 1, 5, 8–10, 16, 23, 26, 33, 68, 70, 72, 96–97, 99–104, 106–107, 110, 112, 114–115, 122–124, 128–129, 132–135, 138–142, 147–149, 152, 155–157, 162–165, 167, 174, 178, 180–184, 187–189, 194–195, 198–202, 205–211
Workshop on Multilingualism (WoM), 1–5, 199–200, 209

national language, 68–70, 72, 77, 90, 100–101, 115, 125–127, 137, 147, 154, 178–179, 208
native language, 99, 130
new speaker, 53–54, 60–62, 209
Norwegian, 44, 48–49, 136–137, 142, 151, 189, 207

official language, 12, 15, 24–26, 44, 50, 68–69, 99–101, 107, 141, 154, 174, 176–178, 194, 200–201, 210

plurilingual, 8, 27, 95–98, 100–102, 105–107, 110, 114–116, 190, 206
  pedagogy, 31, 95, 96
plurilingualism, 5, 8, 95–98, 100, 102, 104, 106–110, 112–114, 205–206
Polish, 27, 151–153, 159, 161, 202
preschool/early childhood education/ kindergarten, 12, 16–21, 28–31, 45, 78, 98, 100, 125, 148, 154, 157, 177, 179, 203
primary school/elementary school, 16, 19–21, 30, 40, 42, 49, 52, 54–55, 98, 126, 131, 134, 139, 148, 152–153, 155, 157–158, 164, 180, 186–187, 192, 199, 203

regional language, 19, 96, 115
Roma (language), 101, 153–155, 178, 208
Roma (people), 13, 99, 101, 153
Romani (Chib), 12, 15–16, 18–19, 23
Romanian, 97, 130, 132, 141, 207
Russian, 97, 100, 125, 127–128, 130–133, 136–137, 141–142, 151–152, 154, 156–157, 184, 207

Sami (languages), 5 7, 12, 15–19, 23, 39–49, 62–64, 125, 155–156, 178, 181, 202–203, 208, 210
Sami people, 5, 13, 15–18, 39–49, 101, 154, 201, 203
school, *see also* preschool, primary school, secondary school, upper secondary school, 15, 17, 19, 22–23, 31, 42, 48–49, 55 77, 98, 101, 151, 201
  independent, 14–17, 21
  public, 15–16, 19, 21, 27, 72, 156–158
  state(-owned), 20, 100, 152

secondary school (post-primary school), 19, 21, 29, 40, 45, 48, 52, 54, 131, 152–153, 159, 180, 182, 186–187, 191, 199, 203
second language (L2), 7, 20, 29–30, 39–40, 42, 44, 46–49, 51, 53, 55, 57, 59–60, 63, 99, 126, 132, 134, 148–149, 151, 155, 159–160, 174, 177, 181, 201, 203–204, 208
  education (programme), 7, 42, 53
  teaching/instruction, 20, 25, 44, 47–48, 59, 177, 203
  learner/student, 51, 53–54, 59–60, 162, 202, 204
Sign language, 15, 26–27, 101, 149, 153–155, 178, 208
slang, 8, 85, 91–92, 205
Slovenian/Slovene (language) 99, 108
socialisation, 101, 141, 163, 165, 201
Spanish, 15, 21, 27, 97–98, 130–132, 136–137, 142, 151–152, 156–158, 183–184, 189, 202, 207
Standard Modern Greek, 124, 141, 207
Swedish, 7, 13, 16–18, 20, 22–24, 100–101
  in Finland, 68–71, 73–82, 100–101, 125–127, 129, 136–142, 151, 154–156, 173, 174, 178–181, 184, 186–189, 193–194, 208
Swedish-medium school/childcare, 7, 68–70, 71, 74–75, 78, 91–92, 125–126, 129, 138, 141, 154–156, 163–164, 179, 205
Swedish immersion in Finland, 156, 174, 179–180, 183–184, 186–187, 189, 194, 209

target language, 40, 133, 156, 200, 203
teacher, 8–9, 20, 30–31, 33, 45, 46, 52, 54, 63, 85–88, 91–92, 96–98, 100–105, 108–116, 121, 123, 130, 135, 139–141, 147–148, 152, 158–159, 162–167, 181, 205–207, 209
student, 8–9, 95, 96–99, 101–115, 122–124, 127–142, 163–164, 186, 205–206
educator, 8–9, 101–102, 105, 148, 163–164, 166
training/education, 6, 40, 49, 53, 55, 60–61, 100, 122–123, 126–127, 142, 147, 162, 165–167, 177, 209

trajectory, 8–9, 121, 123, 126–127, 131–132, 134, 140–142, 173–174, 176, 185, 191, 193–194, 206, 208–210
translanguaging (polylanguaging), 31, 51, 79, 90, 139–140, 175
trilingual(ism), 126, 173, 176, 181, 193-194
Turkish, 83–84, 89, 91, 111

Ukrainian, 27, 130, 132, 202
upper secondary school, 16–17, 153, 178, 191

Welsh, 6–7, 39–41, 49–64, 198, 202–204
Welsh-medium education, 40, 49–51, 53–57, 60–62

Yiddish, 12, 15, 16, 18, 19, 23

For Product Safety Concerns and Information please contact our EU Authorised Representative:

Easy Access System Europe

Mustamäe tee 50

10621 Tallinn

Estonia

gpsr.requests@easproject.com